No Quick Fixes:
Perspectives on Schools in Difficulty

Edited by

Louise Stoll and Kate Myers

 The Falmer Press

(A member of the Taylor & Francis Group)
London · Washington, D.C.

UK Falmer Press, 1 Gunpowder Square, London, EC4A 3DE
USA Falmer Press, Taylor & Francis Inc., 1900 Frost Road, Suite 101, Bristol, PA 19007

First published in 1998

A catalogue record for this book is available from the British Library

ISBN 0 7507 0714 3 cased
ISBN 0 7507 0674 0 paper

Library of Congress Cataloging-in-Publication Data are available on request

Jacket design by Caroline Archer

Typeset in 10/12 pt Times by
Graphicraft Typesetters Ltd., Hong Kong.

Printed in Great Britain by Biddles Ltd., Guildford and King's Lynn on paper which has a specified pH value on final paper manufacture of not less than 7.5 and is therefore 'acid free'.

Every effort has been made to contact copyright holders for their permission to reprint material in this book. The publishers would be grateful to hear from any copyright holder who is not here acknowledged and will undertake to rectify any errors or omissions in future editions of this book.

Contents

Contents

Acknowledgments

In compiling this book, we owe thanks to a large number of people. In particular, we are grateful to Dean Fink, Harvey Goldstein, Denis Lawton, Peter Mortimore, Richard and Gill Rusbridger, Pam Sammons, Adella Shapiro, Paddy Walsh and Chris Watkins for discussions and feedback. Participants in the Interactive Symposium on Understanding Ineffectiveness at the Tenth International Congress for School Effectiveness and Improvement in Memphis stimulated our thinking and broadened our own perspectives. We would also like to thank the Associate Directors and Associates of the International School Effectiveness and Improvement Centre (ISEIC) and our colleagues in Assessment, Guidance and Effective Learning (AGEL) at the Institute of Education for their ongoing support. Staff and pupils in schools involved in case studies of improving schools we have carried out have reminded us of the enormous challenge, complexity and reality of working in schools in difficulties. We are especially thankful to them for opening themselves up to us and sharing their experiences.

Our special thanks to Ashley Hay, Angela Akbar and Karen Cass for the enormous effort they have put into pulling together the manuscript, to Anna Clarkson for her sensitive editorial judgments and to Malcolm Clarkson for encouraging us to proceed with our idea for the book.

Glossary

As much as being a definitive list of abbreviations and acronyms used throughout the book, we hope that the glossary will also provide explanations and equivalent phrases for international readers.

AIP	Accelerated Inspection Process
Appraisal	Teacher evaluation
ATL	Association of Teachers and Lecturers
CES	Coalition of Essential Schools
Dearing	Sir Ron Dearing, who carried out a review of the National Curriculum and its assessments
DEMOS	An independent think-tank
DfEE	Department for Education and Employment
EA	Education Association
EAS	Education Advisory Service
EBD	Emotionally and Behaviourally Disturbed
ESRC	Economic and Social Research Council
Faculty	Staff
GCSE	General Certificate of Secondary Education
GEST	Grants for Educational Support and Training
GMS	Grant Maintained Status (charter school)
Governing Body	School council
Principal	Headteacher
HMCI	Her Majesty's Chief Inspector
HMI	Her Majesty's Inspectorate
HRO	High Reliability Organizations
IALS	International Adult Literacy Survey
ILEA	Inner London Education Authority
ISEIC	International School Effectiveness and Improvement Centre
ISEP	Improving School Effectiveness Project
ISERP	International School Effectiveness Research Project
LEA	Local Education Authority
LMS	Local Management of Schools (site-based management)
LSES	Louisiana School Effectiveness Study
NUT	National Union of Teachers
OD	Organizational Development

OFSTED	Office for Standards in Education
OECD	Organisation for Economic Co-operation and Development
Section 11	Grant from the Home Office for pupils of non-Commonwealth origin
SOEID	Scottish Office Education and Industry Department
SMT	Senior Management Team (school administrators)
SRB	Single Regeneration Budget
Superintendent	Director of Education/CEO
TES	*Times Educational Supplement*
TTA	Teacher Training Agency

Chapter 1

No Quick Fixes: An Introduction

Louise Stoll and Kate Myers

It was with some trepidation and yet a sense of urgency that we decided to focus a book on the topic of schools in difficulty: trepidation because we did not wish it to be viewed as yet another opportunity to 'bash the teachers'; urgency because school failure is a theme that dominates current educational discourse. Yet, to us, and many people with whom we come into contact, there is a lack of clarity over its definition and consequent misinterpretation of appropriate responses.

Having decided to undertake this project, we felt it important to consider the topic from a variety of perspectives, and asked for contributions from people who represented a diversity of interests and roles. These included national and local policy makers and observers; headteachers of primary, secondary and special schools; those in external support roles; colleagues interested in conceptual issues; and those who could offer international perspectives, in order to contextualize the British contributions. Our book is organized in sections that reflect these perspectives. The richness of the contributions have reaffirmed for us the complexity of the topic, through multiple interpretations of reality conveyed through diverse expressions and metaphors. In particular, they highlight the need to:

- clarify definitions;
- consider the implications of the language in current usage;
- broaden our understanding of ineffectiveness through searching beyond the confines of education;
- pay attention to the capacity of different schools to improve and avoid simplistic 'one size fits all' solutions;
- recognize the importance of effective leadership;
- remember the centrality of teaching and learning; and
- take into account that schools exist within a larger context that can enhance or inhibit their effectiveness.

In this introductory chapter, we examine these issues highlighting, where appropriate, contributions of the chapter authors, and consider the impact of current and proposed national policies. At the start of each section, we have also written a brief introduction, to draw out common and conflicting issues raised by the authors.

Our own recent experience has been primarily with British schools. We appreciate that the book's audience will mainly be those who work with, or have an active interest in, British schools, although we hope that the authors' contributions will also resonate with practitioners, policy makers, researchers and students of education in other countries.

We believe it is important to step back and consider why 'failure' is so topical. As Karen Kovacs explains in her chapter, there is increasing concern about low educational and skills attainment in a post-industrial economy and information age, despite ongoing measures undertaken to address failure by member countries of the OECD (see also chapters by David Reynolds and Sam Stringfield). The future of children and young people is too important to leave to chance, but has this always been so? We find ourselves in a rapidly changing world. Despite the fact we have much to be pleased about in terms of an increase in pupils' achievement (Mortimore, 1996):

> Failure is, of course, a relative concept. The current concern about failure should be seen in the context of societies which were not only attempting to educate *all* young people, but were also attempting to prepare them for rapidly changing economies which demanded higher and higher skills, and different kinds of skills, from what was acceptable at earlier stages of industrialisation. (Lawton, 1997, p. 9)

A Variety of Definitions

Failure is often viewed as the opposite of success. In terms of schooling, success is equated with greater effectiveness. To understand failure, or ineffectiveness, it is therefore necessary to define effectiveness. Herein lies a problem. No common definition of school effectiveness exists across OECD member countries (Chapman and Aspin, 1994) or, indeed, within Britain (see Caroline Lodge's chapter). This poses a fundamental problem for school effectiveness and, consequently, ineffectiveness. What do these terms actually mean? Do they mean the same things to different people? To arrive at a definition of a school as effective, forces choice between competing values regarding the purposes of education. However, there is no common agreement about the purpose of education. Furthermore, what educators perceive as important outcomes of schooling may not coincide with views of pupils, parents, governors, the local community or national agencies.

Brouilette (1996) summarizes four common ways of viewing the purposes of education as humanist, social efficiency, developmentalist, and social meliorist. The purpose of education for the *humanist* is to prepare pupils for citizenship so they understand the values and traditions embodied in their societies' institutions. Pupils must, therefore, be sufficiently literate to communicate with fellow citizens and have the knowledge necessary to comprehend current issues and act accordingly. In practice this has tended to be interpreted as emphasizing liberal arts and the 'basics' — grammar, spelling, arithmetic — as well as an understanding of western values and traditions.

To those who advocate *social efficiency*, the purpose of schools is to prepare pupils for jobs, and contribute to the society's economic well-being. The concept of pupils as 'human capital' evolves from this point of view. While this view places an emphasis on the basics and sees education as an 'input–output' process, it also stresses the need for vocational education.

The *developmentalist* position holds that education should help individual pupils to develop their personal potential 'so that they are prepared to be creative, self-motivated lifelong learners who are effective problem-solvers, able to communicate and collaborate with others, and to meet the varied challenges they will encounter in their adult lives' (*ibid*, p. 224). While humanists and developmentalists have similar aspirations for pupils, they diverge on where to put their curricular emphasis. For the developmentalist, to focus too early on what they view as 'cosmetics' would inhibit a pupil's creativity and imagination.

The purpose of education to the *social meliorist* is to bring about a more just society, 'through using the schools to help those children whose background puts them at risk, to get the resources they need to succeed, and through teaching all parents about diverse cultures and ethnic heritages, thus helping them to grow into open-minded, tolerant adults' (*ibid*, p. 224). For example, in Austria, one of the highlighted features of failing schools is ignoring disadvantaged children, while another is gender discrimination (Hiebl, 1995). Those who advocate this view see the humanist approach as narrow, traditional and elitist. Similarly, they perceive the social efficiency perspective as exploitative and replicating social injustice. From a social meliorist point of view, the developmentalist view tends to ignore the social context and social ills which prevent pupils from taking advantage of opportunities.

While, in reality, some people may subscribe to more than one of these positions, in their extreme, they help to explain the definitional dilemma. To the social meliorist, for example, a school which does not actively attempt to overcome barriers for disadvantaged pupils is ineffective. To the humanist, a school which uses more 'progressive' child-centred teaching strategies is ineffective because it denies access to traditional views and skills. It would appear that those who define schooling from the humanist and social efficiency perspectives have in large measure politically defined what society means by the terms effectiveness and ineffectiveness. There are of course other perspectives. The developmentalist would be concerned about schools that did not create effective problem-solvers and the social meliorist would condemn schools that perpetuated a traditional and elitist system.

Effectiveness can be seen through many dimensions. One could argue, for example, that promotion of a healthy lifestyle should be an essential goal of schooling. Similarly, it is argued that success in life is related to emotional intelligence (Goleman, 1996), which influences pupils', and we would argue teachers', self-concepts and motivation. From this perspective, one can claim that an effective school cannot only be about academic outcomes, it must also be concerned with caring, which:

> not only provides the moral purpose for change . . . it also adds the ethic which invites pupils, teachers, principals, parents and all those interested in educational change to join, contribute and persevere on the change journey. (Stoll and Fink, 1996, p. 191)

In short, an effective school also has heart (Hargreaves, 1997). To be caring does not mean that expectations are low: far from it. Steven Pugh, in his chapter, distinguishes between care and caring. In our view, caring teachers expect all of their pupils to do well, and do what it takes to the best of their abilities to help every pupil achieve. 'To do less is uncaring' (Stoll and Fink, 1996, p. 192).

Use of Language

[handwritten annotation: ↑ Teachers have an influential role]

As we were editing the chapters, we were struck by the large number of words that are used to convey the idea of schools in difficulty. These include failing, ineffective, underachieving, schools with problems, struggling, troubled, troubling, swaying, stuck, sinking, sliding, cruising and promenading. Why is there such a plethora of words used to describe schools with difficulties? We believe this reflects the complexity of differences between such schools and the supposed underlying causes for their difficulties (see the chapters by Michael Barber, Kate Myers and Harvey Goldstein, and Louise Stoll and Dean Fink).

If we look at the language of national policy, we see schools requiring 'special measures' (which has a chilling ring of 'the final solution' to it) and schools 'with serious weaknesses', weakness being a defect. What messages do such terms and public labels send out? (see Kate Myers' and Harvey Goldstein's chapter). In visits to such schools, we have heard harrowing stories of shock, desperation, hopelessness and helplessness, similar to the experiences of those facing bereavement. Such sentiments are exacerbated by the twist of the media's knife — or being in the media goldfish bowl, as Vivien Cutler so vividly describes it — with headlines such as 'is this the worst school in Britain?' (see Christine Whatford's chapter) and 'school for dunces' (see Steven Pugh's chapter). In our view the way language has been used by politicians and the media has often exacerbated and prolonged the problem of schools in difficulty (and has also had a negative effect on LEAs; see Rob Watling and colleagues' chapter). It has contributed to low teacher morale and feelings of impotence and, through the drip-feed method of regular exposure to horror stories, encouraged the public to believe that standards are low in the majority of schools, and that a significant minority are in a state of perpetual crisis.

Opening an OECD seminar on combating failure at school in London at the end of 1995, Gillian Shephard, then Secretary of State for Education in England, defended her government's policy on identifying failing schools, though acknowledged the policy was not universally popular:

> Critics have complained that naming schools publicly is unnecessary. Murmur the truth to schools quietly, privately, they argue, and schools will put things right. (p. 3)

There are, however, other ways of dealing with the problem. In Malaysia for example, announcements are only made about schools that are successful. The question is, is blame an effective strategy? The language of blame and recrimination is pervasive and serves the purpose of rejecting any personal responsibility for the problem by pushing it on to others. During the 1997 election campaign, for example, we heard a lot about *zero tolerance*. There was *zero tolerance* of crime and *zero tolerance* of failure in schools. The term suggests virility and decisiveness and allows no room for the 'wimps' and 'fainthearted' or simply for those who may think, 'yes, but it's more complicated than that'. When it is used about schools, the implication is that zero tolerance is for the teachers who 'allow' failure to happen. Compared with the term 'success for all' (Slavin, Madden, Dolan and Wasik, 1996), zero tolerance is negative and recriminating. Most important, it is unlikely to reach the 'hearts and minds' of those who need to be reached if change is really to occur. We are told that warm words are not enough and that zero tolerance of failure is necessary for success for all. According to Michael Barber (in this volume), 'success for all and zero tolerance of failure are synonymous'. We disagree with this view. We suggest that they are related but not synonymous, in the same way as the half full/half empty glass are on one level the same thing, but on another level they convey very different images. Even more important, they are likely to elicit very different responses. There are issues about the way 'failure' is used in this context. Most of us learn through and from our mistakes. 'Zero tolerance of failure' suggests this is not an option and that we must turn away from, reject, punish and blame those who fail. The different 'overtones' of meaning are significant and not just a semantic debate if our desired outcome is bringing about positive change rather than posturing or scoring political points. This is a 'hearts and minds' task. Blaming people does not foster a feeling of wanting to share the problem and contribute to its solution.

Indeed, according to psychoanalysis, blaming people may engender somewhat different responses (Segal, 1997). When people use the mechanism of blaming, in dividing off the responsibility from themselves and pushing it on to another object, the blamer attributes 'badness' to an individual or a group of people and is thus able to demonize them and use them as a scapegoat. When this happens to an individual or group, the foundation of belief in themselves is shaken. One response is to accept the projection and invoke appeasement. A more frequent response is to reject the projection and push it out. This can become a paranoid cycle with both sides believing 'it's not us, it's you', sometimes resulting in warfare. A third response is to do unto others what has been done unto you. So the blamed becomes the blamer and blames everyone else (e.g., in schools, parents, governors, pupils) except him- or herself for the problem.

The mature way to tackle these issues has to be through joint acceptance of the problem and working together to find remedies. The language used to analyse and describe the problem must contribute to whether all parties involved feel able to share responsibility for solving it. Education should be about cooperation, not confrontation.

Alternative Metaphors

The contributors to this book have used an array of metaphors in their reflections on schools in difficulty. Myers (1995) argues that the use of metaphors can be a powerful, illuminating and evocative way to help understand issues by explaining them in a different context (see Caroline Lodge's chapter for further discussion of the use of metaphors).

Notwithstanding Linda Turner's powerful visual of the headteacher as juggler, the most frequent metaphorical allusions relate in some way to health, whether physical or mental. As Myers (1995) has noted, using the health metaphor to describe schools is not new. Indeed, Miles drew on it over 30 years ago in his characterization of a healthy school (Miles, 1965). Sam Stringfield (in this volume) offers an anatomy of ineffectiveness, while Hargreaves (1997) argues that there is too much emphasis on the symptoms of failure, and too little understanding of its pathology.

We are aware that the use of medical metaphors is not unproblematic. Much traditional medicine tends to look at isolated parts of patients, rather than the whole. It is here that holistic and alternative medicine may have something to contribute in that they focus on the whole person and their environment. The school in difficulty rarely only has a problem because of one issue, for example the poor literacy levels of its pupils. Furthermore, trying to change established practices will have a rippling effect on other aspects of the school.

Organizational health inventories have been developed for school self-diagnosis. Hoy and colleagues (1991), who have developed one of these inventories, describe unhealthy schools as:

> ... vulnerable to destructive outside forces ... The principal provides little direction or structure; exhibits little encouragement and support for teachers ... Teachers do not feel good about their colleagues or their jobs. They act aloof, suspicious, and defensive ... finally there is little press for academic excellence. (p. 184)

This description bears some similarity to existing findings of studies of ineffective schools (see, for example, Rosenholtz, 1989; Reynolds, 1996; and Kate Myers and Harvey Goldstein, and Sam Stringfield in this book). Indeed, some schools may not just be unhealthy; they may have a severe mental health problem (Myers, 1995). Many psychotherapists would argue that how people behave at work reflects their own early family experience, and it has been argued that the best metaphor for an effective school is that of the caring family (Stoll and Fink, 1996). So can understandings about family therapy help dysfunctional schools? Although there are clearly differences between small families and large schools, there are interesting and pertinent connections to be made: 'A family is a system that operates through transactional patterns' (Minuchin, 1974, p. 51). Like a dysfunctional family, a school experiencing, and not coping with, difficulties is in effect dysfunctional: the transactional systems have broken down. Bradshaw (1988) describes a body of covert rules that operate unconsciously in dysfunctional families and create distress. These include control; perfectionism and fear of failure; blame (discussed earlier); denial of feelings, perceptions, thoughts, wants and imaginings; a no talk rule; creation of myths, as masks to distract others; ongoing disagreements; and unreliability and lack of trust.

Can therapeutic techniques, however, be used with schools? While there are a number of initiatives that offer therapy for pupils on site and, in some instances, individual teachers have taken the opportunity to discuss their own pupil-related issues with the therapists, as yet, school-wide therapy for whole staff is not commonly available, although both John MacBeath and David Reynolds, in their chapters, describe the psychotherapeutic and counselling techniques used by change agents. We wonder whether it would be of value for some schools to devote time to working with a therapist to help them understand the blockages to effective functioning? In addition to the practical difficulties of size, time and resources, as well as sensitive introduction and handling, it may be that carefully targeted organizational development approaches, such as conflict resolution, would be more appropriate (Watkins, personal communication).

Further thinking is clearly needed to see how useful health metaphors are as an aid to school improvement.

Capacity for Change

It is clear that there are many different types of schools in difficulties. Indeed, there are a variety of ways for a school to be ineffective (Hargreaves, 1995). Reynolds (1996), however, raises the issue of whether ineffective schools have the 'prior competencies' to bring about the necessary changes. It is important to understand the state of readiness of an institution before it can effectively cope with change (see John MacBeath's chapter). Myers (1995) reminds us, we have a tendency to reinvent the wheel, for it was over twenty years ago that Derr (1976) wrote, with reference to organizational development in schools, 'The organization should, for example, possess a certain "readiness", in order to employ organization development' (p. 229), and only a few years later that Fullan and colleagues (1980) reiterated the need to focus on readiness conditions:

> Classical OD (organizational process and problem oriented approaches) . . . seem to depend on fairly stable environmental conditions, and a certain level of favorable attitude and initial propensity for collective problem solving. Thus, this form of OD probably does not represent the most appropriate strategy for change in turbulent urban school districts. (pp. 151–2)

What is certain, is that not all schools are at the same stage of readiness for change, and this has little to do with their perceived state of effectiveness. The high-achieving intake but cruising school (see Louise Stoll and Dean Fink's chapter), sitting 'comfortably' at or near the top of the league tables, may lack the necessary prerequisite conditions for deep, meaningful and lasting change to take place no less than the inner-city school that has just failed its Office for Standards in Education (OFSTED) inspection. Similarly, capacity for change may be in some way linked to the size of the school. Change in secondary schools is inherently more difficult than in primary schools (Louis and Miles, 1990; see also the chapters by Michael Stark, Christine Whatford and Vivien Cutler). Building the capacity for change is extremely complex, as acknowledged by the Department for Education and Employment (DfEE) and OFSTED (1995):

> . . . in [some] cases, where all the elements for success appear to be present, there may be an indefinable characteristic which prevents improvement. The improvement of a school is more an organic process than a mechanical one, and consequently there is an element of unpredictability inherent in it. (p. 19)

Leadership

Many of the contributors to this book have referred to the importance of leadership. Leadership applies at all levels, within the LEA as well as the school, but the role of the head seems to dominate most discussions. Aspects of leadership are often intangible but we know that an effective leader has a vision and is able to convey this vision to different groups who are involved with the school including staff, pupils, parents and governors. The invitational process through which this is achieved, based on communicating messages to people which inform them that they are able, responsible and worthwhile (Stoll and Fink, 1996), helps to unify these groups and give them a common mission. In a school experiencing difficulties, the vision often has to be conveyed to groups that are disparate as well as different. In-fighting among the staff/governors is not unknown in these schools and, instead of uniting with the leader, the groups may well use the leader to address old scores and grievances among themselves. In addition, a core leadership skill in schools with difficulties is the ability to build, and sometimes rebuild, staff confidence (see, particularly, the school perspective chapters).

Being a headteacher in the best of situations can be a stressful and lonely job. It takes a particularly confident, experienced and resilient person to cope with leadership in difficult circumstances. External support is often essential. It seems that many schools under special measures have appointed a new headteacher just before or soon after the OFSTED inspection and this is seen as a key reason for their subsequent improvement (OFSTED, 1997), but according to the same source, another characteristic of 'improving failing schools' is that they have:

> been well supported by their LEAs who have acted swiftly to provide good and timely support to schools; [and] received extra financial support either from their LEA or in the case of grant maintained schools from the Funding Agency for Schools. (OFSTED, 1997, p. 6)

We wonder whether if this sort of support had been available to some of the previous incumbents, there would have been quite so much turnover in headteachers.

The Centrality of Teaching and Learning

The chapters in this book reinforce the vital importance to improvement of focusing on teaching and learning. What is of most concern to teachers is what goes on between them and the pupils in their classes and classrooms. They do not have the time to participate in meetings and decision making for the sake of it. Indeed, school effectiveness research suggests that the classroom effect is greater than the whole school effect (Scheerens, 1992), yet it appears that a lot of attention is diverted to management solutions, including school development plans, league tables, and whole school target setting, with less thought and energy given to the potential of teacher development and action research related directly to improved classroom practice.

critical

Changing practice, however, is notoriously difficult, and requires time and effort to develop new skills, as well as the will to change (Miles, 1987). In schools with difficulties, although this is the central issue, if the internal capacity to cope with change is missing, consequently it is often impossible to focus immediate attention on teaching and learning (Stoll and Fink, 1996). This poses a dilemma for those involved: knowing that classroom practice has to change but realizing that appropriate internal conditions and structures have to be in place to allow this to happen.

From our and others' experience, putting into place the basic competencies (aided, often by significant staff changes, including a new headteacher, and significant resources) may be accomplished relatively swiftly (see Michael Stark's chapter). What often still remains, however, is an unmotivating and unchallenging teaching and learning experience for pupils. This is where there are no quick fixes. It is the most complex aspect of the change process (see the school perspectives and the chapter by James Learmonth and Kathy Lowers), and takes the greatest time because it involves intensive staff development, new learning, and frequently, the need for a fundamental shift in beliefs about ways of working with pupils and their ability to learn (see John MacBeath's chapter).

Context of School Improvement

Interestingly, if we look at other OECD countries, we find a distinct difference between those who emphasize *failure of pupils* (most countries) and the few, including England and Wales, who talk in terms of *school failure* (see chapter by Karen Kovacs) and view the concept as part of their strategy for improving schools. It should be noted that the title of the OECD activity on this topic is 'Combating Failure *at* School' (our emphasis). This suggests that if pupils have difficulties, the context and something within the pupils themselves may, at least in part, be responsible for the failure of pupils at schools. This contrasts with the view that pupils have difficulties because *of* the failure of schools. When the failure of pupils is emphasized, it is possible to provide programmes to match the diagnosed needs of the identified groups or to make fundamental changes to the context (e.g., housing and employment) so that the failure does not reoccur. When failure of the school is emphasized, the external contest is not considered. Indeed, it is believed anyone who suggests the context may contribute to the schools' problems is complacent and has low expectations of the pupils.

School effectiveness research has demonstrated that schools in similar areas can have different effects on their pupils' life chances; that, indeed, school can make a difference. In taking up these important research findings, some policy makers, however, have construed this to mean that the school is responsible for the success or otherwise of its pupils. There is some truth in this, but only to a limited extent. School explains a relatively small percentage of the difference in pupils' *overall attainment* (8–12 per cent, Reynolds, Sammons, Stoll, Barber and Hillman, 1996). In terms of *progress*, the effect is larger (nearer 25 per cent, see Mortimore, Sammons, Stoll, Lewis and Ecob, 1988) and greater than that attributable to social and individual background. It remains important, however, to recognize that schools exist within a wider social context. As Lawton (1997) cautions, the research evidence that schools make a difference 'should not, however, be used as an excuse for societies being complacent about such social problems as gross poverty and inadequate levels of housing' (pp. 17–18). Furthermore, the pressure on schools created by social deprivation is exacerbated by free market choice that promotes competition and creates 'winners and losers' (Riley and Rowles, 1997). It seems clear that education policies related to improving schools in difficulty are most likely to succeed when taking the wider national and community interest into full account and when properly coordinated with other policies (OECD, 1997).

Schools in difficulty, particularly those in disadvantaged areas, need coordinated support strategies. Education ministries need to join with health and social service ministries, local communities and school psychologists, to support schools. Examples are seen in a range of American restructuring initiatives that, among other objectives, incorporate partnerships between education, the community and social services. For example, the National Alliance for Restructuring Education, with its goal of all young people reaching high standards of achievement:

> . . . is interested in creating a web of supports and services for children and families, and in engaging parents, guardians and the public in the education of their children. Because the problem is larger than the schools alone, the solution must encompass entities outside of schools, as well. (Rothman, 1996, p. 181)

Similarly in south London, schools, three LEAs, the local health authority, specialist agencies and local communities are working together on the Healthier School Partnership Project to support the development of schools as health promoting institutions and establish and sustain healthy alliances between schools and their local communities (Toft, 1996). Earlier we noted the importance of health in relation to schooling, but it too is subject to context. The risk of developing physical, psychological or social health problems is greater for those sectors of populations with the least social status, social capital and human capital resources (Aday, 1994).

Social issues can have a profound impact on pupils and their orientation to education. Take the 8-year-old boy in the Glasgow school whose mother never came to see his teacher when requested. After the third occasion, the teacher asked the boy for the reason, to be told that she never leaves the house because she has been afraid to go out since they witnessed a murder. Each day when the boy returns from school, they lock themselves into their home. Such experiences are not un-common in some communities, so it is not surprising that a national policy document tells us:

> ... there is certainly a link between socio-economic deprivation and the likelihood that a school will be found failing ... 7 per cent of schools with disadvantaged pupils have been found to be failing, compared to the national 'failure rate' of 1.5–2 per cent. (DfEE and OFSTED, 1995, p. 12)

[handwritten margin note: Social class]
[handwritten note: ofsted]

However, we do not see this as a reason to blame these schools. Some countries target funding to assist schools where a high proportion of students come from backgrounds likely to create barriers to educational achievement. This is similar to the post-Plowden Educational Priority Area scheme. We hope the new Labour government's proposal to establish Education Action Zones will provide opportunities to target resources to specific areas of deprivation.

[handwritten note: ↑ underperforming schools need resources]

Consequences of Policy

In recent years, government policy in England and Wales has introduced local management of schools (LMS), the national curriculum, new vocational courses and qualifications, assessment, appraisal, open enrolment, league tables and a new inspection system. These changes have taken place at the same time as a reduction of the powers and budgets of LEAs and consequently a reduction of support they are able to offer to schools (see the chapters by Christine Whatford, and Rob Watling and colleagues). Many of the changes have encouraged competition rather than coopera-tion between schools thereby reducing another avenue of support. The issue of better resourced grant maintained schools competing for pupils with maintained schools has exacerbated this situation in some areas of the country. Several of the schools that have hit the headlines after being deemed requiring special measures have found themselves in difficulty at least in part as a consequence of local and govern-ment policies.

[handwritten margin note: not positive changes]

Another change has been a new role for governing bodies, for which many are still unprepared. In studies of experiences of failing schools, Earley (1996a) and Riley and Rowles (1997) found that their governing bodies had often not been operating effectively and had a limited understanding of their role in relation to helping the school raise achievement (see also David Reynolds' and Michael Stark's chapters). Investment is clearly needed at a national level in training for governing bodies to help them undertake their role effectively.

[handwritten margin note: quote against "ofsted"]

The sometimes devastating impact of OFSTED inspections on staff morale (see chapters by Linda Turner, and James Learmonth and Kathy Lowers), the 'development paralysis' that is caused purely by the knowledge of an impending inspection (Stoll, Myers and Harrington, 1995), and their enormous cost — estimated by Earley (1996b) to be over £100 million per year, or approximately £30,000 for an average size secondary school —, must lead to serious questioning of their overall usefulness as a means of real and lasting improvement. An alternative, less costly strategy is required: one that also validates schools' own self-evaluation (see, for example, the Triennial School Review process carried out in the state of Victoria, in Australia; Victoria Office of Review, 1997).

Conclusion

Having assembled the book, read and reread all the contributions and other relevant literature, and listened to the viewpoints expressed by participants from at least ten countries at an interactive international symposium on 'Understanding Ineffectiveness' at the Tenth International Congress for School Effectiveness and Improvement, we remain convinced that our book title is apt. There are urgent political pressures to speed up the change process. However, for real, deep and lasting improvements to teaching and learning, supported by the commitment, development and self-efficacy of the teaching profession, resources, time, and political commitment are needed. For those who seek easy ways out, the words of the OECD (1997) should be heeded:

> Is failure endemic or is it that the right counter-measures have yet to be discovered and tested? Is it that the right counter-measures are known or, indeed, in operation, but have not so far been applied with the right balance in the right way ... ? Is it simply beyond the capacity of education systems and schools in their present form to deal with the problem? ... Is failure, preponderantly, an environmental problem? The fact that, after all the efforts of the last three decades and longer, these questions must be asked demonstrates that there are no easy solutions ... to the problem of school failure. (p. 9)

In short, in our view, there are no magic answers and no quick fixes.

References

ADAY, L. (1994) 'Health status of vulnerable populations', *Annual Review of Public Health*, 15, pp. 487–509.

BRADSHAW, J. (1988) *Bradshaw on The Family: A Revolutionary Way of Self-Discovery*, Florida: Health Communications Inc.

BROUILETTE, L. (1996) *A Geology of School Reform: The Successive Restructuring of A School District*, New York: State University of New York Press.

CHAPMAN, J. and ASPIN, D. (1994) 'Securing the future: An overview of some problems, issues and trends arising from the OECD activity on "The Effectiveness of Schooling and of Educational Resource Management" ', Paper prepared for Directorate for Education Employment. Labour and Social Affairs, Organisation for Economic Cooperation and Development, Paris.

DERR, B.C. (1976) ' "OD" won't work', *Schools, Education and Urban Society*, **8**, 2, pp. 227–41.

DfEE and OFSTED (1995) *The Improvement of Failing Schools: UK Policy and Practice 1993–1995*, London: Department for Education and Employment and Office for Standards in Education.

EARLEY, P. (1996a) 'Governing Bodies, External Inspections and "Failing Schools"', Paper presented to the European Conference on Educational Research, University of Seville.

EARLEY, P. (1996b) 'School improvement and OFSTED inspection: The research evidence', in EARLEY, P., FIDLER, B. and OUSTON, J. (eds) *Improvement Through Inspection? Complementary Approaches to School Development*, London: David Fulton.

FULLAN, M., MILES, M.B. and TAYLOR, G. (1980) 'Organizational development in schools: The state of the art', *Review of Educational Research*, **50**, 1, pp. 212–83.

GOLEMAN, D. (1996) *Emotional Intelligence: Why it Can Matter More Than IQ*, London: Bloomsbury.

HARGREAVES, A. (1997) 'Rethinking educational change: Going deeper and wider in the quest for success', in HARGREAVES, A. (ed.) *Rethinking Educational Change with Heart and Mind*, ASCD Yearbook, Alexandria, VA: Association for Supervision and Curriculum Development.

HARGREAVES, D. (1995) 'School culture, school effectiveness and school improvement', *School Effectiveness and School Improvement*, **6**, 91, pp. 23–46.

HARGREAVES, D. (1997) Presentation to the Symposium on 'Ineffective Schools', Annual Meeting of the International Congress for School Effectiveness and Improvement, Memphis.

HEIBL, W. (1995) 'Combating Failure at School in Austria: Improving the Performance of Schools as Institutions', Paper presented at the OECD Seminar on Combating Failure at School, Institute of Education, London, November.

HOY, W., TARTER, C.J. and BLISS, J.R. (1991) 'Organizational climate, school health and effectiveness: A comparative analysis', *Educational Administration Quarterly*, **26**, 3, pp. 260–79.

LAWTON, D. (1997) 'Promoting Improved Teaching and Learning: Policy Lessons', Background Paper for OECD Seminar 'Combating Failure at School' (mimeo).

LOUIS, K.S. and MILES, M.B. (1990) *Improving the Urban High School: What Works and Why*, New York: Teachers College Press.

MILES, M.B. (1965) 'Planned change and organizational health', in CARLSON, R.O. (ed.) *Change Processes in the Public Schools*, Eugene, Oregon: Center for Advanced Study of Educational Administration.

MILES, M.B. (1987) 'Practical Guidelines for Administrators: How to Get There', Paper presented at the Annual Meeting of the American Educational Research Association, Washington.

MINUCHIN, S. (1974) *Families and Family Therapy*, London: Tavistock Publications.

MORTIMORE, P. (1996) 'High Performing Schools and School Improvement', Paper presented at the conference 'Schools of the Third Millennium', Melbourne, Australia, February.

MORTIMORE, P., SAMMONS, P., STOLL, L., LEWIS, D. and ECOB, R. (1988) *School Matters: The Junior Years*, Wells: Open Books. Reprinted (1994) London: Paul Chapman.

MYERS, K. (1995) 'Intensive Care for the Chronically Sick', Paper presented at the European Conference on Educational Research, University of Bath.

OFSTED (1997) *From Failure to Success: How Special Measures Are Helping Schools Improve*, London: Office for Standards in Education.

OECD (1997) *Combating Failure at School: Dimensions of the Problem, Country Experiences and Policy Implications*, Paris: Organisation for Economic Cooperation and Development.

REYNOLDS, D. (1996) 'The problem of the ineffective school: Some evidence and some speculations', in GRAY, J., REYNOLDS, D., FITZ-GIBBON, C. and JESSON, D. (eds) *Merging Traditions: The Future of Research on School Effectiveness and School Improvement*, London: Cassell.

REYNOLDS, D., SAMMONS, P., STOLL, L., BARBER, M. and HILLMAN, J. (1996) 'School effectiveness and school improvement in the United Kingdom', *School Effectiveness and School Improvement*, **7**, 2, pp. 133–58.

RILEY, K. and ROWLES, D. (1997) *Learning from Failure*, London: Haringey Council.

ROSENHOLTZ, S.J. (1989) *Teachers' Workplace: The Social Organization of Schools*, New York: Longman.

ROTHMAN, R. (1996) 'Reform at all levels: National alliance for restructuring education', in STRINGFIELD, S., ROSS, S. and SMITH, L. (eds) *Bold Plans for Restructuring: New American School Designs*, New Jersey: Lawrence Erlbaum Associates.

SCHEERENS, J. (1992) *Effective Schooling: Research, Theory and Practice*, London: Cassell.

SEGAL, H. (1997) *Psychoanalysis Literature and War Papers 1972–1995*, London: Routledge.

SHEPHARD, G. (1995) *Speech to the OECD Seminar on Combating Failure at School*, London, Institute of Education, 20 November.

SLAVIN, R.E., MADDEN, N.A., DOLAN, L.J. and WASIK, B.A. (1996) 'Success for all: A summary of research', *Journal of Education for Students Placed at Risk*, **1**, 1, pp. 41–76.

STOLL, L. and FINK, D. (1996) *Changing Our Schools: Linking School Effectiveness and School Improvement*, Buckingham: Open University Press.

STOLL, L., HARRINGTON, J. and MYERS, K. (1995) Two British School Effectiveness and School Improvement Action Projects', Paper presented to the Eighth International Congress for School Effectiveness and Improvement, Leeuwarden, The Netherlands, January.

TOFT, M. (1996) *Healthier School Partnership: Project Handbook*, London: Lambeth, Southwark and Lewisham Councils.

VICTORIA OFFICE OF REVIEW (1997) *An Accountability Framework: Quality Assurance in Victorian Schools*, Melbourne: State of Victoria Department of Education.

Part 1

Policy

The two chapters in this section focus on central government policy.

The last Conservative Government established clear policies to deal with schools in difficulties, although some commentators believe that schools found themselves in difficulties at least partly *because* of some of the other policies of that government.

The Dark Side of the Moon: Imagining an End to Failure in Urban Education, the first chapter, was Michael Barber's TES/Greenwich lecture, originally delivered in May 1995. An academic commentary about the Conservative Government's policy on this issue, it is reproduced here in full because we believe it was an important paper of its time. For *No Quick Fixes*, the author has added *Second Thoughts*, his reflections almost two years on, about the lecture and his perception of its impact.

In the lecture Michael Barber addressed the issue of failure head-on, welcoming the government's move to shifting autonomy and accountability to schools (for an alternative view see Myers and Goldstein in this volume). His prediction of the number of schools that would become 'failing' is verified by Michael Stark in the following chapter.

It was in this talk that Michael Barber took up Matt Miles' and Michael Fullan's idea of the importance of using both pressure and support — a phrase subsequently much used by Prime Minister Tony Blair in his successful election campaign. Michael Barber also discussed the importance of effective LEA support and suggested that external intervention in a school's affairs should be in inverse proportion to its success. The issue of closing schools was explored and 'fresh starts' were flagged, subsequently to become Labour Party and now the new government's policy.

In *Second Thoughts*, Michael Barber, explains why he chose the theme of failure for his lecture. While reflecting that he should have included an analysis of the impact of school management, broadly he stands by his words in 1995. He explains why the lecture made a greater impact than he had anticipated, discussing the consequences — one of which was being handed the poisoned chalice of becoming a member of the first Education Association which ultimately closed down Hackney Downs school. His chief regret about the lecture is that it might have contributed to politicians from all parties vying with each other to focus on underperformance which has contributed to the demoralization of the teaching profession. This is an important concession and raises the issue about the causes of 'failure' and the consequences and costs of continually concentrating on it and 'talking it up'.

Michael Stark is a civil servant, responsible for carrying out the Conservative and now Labour Government's policy on school effectiveness. His chapter, *No Slow Fixes Either: How Failing Schools in England are Being Restored to Health*, is an optimistic account of many of the themes discussed in Michael Barber's. Having worked with over 250 schools that are in, or have been through special measures, he believes that although failing is always traumatic for those involved, public identification tends to speed rather than delay recovery and is often a precondition for it. He discusses the role of governing bodies and LEAs and suggests that the core purpose of support is to rebuild the school's capacity to regenerate itself. Michael Stark concludes the chapter by stating 'that most schools have not been destroyed by special measures: in most cases they have been revived by them'.

The chapters read together give a fascinating account of concern about and attempts to address failure in the mid- and late 1990s. Both authors conclude that the Conservative Government's policy on school failure has, in Michael Barber's words, 'proved to be a tremendous success'. No independent evaluation of this policy, however, has yet been carried out (see also Karen Kovacs' chapter). Both chapters also raise an enormous number of issues, not least the amount of resources needed to sustain the special measures programme. Once deemed as requiring them, additional support (human and material) is triggered from the GEST budget. The question about how important these resources are to improvement needs to be addressed. Indeed, would all the special measures schools be in this situation had the legislation allowed the LEA to offer the additional support or intervene more forcefully before the inspection? In some, if not all, cases are we using a sledgehammer to crack a nut?

As this book goes to press, a new Labour Government has just been elected. We wait with interest to see if the emphasis and the content of the policy dealing with failing schools will be significantly altered. In our view, *every* child has a right to the best possible education. For this to occur, attention must be paid to the contextual causes of failure that lie outside the remit of the school, as well as what occurs within school.

Chapter 2

The Dark Side of the Moon: Imagining an End to Failure in Urban Education[1]

Michael Barber

The Importance of Failure

It is a paradox but it's true. I have chosen to discuss failure in this TES/Greenwich lecture because I believe the education service is increasingly successful. I began to wonder what the policy implications would be of asking the earth-shatteringly simply question: could we have an education service in which there were no more failing schools? I ask this question not only because it is intrinsically important but also because it uncovers questions which hitherto, to use Roland Barthes' phrase, have been non-discussibles. They are, in my terms, on the dark side of the moon.

A number of the elements of success are falling into place, or will do so within the foreseeable future. There is, for example, recognition across the political spectrum that an education service which provides success for virtually everyone is essential to our economic, social and democratic fortunes in the twenty-first century.

Similarly, the government's insistence on shifting both autonomy and account-ability to school level is a step forward: school improvement has become a task for the schools. It seems amazing that we ever believed anything else, yet for the best part of 150 years we did. Now we can acknowledge that other organizations — LEAs, universities, OFSTED and government — are there to create a context in which schools are enabled and encouraged to improve themselves, not to attempt to impose improvement.

The new openness about performance data which has resulted from the publica-tion of results and inspection reports has also played a part in changing attitudes. Though both performance tables and the inspection process remain flawed, they have unquestionably led headteachers to give a new priority to school improvement.

For all these reasons there has been a welcome explosion of interest in the lessons of the research on school effectiveness and school improvement which Peter Mortimore reviewed in the first TES/Greenwich lecture three years ago. As colleagues in many other universities and in LEAs will agree, the demand from schools for information, consultancy, training and advice in the field of school improvement is burgeoning. In the past, as Peter Mortimore has often remarked, this country led the world in the study of school effectiveness but lagged behind in applying its lessons. This is no longer true. Furthermore, the interest in school effectiveness and school improvement goes far beyond schools. Many LEAs, re-lieved (if involuntarily) of many of their day-to-day administrative functions, have begun to develop a forward-looking, creative role promoting and encouraging school improvement. Birmingham, Nottinghamshire, Lewisham and Greenwich are all good examples but there are many more. At the heart of the strategies of these LEAs is an understanding of what the research says about what works and a determination to build upon it. There is an eagerness and impatience to bring about improvement in some urban schools and LEAs which is intoxicating.

And school effectiveness fever can be found at national level too. The Depart-ment for Education has a School Effectiveness Division which displays a refreshing humility and whose decisions are evidently informed by research. The OFSTED framework, though far from perfect, is laced through with an understanding of school effectiveness. The Secretary of State made history recently by making an entire speech on school effectiveness and has demonstrated repeatedly her know-ledge of the issues. Meanwhile David Blunkett, Labour's education spokesperson, has demonstrated his commitment to higher standards in urban areas and revealed a grasp of school effectiveness and school improvement in several speeches, such as the one he made recently at the Secondary Heads' Association annual conference.

There is even evidence, following the recent spate of teacher conferences, that, sooner or later, the necessary funding for a study of improvement strategy may be forthcoming. Gillian Shephard invited educators to join her in campaigning for more resources for education. 'I want you to help me to see if we can make things better next year,' she told the Secondary Heads' Association. David Blunkett in his speech to the same conference said that he wanted a ten-year strategy for improvement, which linked resources to targets and established three-year funding horizons.

The knowledge that schools make a difference is a liberation. On the shifting sands of the old world view, in which schools made no difference and were essen-tially agents of social control, it was impossible to construct an argument for teach-ing to become a profession of ambition and status. How could it be if its members made no difference? The school effectiveness literature, by contrast, provides a rock on which to build a profession for the future, a task which, incidentally, we have barely begun.

It is this, perhaps irreversible, shift towards school improvement, that makes it important to have a frank and open debate about failure. Such a debate is an essential step on the road to being able to say and to mean that we want every school to be a successful school. Unless we debate failure, that slogan will never be more than vacuous and we — as educators — will be open to the charge of intellectual dishonesty. In other words we can only even come close to ending failure if we acknowledge its existence and face it squarely. It will be with us for ever if we pretend either that it does not exist or that it is inevitable. It does and it isn't.

Of course, creating a truly successful education service in the next century will involve changing more than just the education service. It will involve nothing less than changing the culture, and two aspects of it in particular. The first is the widespread view among parents that a substantial degree of mediocre or inadequate education is inevitable and that failure, like the poor, will always be with us. The second is that peculiarly British strand of culture which suggests that the extent of success is defined by the extent of failure. The more people that fail, the greater the success of those who succeed. This is the view that leads to every annual improvement in GCSE performance being interpreted as evidence of a fall in standards. It is the crystalline heart of the culture of low expectations. Changing these deep-seated cultural attitudes involves necessarily an open debate about the nature of failure and the solutions to it.

We as educators might be expected to be found in the vanguard of a campaign to this poverty-stricken culture. In fact all too often we reinforce it.

When the education service is accused of failure, the (perhaps understandable) tendency of many educators is to deny it or minimize it. When David Blunkett spoke recently of the need to deal vigorously with failing schools — of which much more later — one union leader was quoted as saying that if schools had sufficient support from government they would never fail (*The Guardian*, 12 April 1995). This view is untenable. Worse still, by suggesting that the only variable is government support, it implies that the quality of teaching is insignificant. It therefore belittles, by implication, the entire profession.

Another union leader argued that, 'dealing with a small number of schools in deep trouble is not the important agenda' (*The Daily Telegraph*, 12 April 1995). One might comment, in populist tone perhaps, that for the pupils and parents concerned it is the only agenda. More fundamentally the comment fails to recognize that a small number of seriously failing schools not only damage the reputation of the teaching profession and education as a public service but reinforce the low expectations of education which are a characteristic part of this country's inheritance.

Much the same can be said of the response to Chris Woodhead's remarks (*The Daily Mail*, 5 September 1994) that 30 per cent of teaching is unsatisfactory or poor. I was probably not alone in arguing that he ought to have stressed that 70 per cent of teaching was satisfactory or better. Of course, the positive facts should be put on the record (as in fact they were), but it struck me, on reflection, that my response was both defensive and complacent. Was I really willing to accept that 30 per cent of lessons are inadequate? Does this not make a mockery of the idea of pupils' entitlement? Is this not playing straight into the hands of those who believe that failure will always be with us? Does it not contribute, indeed, to what Stephen Ball with his usual verbal felicity, has described as 'the discourse of derision'? (Ball, 1990).

We would after all be appalled if an air traffic controller attempted to reassure us by telling us that the other nine planes landed safely. We ought to be aiming to emulate as far as possible the levels of reliability achieved in other types of service (Stringfield and Herman, 1994). While managing a successful school is infinitely more complex than controlling air traffic and depends on what might be described as a large number of unpredictable variables (otherwise known as children), failure in education can be just as catastrophic as failure in the airline industry. It differs only in that it happens more slowly and that no one has yet made the movie.

Defining Failure

Failure is relative. It is often defined in relation to some expected norm. Peter Mortimore has carefully defined an effective school in relative terms. It is, he says, 'a school in which students progress further than might be expected from a consideration of its intake' (Mortimore, 1991, p. 9).

An ineffective school could be defined in similar, but opposite, relative terms as a school in which students fail to progress as far as might be expected from a consideration of its intake. This definition would leave us looking at perhaps 20–30 per cent of schools. Many of these schools are underperforming but nevertheless have within them the capacity for improvement. In other words, the prescriptions of the school improvement literature, whether the Hopkins model or the Brighouse model or another, are likely to succeed.

However there are schools where the underperformance is more serious. OFSTED has two categories for these. There are those schools, which on the basis of OFSTED inspection, have been found to be failing and there are others which, while not technically failing, have been found to have serious weaknesses. The rest of this lecture focuses on these two categories and uses the term 'failing schools' for the former and 'struggling schools' for the latter. Let us assume for a moment that OFSTED inspection is broadly reliable. Such evidence as there is suggests incidentally that OFSTED errs, if anything, on the side of leniency, giving schools the benefit of the doubt in cases of failure.

So far 50 schools have been identified as failing, schools where at least 8,000 children are being failed. Of these, nineteen are secondary schools, two are middle, twenty-six are primary and three are special. The proportion of failing primary schools will increase inevitably as the proportion of primary inspections increases. Contrary to public perception by no means all of these are in urban areas. A number, for example, are in Norfolk, which no doubt means they will receive especially careful attention from the Secretary of State herself. As the inspection process rolls on the numbers will no doubt increase. At the moment between 1 and 2 per cent of all schools inspected have been identified as failing. If that percentage remained constant, between 250–500 schools would be found to be failing across the whole of England and Wales, if the four-year inspection cycle is completed.

In terms of struggling schools, the rate is running in the region of 5–10 per cent which, if maintained, would cover between 1,250 and 2,500 schools in total. Numbers alone dictate, therefore, that the policy for struggling schools should be different from that for failing schools.

If it is possible to summarize the difference between a 'struggling' and a 'failing' school it lies surely in the extent to which the school is capable of sustainable self-generated improvement.

In the case of a struggling school this capacity is clearly limited, otherwise it would surely not be found to be struggling at all. On the other hand, some elements of the capacity must be in place, or the school would be failing. It might, for example, have a core of staff committed to and capable of driving improvement. Its weaknesses might be due to a relatively small number of staff. Perhaps the gap between positive aspirations and day-to-day reality, though still wide, is narrowing. Whatever the precise picture, there must be within the school substantial will and some capability to improve [see also, Stoll and Fink in this volume]. These provide a foundation on which a strategy for improvement can be built with the support of, and pressure from, external agencies, such as the LEA, the DFE and OFSTED.

On the other hand, in the failing school these qualities will be in short supply. Even with the support of external agencies in these circumstances there is no firm foundation within the school on which to build improvement. The pressure that results from being found to be failing and from the threat of closure may provide a turning point — as has happened in a number of recent cases — or it may simply reinforce the school's incapacity, but some kind of substantial intervention is necessary.

The research evidence on the nature of failure is limited. The tendency has been to assume that a failing school is simply one which does not have the characteristics of an effective school. However, as David Reynolds — quoting Kate Myers [see also, Myers and Goldstein in this volume] — has argued, it is almost certainly more complicated than that:

> Rather than seeing ineffective schools as 'not having success characteristics', it might be more productive to see them as 'having failure characteristics', and to view them as having factors not seen in the effective schools it may be that the schools have *antithetical* characteristics. (Reynolds, 1995)

He goes on to list some of these. They include such characteristics as believing that change is someone else's job and that 'the way we've always done things' is the way to carry on doing them, potentially effective staff hiding behind the norms of an ineffective group, anxiety about taking risks, blaming children and their communities for poor standards, a fear of outside intervention, and numerous personality clashes, feuds and fractured relationships.

In these circumstances, Reynolds is surely right to argue, the school improvement strategies that help quite good schools become excellent or moderate schools become better are unlikely to work. The state of affairs is more intractable than this kind of response implies. A prior step is needed in which, through a combination of pressure and support, the school itself decides it wants to change and a critical mass for making change happen is created among the staff. Before discussing how this might be done, it is necessary to look at the process we have in place for identifying failure.

Identifying Failure

Tucked away in Michael Fullan's magisterial review of thinking about educational change (Fullan, 1991) there is a policy insight, the importance of which has not yet, in my view, been fully recognized. He describes the pressure–support paradox. The implementation of effective change, he argues, requires those whose responsibility it is, to be simultaneously supported and under pressure. The agents of change should be encouraged, consulted and invested in; their achievements should be celebrated and their commitment acknowledged. However, support alone is not enough. Agents of change, especially in education, are busy people; doing what they do already takes up all the hours God sent. Unless there is substantial pressure for change, as well as support, they are unlikely to give priority to implementing change which by its nature creates uncertainty, anxiety and yet more work, at least in the short term.

Like so many brilliant insights this is a blinding flash of the obvious. It helps to explain so much. One could for example summarize the history of education over the last forty years in terms of the pressure–support paradox. We had thirty years of support without pressure, then ten years of pressure without support. Now we need both.

For teachers to counter the pressure for change from central government by demanding support is to fall into a trap. Demanding support alone sounds self-interested, complacent and defensive. The effective critique examines the balance of pressure and support and the details of both sides of the paradox. It argues not for support in place of pressure but for a judicious mix of the two.

Since this lecture focuses on failure it inevitably discusses the pressure side of the paradox in more depth than support. This should not be taken to mean that support is not important. Consultation of teachers, celebration of success, steady investment in their professional development and in education as a whole are all important. For the purposes of this lecture I am assuming them.

With my back thus covered, at least a little, I want now to examine OFSTED's role, since it is clearly crucial to the pressure side of the paradox.

Responsibility for defining and identifying school failure rests, at national level, with the Office for Standards in Education. There is a local level of responsibility for identifying failure too, which lies with LEAs and is dealt with in the next section. OFSTED has, on the whole, had a bad press, at least among educators. There have been some problems with the inspection process and Her Majesty's Chief Inspector is inclined to be provocative.

Nevertheless, it has changed the educational landscape for the better. The framework for inspection has been welcomed by governors, headteachers and teachers and appears to be making a positive contribution to school improvement. The evidence suggests that in the period between the arrival of the [inspection] handbook and the call of the inspector, schools improve as a result of a process of more or less formal self-review. On the whole, inspections run smoothly, and post-inspection action plans promote further improvement though not of the same significance as that prior to inspection. 'Improvement before inspection' might be a better summary of OFSTED's impact than 'improvement through inspection'.

Some inspection reports suffer from an excess of blandness: there has been too much emphasis on paper policies and the extent of improvement following inspection is disappointing. Nevertheless the overall effect has been beneficial, certainly if the staff and governors of schools where inspection has already taken place are to be believed.

Whether the level of benefit is worth the investment in time, money and energy in the OFSTED process is another matter. A number of significant improvements could be made which would improve both the effectiveness and efficiency of the process particularly in relation to failure. Some important critiques of OFSTED's performance are now appearing, of which the most important is probably David Hargreaves' article in the *Cambridge Journal of Education* (Hargreaves, 1995). A number of themes emerge from these critiques. For example, if the self-evaluation prior to inspection is the most beneficial aspect of the process, it surely makes sense to enhance its status. The involvement of an external consultant in the process, appointed by the school, might be encouraged. The self-evaluation report might be published. Then the external inspection could for many schools simply be a check on the validity of the self-evaluation and on the schools' ability to improve itself. This form of external inspection would be lighter and cheaper.

A full scale inspection would only be necessary in three sets of circumstances: firstly, where there was variance between the self-evaluation findings and those of the check; secondly, where the school appeared to lack the potential to generate its own improvement; and thirdly, where available published data suggested the school might be providing an unacceptably low standard of education. The OFSTED database, building on recent work undertaken for it by the Institute of Education in London (Sammons, Thomas, Mortimore, Owen and Pennell, 1994), would already be adequate for making these decisions, though with time the performance data available will become more refined.

By thus reducing the number of full inspections required, sufficient national resources should become available for developing what might — ambiguously — be called a strategy for failure. Firstly, inspections of those schools which are subjected to full inspection could be more thorough than those available at present. This might make it possible to reach judgments on some of those antithetical characteristic factors described so vividly by David Reynolds. Secondly, more thought and time could be given to the process of developing a follow-up action plan. Schools could receive a limited one-off post-inspection payment to assist with their action planning and its implementation. Thirdly, follow-up inspections after six months, a year and eighteen months could be similarly thorough and focus specifically on the school's capacity for self-renewal. Fourthly, there could be investment in national research into the whole question of the nature and character of school failure and the range of strategies most likely to succeed in tackling it. This in turn would inform the process of developing follow-up action plans in failing or struggling schools.

With this kind of strategy in place a further reform of inspection would be necessary perhaps four years or so from now. The standards set out in the OFSTED framework, which define success, should be ratcheted up. Our tolerance of underperformance would be reduced. As David Hargreaves put it:

> OFSTED should identify and promote help for the worst schools, since only by progressively eliminating the worst schools — an endless task — can national standards and levels of achievement indisputably rise over a sustained period. (Hargreaves, 1995, p. 122)

Thus around the turn of the century or a little before we would raise our expectations of the school system as a whole. The cycle of identifying and tackling failure would then begin again in relation to the new higher standards. In short, we would have invented a Reading Recovery approach to school failure.

Avoiding Failure

The primary responsibility for promoting success and avoiding failure lies with the school. It is assumed for the purposes of the argument here that the vast majority of schools have both the will and the ability to drive their own improvement. However, their ability to do so can be greatly enhanced by a local authority, as many LEAs are demonstrating in practice.

There are numerous positive steps LEAs can take to promote school improvement and thus to reduce the likelihood of school failure. In the context of this lecture there is insufficient time to go into detail but a rapid sketch, drawing on recent evidence and real examples, can be attempted.

A good LEA provides local leadership. It promotes the importance of education in the community and builds up the confidence and status of those who work in the sector. Where possible it links education to other related services such as leisure and social services. It has a strategic development plan, perhaps stretching up to or into the twenty-first century. It has its own targets for pupil performance which relate to both rate of improvement and the absolute performance it hopes its citizens, young and old alike, will achieve. It uses its moral authority to create learning networks by linking the efforts of universities, Training and Enterprise Councils, employers, FE institutions and community organizations in relation to school improvement. Though none of these owes allegiance to the LEA, they tend to perceive its role in relation to school improvement as *primus inter pares*. In Brent, for example, the GM schools have been willing to work with the LEA for this purpose.

The good LEA is a source of excellent performance data for schools: value-added analyses which show not only how whole schools compare with other schools, but also break down figures by race, gender, age and, where appropriate, department; pupil and parent attitudinal data which explore other important educational outcomes such as peer group attitudes, pupil relationships and parental support; and financial data which shows how a school's resource allocation compares to that of other schools.

There are many other important responsibilities of LEAs in relation to, for example, special educational needs and admissions which are important and which I am aware of skating over. The central point of my argument here is that unless an LEA is successfully promoting school improvement, its contribution to dealing with school failure is likely to be contentious and lacking in credibility.

The LEA also has a clearly defined role in relation to failing schools. At this point, I want to highlight a significant weakness in the present arrangements.

At present the LEA can only intervene at all once a school has been designated as 'failing' [see, also, Whatford in this volume]. This means that some urban LEAs find themselves in the peculiar position of observing the decline of a sch has not yet been inspected or been found to be failing, while being u anything about it other than exhort the governors, who in some cases n of the problem. Whatever else the story of Kingsmead school in Hack.., it showed beyond doubt the weakness of an LEA in relation to a school where the governors support the headteacher.

On the whole the autonomy that schools have under the LMS arrangements has proved beneficial. Indeed I would argue that in some respects it might be extended. On the other hand, if in the occasional case, that autonomy turns out to be a licence to fail, then it is clearly problematic. For this reason I would propose that the general policy principle should be that *external intervention in a school's affairs should be in inverse proportion to its success*. This principle underpins the proposals in this lecture.

Where an LEA believes a school is underperforming it may embark on an inspection of the school. This kind of inspection, though useful for collecting evidence, has none of the statutory force of an OFSTED inspection. If an LEA does have evidence, on the basis, for example, of published performance data, parental complaints or an LEA inspection, that a school might be struggling, it is absurd — and an affront to the pupils — that intervention can only come after the next OFSTED inspection, which might be years away. In these circumstances, the LEA ought to be able to trigger an OFSTED inspection, provided it can make a convincing case based on objective evidence. In deciding whether the LEA's case was a good one, OFSTED should consider whether the LEA had offered clear improvement advice, founded in research, which the governors or the head had chosen to ignore. If this was the case a school would have to think carefully before rejecting advice. The power to trigger an inspection would thus provide the LEA with leverage which paradoxically would mean that it was used very rarely.

Tackling Failure

I want to look at tackling failure in two subsections: the first dealing with struggling schools, the second with failing schools.

Struggling Schools

If there are likely to be between 1,500 and 2,500 in the struggling category, there can be no realistic prospect of their receiving extensive additional resources to assist their improvement strategy, but four steps, currently not possible or only partially possible, could make an important contribution.

The first would be to provide the LEA with the power to trigger an inspection as described in the previous section. This could help to avoid struggling schools sliding into the failing category. Its main impact therefore would be prior to a timetabled inspection.

Secondly, the action plan for a struggling school, and the process of arriving at it, needs refinement. Though, under my definition of 'struggling' I have assumed the school has some potential for self-renewal, it is unlikely to be as effective in the action planning process as a better school, yet it needs an effective action plan all the more. There is, therefore, a case for a specific limited sum of money being made available to enable the school to buy expert advice, from the LEA or else-where, on the construction of its action plan.

The evidence suggests that an action plan needs to synthesize the generic research findings on school improvement with detailed knowledge and understanding of the school in question. Charles Teddlie, who is jointly responsible with Sam Stringfield, for the important Louisiana School Effectiveness Study, argues:

> An ineffective school did not get that way overnight. Each has a unique history. While the school leadership team will develop the goals for the improvement process, it may be . . . incapable of assessing the school culture and personal relationships to which Reynolds (1991) referred . . . The adaptation of generic school effects principles, together with information gleaned from contextually specific studies, to a particular situation will result in a plan unique to that school. (Teddlie, 1994, p. 6)

This suggests that while the school must have ownership of the action plan, the inputs of an outside expert and of OFSTED would be crucial. The question remains as to who should pay. The DfEE has suggested that LEAs, through GEST, might consider doing so, but the redirection of OFSTED's resources described earlier in this lecture might provide a more secure form of funding.

The research also suggests that action plans need to include a variety of success criteria. Clearly test and/or public examination results provide the most important source of data for success criteria, but the evidence suggests that they can take some time to shift significantly. It is therefore important that success criteria based on other data such as student and teacher attitudes, and truancy figures and other changes in behaviour, ought also to be included (Reynolds, 1995). The key is to measure improvement and to ensure some early evidence of progress, which can help build confidence and create an upward spiral.

The third necessary step is to arrive at a formal post-inspection procedure for dealing with the sensitive issue of failing teachers and, in some cases, failing headteachers. The evidence of inspections to date suggests that in a substantial number of cases a school's underperformance may be attributed to a small number of poor teachers. As David Hargreaves argued in his DEMOS pamphlet:

> The departure of incompetent heads, who sell their teachers short, and incompetent classroom teachers, who sell students short, would probably make the single most important contribution to raising standards . . . (1994, p. 25)

 The evidence at present suggests that following some OFSTED inspections, headteachers and teachers are taking early retirement or leaving their posts for other reasons. Some of those leaving are, however, perfectly good teacher, teachers who have succumbed to the pressure of inspection, and whose a major loss, not a gain. There ought to be a fairer process than this. It mi, for example, the inspection team giving a confidential report to the I where they had concerns about the performance of specific individuals. their word would not be taken at face value, but their report might begin a formal competency procedure which would end in a return visit some months later, at which clear decisions should be taken. In schools where management was aware of differences in teachers' performance and followed up any concerns as part of their day-to-day role, a post-inspection procedure of this kind would hardly be necessary, but in struggling schools this pattern of management may not be fully in place.

Tim Brighouse and Bob Moon are due shortly to put forward much more thoroughly worked-through proposals than has been possible here. They need to be given serious consideration.

Fourthly, it is important that there are follow-up inspections at regular intervals in struggling schools. These can either provide the external validation of improvement which is so important to building confidence, or, where progress has not been made, ensure that the strategy is reconsidered. To ensure that all struggling schools receive thorough, effective follow-up would be another benefit of the redirection of OFSTED's resources suggested earlier.

Failing Schools

Our definition of a failing school assumes that it has a very limited capacity for self-renewal. By definition, therefore, the fate of a school in these circumstances — 'in need of special measures' in government jargon — is to a large extent in the hands of external agencies in the early stages after an inspection.

Once a school has been found by OFSTED to be failing, it must, like any school after an inspection, produce an action plan. The LEA then has ten days to produce its commentary on that plan. This must specify whether the LEA intends to use its powers to appoint additional governors or to suspend the school's delegated budget. It should also set out the LEA's views of the school's action plan and whether it intends to provide additional resources to support the turn-round process. Alternatively the LEA may take this opportunity to decide to close a school under the normal statutory procedures. As Gray and Wilcox (1994) have pointed out, 'we are very reluctant in Britain to close schools down; it also happens to be rather difficult to do this' (p. 253).

However, this reluctance may be beginning to change. David Blunkett's recent speech to the Association of Teachers and Lecturers conference put school closure back in the headlines. His speech certainly gave notice of New Labour's determination to drive for higher standards and to take school failure seriously, but what he said about closure — as opposed to 'fresh start' — is an affirmation of what is in fact already happening. A significant proportion of those schools that have been identified as failing are already being closed. Six out of the first batch of fifteen are in this category, including a number in London. The proportion of failing schools that are eventually closed will ultimately be smaller than this since the early round of inspection included a number of well-known cases of persistent failure but, where there are alternative school places available, it is certainly an option worth considering. For the pupils it may be the best option. More likely, in most cases, will be the construction of an action plan designed to improve the school. Here the points made about struggling schools apply too.

The difference in the case of a failing school is that the input from outside needs to be significantly greater. The threat of closure or the power to establish an education association are important levers in ensuring sufficient pressure for change. For this reason the fact that the power to establish an education association has not been used, should not be seen as an argument against the government having it as an option. On the contrary, it is evidence of the care and sensitivity with which the DfEE, to date, has approached the issue. The power provides leverage over the school and over the relevant LEA. This may seem a harsh view particularly since a number of LEAs, such as Hammersmith and Fulham, have led the way in constructively addressing failure [see Whatford's chapter]. However, there may be cases where the LEA is so heavily implicated in a given school failure, that it could not easily achieve sufficient distance from the school or its own errors. The pressure the DfEE can apply in these circumstances is important. The early evidence suggests that in a number of cases this balance of responsibilities is leading to more or less cooperative action for improvement involving the school, the LEA, OFSTED and the DfEE. Some of those schools originally identified as failing have made sufficient progress to 'come off the list'. Others are moving towards this more cheerful state of affairs. In each of these cases it is a tribute to the efforts of the various agencies, but above all to the staff in the schools who have led the improvement process. There is a fascinating story to tell about the school level micropolitics of turning round a failing school, but that is for another occasion.

Certainly the balance of pressure and support has been the decisive factor in these successes. It may be that in the case of failing schools a limited amount of additional funding beyond that for the action plan would provide a further catalyst for improvement in some circumstances. It might, for example, pay for some visible one-off improvement in facilities or equipment, or for temporary additional staffing for a specific purpose. However, any such funding should be integrally related to the overall action plan and time limit, with a clear explanation of how the school would continue its improvement without any additional funding. Any suggestion of rewarding failure needs to be avoided.

Even if action plans prove to be effective in general, there will be some failing schools that remain impervious to any improvement strategy for whatever reason. They are likely to be schools that have to a high degree the 'failure characteristics' and the characteristics 'antithetical' to effectiveness which Kate Myers and David Reynolds has described.

At present we have no experience of this situation in the 1990s context and the policy framework may not be prepared for it, but it will happen and, in terms of imagining an end to failure, it is important. Above all, it is important because the pupils at such schools would still be receiving an inadequate education as they would have done, by the time this situation was reached, for several years. Time would be of the essence and something would have to be done.

One option would be for the government to use its powers under the 1993 Education Act to set up an education association. This might be the appropriate response if the school's failure to improve since its inspection had been primarily the responsibility of the LEA, for LEAs are the primary victims of the education association arrangements. It may be important for central government to have the power to act in these circumstances but they are likely to be highly unusual.

Though formally the post-inspection strategy would have been the responsibility of the school and the LEA, in practice OFSTED and the Department of Education would have been involved too. The post-inspection strategies of failing schools to date have in practice been developed through a process of negotiation involving the school, the LEA and the national agencies. In some cases these strategies have worked. But if they have not worked, what will an education association be able to do that has not been done already? The answer is, unless it could command significant extra resources and personnel powers, not much.

If the education association option is unlikely to work, the only other option currently available is closure. But as an option in these circumstances it has limitations. It is a slow and cumbersome process. Due process and the rights of staff and community to consultation are important but the uncertainty is damaging to the school and there ought to be extreme concern, by this stage, for the entitlement of the young people to a satisfactory education. It might therefore be necessary to provide for a more streamlined process for closure and dispersal in these very specific circumstances.

But this is not the only problem. What if there is a clear need for school places in that area? What if, as a result of the dispersal of the pupils, some would have to make long or inconvenient journeys across many late twentieth-century inner-cities? What if they are on an outer rim estate cut off from the rest of the world? If, as is likely, truancy is already rife and the experience of school for most of the young people has been less than inspiring, would they be likely to make those tortuous journeys? Or would they be more likely to swell the ranks of 'the disappeared', those young people who no longer attend school at all and vanish from the social statistics until they reappear, if they ever do, in the crime statistics?

The idea of a 'fresh start', floated by David Blunkett at the ATL conference, would surely be worth considering in these specific circumstances. The school would be closed by the LEA (with the approval of the DFE) and a new school opened on the same site. Careful attention would need to be given to the transition phase but the fact that this would need to be done quickly, perhaps over an extended summer break, is an advantage, not a disadvantage. Any deficit accumulated by the old school would be written off, thus providing the new school with a financial clean slate.

The change would need to be more than cosmetic. A name change and a few computers would probably not be enough. It would need to be a new school with a new governing body. The professional leadership would need to be of the highest calibre. It would need to draw on the latest research and use innovative approaches to teaching and learning. All its staff would need to be newly appointed though, of course, staff from the closed school would be entitled to apply. Above all it would need some additional revenue funding in order to attract highly qualified and committed applicants for posts in what might inevitably be a risky venture. For its first year, the school would also need to draw on a 'critical friend', a person expert in the process of school improvement, who would be a source of advice, ideas, affirmation and constructive criticism. The project would need to be perceived by the newly appointed staff, the pupils and the local community as an ambitious, exciting, innovative and bold attempt to create success in difficult circumstances.

The idea needs further refinement, thought and debate, but as the final step in a national policy to bring an end to failure it seems to me to have considerable potential. Certainly, the 'fresh start' idea and (no doubt much else) that has been discussed in this lecture will be controversial. The problem for its critics, at least to date, is that they provide no serious alternative. In other words, by implication at least, they are prepared to tolerate continuing failure. They see it as inevitable. On the brink of the twenty-first century, this seems to me to be unacceptable.

The End of Failure

I have a sense of emerging into the sunlight after a long and difficult journey through the shadows. I want to conclude by emphasizing that my chief aim in this lecture is to be positive. The issues of educational policy in the 1990s are riddled with paradox, the question of failure more than most. Let me add to them.

It is only because of the growing evidence of success that it is possible now to give serious thought to the question of failure. Conversely by imagining what it would take to deal with failure, we can encourage success. A policy which is thorough in its approach to failure, will make failure less likely. For these reasons the shallow, false dichotomy that we should focus on promoting success, not tackling failure, should be unmasked. A policy for tacking failure is a necessary element of any credible strategy designed to promote successful schools for all.

By working steadily to deal with failure wherever it occurs, and by ratcheting up expectations over a period of time, failure as defined today can be reduced, and ultimately eliminated. There is evidence in many urban areas of schools and LEAs dedicating themselves to improvement against previous performance and to promoting effectiveness. More schools than ever in urban areas are implementing successful improvement strategies. More LEAs than ever are recognizing, and exploiting, the wealth of opportunities open to them for promoting improvement. More teachers than ever, and their leaders, are recognizing that school improvement is the only issue of substance on the agenda. The debates about funding and class sizes are subsets of a much wider debate about quality.

Central government — in spite of this year's hopefully temporary abdication of responsibility on funding — is demonstrating an increasing understanding of the school improvement issue as the performance of the DFE's School Effectiveness

Division shows. The Labour Party, through its formidable education spokesperson, has demonstrated both its grasp of the issues and its determination to raise standards and expectations especially in urban areas.

There are therefore many grounds for optimism. It ought to be possible to put the destructive bitterness of the early 1990s behind us. An open, serious, professional debate about failure is now possible. It can contribute to overthrowing the nineteenth-century cultural attitudes which have dogged British education in the twentieth century. Perhaps as a result we can end, or virtually end, failure, in the twenty-first century and ensure that all pupils receive the quality of education, to which they are entitled. The first step is to throw a steady beam of light on the dark side of the moon.

May 1995

Second Thoughts

When I wrote this TES–Greenwich lecture, which was originally delivered in May 1995, I knew it would be controversial. School failure was not something that people talked about. There had been the occasional piece of research on the subject — David Reynolds had written about it for example — but generally the research had sought out successful schools and identified their characteristics.

Three things prompted me to take up the theme of failure. The first was the direct experience of inner London education I had had as Chair of Education in Hackney. I had seen during that time the heroic efforts of some schools in difficult circumstances to provide a good education for their pupils and, at the other end of the scale, the sacrifice, in a handful of schools, of children's interests to those of teachers. The primacy of teachers' interest in these cases was dressed up in a sub-Marxist language which purported to promote equal opportunities but in fact patronized young people by justifying their underperformance.

The second was the government's 1993 legislation on school failure which was just beginning to impact on the system. As a union official at the time I had been unimpressed with much of the interminable 1993 Education Act, but I had always been a strong supporter of the new powers it gave ministers to take over failing schools. In fact, I had advocated precisely this in a book published in 1992, but no-one had noticed.

The third was a chance conversation with a friend in the early weeks of 1995 when I was just beginning to think about my TES–Greenwich lecture. I asked this friend, as a strategic management consultant, what he thought would make a good theme, and he said simply, 'Could you design a policy under which there were no more failing schools?' In the lecture I tried to do just that.

In the course of writing it, a very obvious thought occurred to me: that those of us who work in education are wedded to all sorts of phrases which we use but don't mean. We love to talk about 'success for all' but all too often it is no more than warm words. If we mean it we have no choice but to seek to eliminate failure. The truth is that 'success for all' and 'zero tolerance of failure' are synonymous.

Looking back at the text I can see weaknesses. The OFSTED inspection system, as Chris Woodhead himself has admitted, has some way to go before we can have complete confidence in the objectivity of inspectors, who are still too likely to give the benefit of the doubt to schools that are seriously underperforming. My lecture is inadequate in failing to provide an analysis of the impact of school management. Some of the schools that have recovered from failure most rapidly are those where all that was required was a change of headteacher, whereas implicit in parts of my lecture is an assumption that the whole school must take responsibility for what in some cases is no more than a failure over leadership. Broadly, however, I stand by the analysis and the conclusions I reached.

The TES–Greenwich lecture made a greater impact than I had anticipated. This was partly because at Easter that year David Blunkett was unpardonably jostled by a group of left-wing activists at the NUT Conference after he had advocated closing and re-opening failing schools, giving them what he called 'a fresh start'. It was also because I was the first to calculate what number of schools would be likely to fail by the time OFSTED completed its four-year inspection cycle. The estimates have proved to be accurate. Moreover, the government policy on school failure, for which this lecture provided critical support for the first time from within the education establishment, has proved to be a tremendous success.

A number of consequences flowed from the lecture. For me personally the most significant was that I was offered, when it came up, the poisoned chalice of joining the Hackney Downs Education Association or 'hit squad' as the press preferred to call it. Our eventual decision to close the school was highly controversial and may never be forgiven in some quarters but I had no doubt at the time that it was right and events since then have borne out our judgment. The boys, now at Homerton House school, are thriving. Only those who put the interests of the staff ahead of the pupils can dispute our conclusions. Even they would have to recognize that the staff are better off too out of a school which had such a poisoned inheritance, that saving it would have been beyond even an army of saints.

Following the lecture, but not necessarily a consequence of it, politicians of all parties firmed up their stance on school failure. Overall this was in my view a positive development. It had, however, a dark side and if my lecture contributed to that, it is my chief regret about it. For a year the focus of political and media debate was on underperformance. At times the politicians seemed to vie with each other in a scramble to identify failure and advocate new, tough means of eradicating it. Caught in this gale of criticism, the teaching profession became demoralized. Its leaders proved unable, in the deafening roar, to point out the very real achievements of schools. Fortunately the climate is shifting back again now but it has taken its toll.

There are three lessons to learn from this experience. One is that educational success is now seen across society as so important that failure, where it occurs, will remain a legitimate part of public debate. The second is that we, who work in education, need to understand that only by acknowledging failure can we expect the genuine success of the majority to be recognized. Put another way, pretending that failure does not occur is an unsustainable position which damages the whole profession. Thirdly, the profession itself needs to put forward proposals for addressing underperformance because the only alternative is that someone else will. There are real opportunities ahead for the education service, which I believe is emerging from a difficult few years stronger, wiser and more assertive than it was.

Note

1 *The TES–Greenwich Education Lecture 1995 given at Woolwich Town Hall, London on Thursday May 11 1995.*

References

BALL, S. (1990) *Reforming Education and Changing Schools*, London: Routledge.

FULLAN, M. (1991) *The New Meaning of Educational Change*, London: Cassell.

GRAY, J. and WILCOX, B. (1994) 'The Challenge of Turning Round Ineffective Schools', Unpublished paper for ESRC Seminar Series on School Effectiveness and School Improvement. (Subsequently published in GRAY, J. and WILCOX, B. (eds) (1995) *Good School, Bad School: Evaluating Performance and Encouraging Improvement*, Buckingham: Open University Press.)

HARGREAVES, D. (1994) *The Mosaic of Learning: Schools and Teachers for the Next Century*, London: Demos.

HARGREAVES, D. (1995) 'Inspection and school improvement', *Cambridge Journal of Education*, **25**, 1, pp. 115–23.

MORTIMORE, P. (1991) 'The nature and findings of research on school effectiveness in the primary sector', in RIDDELL, S. and BROWN, S. (eds) *School Effectiveness Research: Its Messages for School Improvement*, Edinburgh: HMSO.

MORTIMORE, P. (1992) 'Bucking the Trends: Promoting Successful Urban Education', TES–Greenwich Lecture.

MYERS, K. (1994) 'Why Schools in Difficult may Find the Research on School Effectiveness and School Improvement Inappropriate for their Needs', Unpublished assignment for Doctorate of Education course, University of Bristol.

REYNOLDS, D. (1991) 'Changing ineffective schools', in AINSCOW, M. (ed.) *Effective Schools for All*, London: David Fulton.

REYNOLDS, D. (1995) 'The Problem of the Ineffective School: Some Evidence and Some Speculations', Unpublished paper for ESRC Seminar Series on School Effectiveness and School Improvement (Subsequently published in GRAY, J., REYNOLDS, D., FITZ-GIBBON, C. and JESSON, D. (eds) (1996) *Merging Traditions: The Future of Research on School Effectiveness and School Improvement*, London: Cassell.)

SAMMONS, P., THOMAS, S., MORTIMORE, P., OWEN, C. and PENNELL, H. (1994) *Assessing School Effectiveness: Developing Measures to Put School Performance in Context*, London: OFSTED and Institute of Education.

STRINGFIELD, S. and HERMAN, B. (1994) 'Observations of Partial Implementations of the Coalition of Essential Schools: The Need for Higher Reliability Organizational Methods', Paper presented at the Annual Meeting of the American Educational Research Association, New Orleans.

TEDDLIE, C. (1994) 'The Louisiana School Effectiveness Study: Research Results and Implications for School Improvement', Unpublished Research Seminar Paper, University of Newcastle.

Chapter 3

No Slow Fixes Either: How Failing Schools in England are Being Restored to Health

Michael Stark

Introduction

The strategy adopted in Britain over recent years for raising the standards of pupil performance is unique among developed countries in two ways. First, it identifies the *school* — rather than the nation, or the individual pupil — as the level at which large-scale and lasting improvement is most likely to be achieved. The strategy seeks, therefore, to enhance the capacity of the school to improve the quality of its own teaching and learning, by effective management planning within a regular cycle of review. Second, however, it accepts that at any moment a small proportion of schools are failing to provide an acceptable standard of education, and are incapable of spontaneous self-improvement. The strategy, therefore, provides (most explicitly in England and Wales, but implicitly also in the rest of the UK) for special measures to assist the process in those schools.

Inevitably, public attention has focused on this small proportion of schools that, in the words of the Education Act 1993, are 'failing to provide an acceptable standard of education': an adverse inspection report on a particular institution provides a dramatic story. But in fact there is much good news arising from intervention in these schools. This chapter reviews the first three years of the 'special measures' regime inaugurated by that Act.

Special Measures

The special measures arrangements, which will be familiar to most readers, form part of a wider, comprehensive strategy for the improvement of all schools in England and Wales. Every publicly funded school is regularly inspected, in the first instance within a four-year cycle, and its report published. Inspectors identify failing (and in future seriously weak) schools in the report. The governors of *every* inspected school must produce an action plan; but at a failing school the plan has to be submitted to the Secretary of State, with a parallel statement from the Local Education Authority (LEA) — and, if a church school, the diocese — commenting on the governors' plan, and explaining what help will be offered to turn the school around. The Secretary of State can either transfer the school to the control of an Education Association (a group of appointed commissioners) or leave the school and LEA to implement the plan, sometimes after requesting revisions or amendments.

When these arrangements came into effect in 1993, the general attitude of schools and LEAs was hostile. It was asserted that (a) publicly identifying failing schools would damage them, not improve them; (b) improving such a school could only be done over many years; and (c) the government would be tempted to intervene often, and usually without success. Three years on, these fears have been largely dispelled. To take them in turn.

Does Public Identification of Failure Prevent Recovery?

The announcement that a school is failing is always traumatic for its staff, worrying for its parents and unsettling for its pupils. But by January 1997, well over 250 schools had been through this shock. OFSTED and DfEE, having worked closely with each school, are perhaps best placed to reach an overall judgment. It is our joint conclusion that the public identification of unacceptable standards tends to speed rather than delay recovery, and indeed is often a precondition for it.

As academic commentators have pointed out, the characteristics of a grossly ineffective school are not just the inverse of the characteristics of an effective one: there is usually at their core some serious breakdown in leadership, relationships or ethos. Such dysfunctions have to be put right before any of the normal school improvement techniques will work, and often a public declaration of failure is a prerequisite for that action. Several case studies of schools that have come out of special measures, recently carried out for the DfEE, indicate that this was the moment at which key people involved with the school themselves recognized the need for urgent action, and began to see this as an opportunity rather than a threat.

Is Improvement Necessarily Slow?

By initiating the policy, Ministers stated a general target of two years within which time a failing school should be: restored to health; making substantial progress towards leaving special measures; or, in some cases, heading for closure. Events have proved this to be a realistic aim. Schools under special measures tend either to move quickly towards closure, or to improve quite rapidly.

At the end of 1996, of the ninety schools whose progress had been monitored by revisits from OFSTED, seventy-seven (86 per cent) had been identified as making good progress — sometimes impressively good — of which fourteen (16 per cent) had been declared by HMCI to be no longer failing. Some twelve schools had closed and others were moving towards closure; this too may be counted a success where the pupils are able to transfer to better schools within suitable reach. There remained a group of ten or so secondary schools in London and other cities where progress was notably slower: but even here there was evidence of some improve-ment. No school had got worse across the board than at the time of inspection.

By the same date, fourteen schools had been declared by HMCI to be once again providing an acceptable level of education: two secondary, eleven primary and one special. Of these, thirteen were returned to health within two years, and one had taken twenty-seven months. The progress of other schools revisited by OFSTED suggested that most primary schools would take between fifteen and twenty-four months, with some recovering faster, and a few taking perhaps up to thirty months. The limited evidence there is so far on the recovery of special schools suggests that they recover on much the same timescale [see Pugh's chapter in this volume]. The recovery of secondary schools might take just a few months longer: OFSTED revisits suggested that on average they are likely to leave special measures after between twenty-four and thirty months. Again, some will be faster (Northicote Secondary recovered in sixteen months) and a very few with unusually deeply rooted problems may take up to three years.

It should be noted that we are talking here of a return to competence, rather than the achievement of excellence. As our experience increases, it seems likely that school recovery and school improvement are two different processes requiring often rather different kinds of change. The emergency measures needed to turn around a failing school seem to differ from the measures that a good school might take to improve itself further.

A medical analogy may be helpful. The treatment that a sick person needs to recover is different from the regime that will make an ordinary person fit. Indeed, a fitness regime imposed on invalids may make them worse. The same seems to apply to schools; competence must precede excellence. One LEA reacted to the failure of a secondary school with a programme to create instant excellence: curricular specialization, a selective intake, a longer school day, and other ambi-tious measures. It did not work, because the basic infrastructure of the school, including its leadership, was not sound and could not cope with the strain. The school has now reverted to a more conventional pattern, concentrating on getting the basics right.

Three Stages to Transformation

Our experience suggests that there are broadly three stages to the transformation of a failing school. The first is acknowledging failure: facing up to the problems, taking charge of the situation, preparing a sound action plan for recovery and establishing commitment. This will typically take about three months. The second stage is to implement the action plan to re-establish the basic competencies of the school: restore leadership, institute sound management, and improve standards of teaching and learning. This period, typically eighteen months to two years (but longer in particularly problematic cases) corresponds to the government's rule of thumb for schools' progression out of special measures. Only then can the school embark on the third stage, progression towards excellence.

Attitudes Towards Failure

With three years' experience it is striking how far attitudes towards school failure have changed. In this country it is now much more generally accepted, not just that pupils come first and are entitled to achieve, but also that there are objective measures which go a long way towards defining what constitutes an acceptable level of achievement. The capacity to compare pupils' performance against a common baseline of National Curriculum assessment and national examinations takes us close to the point at which we can measure progress consistently between each different stage of the performance of the national cohort, and hence compare the performance of the children with the same prior attainment at different schools. This has thrown the disparity of performance between schools with similar intakes into much sharper relief.

Meanwhile the universal inspection of schools to a common set of criteria, and the special measures policy itself, have helped shift opinion, by proving that substantial improvements can be made at even the weakest schools. The recovery of failing schools after decades of weakness has brought new hope to other schools in like circumstances. It has fostered, too, a welcome interest in the much larger category of schools that, though not failing, have serious weaknesses which prevent an entirely independent regeneration. A good example is Lambeth. Early in 1996, HMCI (Her Majesty's Chief Inspector) announced that he was sufficiently worried by the picture uncovered by inspections to accelerate the inspection of all remaining schools in the borough (the same was also done for Waltham Forest) [see chapter by Watling, Hopkins, Harris and Beresford in this book]. The emerging findings revealed a fascinating diversity of quality within a small borough. By the end of the school year 1995–96, seven failing schools had been announced (most are now making good progress). But alongside them the inspectors had found a wide range of schools: some weak, some sound and at least four of high quality. This was not because schools in the leafy suburban parts of the borough were all doing better than those with disadvantaged intakes. An example highlighted in HMCI's Annual Report for 1995 was Sudbourne Primary in central Brixton, with a high proportion of pupils from deprived backgrounds and starting from a low educational baseline. The inspectors found 'committed, devoted staff' led by 'a calm and greatly admired headteacher'. Despite what the inspectors described as 'daunting difficulties' — including three staff on long-term sick leave — teaching was sound and standards were good. Sudbourne is by no means an isolated case, either in Lambeth or in England.

Is Frequent Government Intervention Inevitable?

As the previous sections demonstrate, the pattern has been one of steady and often rapid improvement under special measures. It has been achieved through much pain and effort and has often required injections of new leadership and resources, but it has generally been within the existing legal and funding control, whether county, voluntary or GM. As a consequence, the government has so far only twice needed to intervene directly: at Hackney Downs and Stratford schools.

Hackney LEA decided to close Hackney Downs (a boys' secondary school) when a very critical OFSTED report judged it to be failing. In anticipation of closure, admission of new pupils stopped and numbers fell to a low level, physical maintenance ceased and the school ran down. A month before it was due to close, the authority, in the face of a local campaign, reversed the decision. The school was by that stage in a very poor state, and the Secretary of State decided to place it under the control of an Education Association, with a remit to report rapidly on its viability. The report advised that the school was not viable on financial, management, educational or planning grounds, and it closed in December 1995 [see also Barber in this volume]. A legal challenge was rejected by the Divisional Court and, subsequently, by the Court of Appeal. Arrangements were made for pupils to transfer to a neighbouring, improving school with spare places.

At Stratford GM School the Secretary of State used her parallel powers in May 1995 to remodel the governing body and appoint five additional governors. Subsequently the school improved markedly, and it came off special measures in December 1995.

Ministers have considered intervention in a number of other cases but so far they have been content to allow the schools to proceed with their action plans, with the help of their LEA, diocese and other interested parties. The general improvement of schools under special measures described above appears to justify this approach. However, Ministers retain the power to intervene when the best interests of the pupils, in all the circumstances, warrant it.

So the government's role has been much more one of encouraging the existing parties both within and outside the school to take responsibility for radical and urgent improvement, but not to attempt to do the job for them.

Raising Expectations

At one of the public consultation meetings organized by the North East London Education Association, a teacher at Hackney Downs School stated an opinion which, quoted in the Education Association report (1995), encapsulated the negative attitudes of several decades:

> It is all very well talking about educational quality, but this is a working class area.
> (p. 22)

Happily this approach, which blames educational failure on the children and parents rather than on the school, has been largely overtaken by the belief that it is for schools to achieve the best results of which their pupils are capable. Expectation, expressed both as absolute levels for achievement and as progress (or 'value-added'), have risen sharply. The evidence available to OFSTED and the DfEE suggests that expectations are rising particularly rapidly in schools under special measures.

The Quality of Teaching

A key element in the recovery of a failing school is a rapid improvement in the quality of teaching. The typical pattern is that a small number of staff leave and the competence of those who remain is raised by targeted teacher training. Of those who leave, some go of their own volition, and some accept early retirement, usually arranged in conjunction with the LEA. But only in around 20 per cent of cases have formal competence proceedings been instituted. It seems to be a common belief amongst headteachers and LEA staff that competence proceedings are long, drawn out, and damage staff morale. This is not altogether true. If competency proceedings are carefully prepared and agreed procedures properly adhered to, matters can be expedited quite swiftly — unless members of staff go off on long-term sick leave, which is becoming quite a common phenomenon. Second, anecdotal evidence suggests that capable staff are not necessarily resentful when capability proceedings are initiated against less competent colleagues whose burden they have been carrying.

However, there is a limit to the number of staff that it is possible and desirable to remove. All experience so far shows that intensive teacher training supplemented by classroom monitoring will lead to substantial improvements in the quality of education in schools under special measures. Here again, LEAs' advice and training expertise can be very helpful. But the crucial factor is the attitude of the staff: if they are not committed to the change the training is designed to effect, the school will not improve.

The recovery of a school depends above all on the quality of the teaching; and all the evidence from schools monitored shows that this can improve substantially, in all types of school, within eighteen months to two years. Those who suggested that schools would take many years just to reach a position of competence seriously under-estimated the professional abilities of teachers.

Leadership: Headteachers

The 1993–96 experience of special measures confirms the belief strongly supported by academic research: the leadership provided by the headteacher is crucial to the success of a school. In just over half of cases thus far, the head has changed within a term or two before (25 per cent) or after (75 per cent) the school's failure. In some of these cases, as well as in the case of other schools which did not fail, the 'new broom' head was appointed in the run-up to an inspection in the hope of turning the school around. In a substantial number of cases, a headteacher who has been at the school for some years has remained at the helm. Some of these have moved on a year or two later. Others have stayed with the school and led it to substantial improvement — in several cases, actually leading it off special measures.

It would be wrong to pillory all the departing heads as incapable; analysis shows many reasons why their leadership may have faltered. Some newly promoted appointees found themselves ill-suited to a particular school. Some failed to adjust to the different demands of their pupils or qualities of their staff. Some longer-serving heads failed to adapt to new demands, for example, the National

Curriculum, LMS or other changes. Some were struggling bravely with serious illness or domestic difficulties. Some had just run out of energy. Whatever the cause, experience shows that an inadequate head will not cope well with the extra demands of a failing school.

All heads, existing or new, who have led their schools to improvement and/or recovery have demonstrated a key set of skills. These can be characterized as:

- *strategic skills*: formulating (or helping governors to formulate) an overall vision for the future of the school: and within it, identifying strategic targets and prioritizing between them;
- *monitoring skills*: keeping tabs on the crucial points where improvement is needed, including classroom observation of colleagues' teaching as a constructive rather than oppressive technique;
- *collegiate skills*: enabling the governors to work as a cohesive, focused unit; creating a sense of common purpose and identity amongst teaching colleagues. This includes the crucial trait of being 'approachable';
- *staff management skills*: including gaining the cooperation and respect of colleagues, and if necessary taking and implementing tough decisions about early retirement and competency proceedings;
- *staff development skills*: planning the personal development of other teachers to give them the skills they need to raise standards;
- *resource management skills*: relating limited means (financial and staffing) to strategic ends, and matching the priorities, and ensuring proper resource control; and
- *ambassadorial skills*: representing the school's interests to the LEA, diocese, or other body, and negotiating their support; and more widely, presenting its public face to parents and the local community (particularly to local newspapers) to regenerate public confidence.

Charismatic, dynamic and inspirational personalities are scarce in any walk of life, but already several have emerged at failing schools: usually in inner-city secondaries needing major injections of new morale. Such heads have succeeded impressively, but the experience so far confirms that charisma on its own is neither necessary (because capable leadership generates a magnetic field of its own) nor sufficient (because vision has to be translated into effective systems which the whole school operates consistently).

Much the same was observed by the editors of *Success Against The Odds*, a study of eleven successful schools in disadvantaged areas (National Commission on Education, 1995):

> The word 'understated' is used [in the case studies] much more frequently than the word 'charismatic'. Headteachers use quiet encouragement to persuade everyone in the school to share ownership of the vision . . . there is a clear sense in which the headteachers have an impact by setting an example to the rest of the school, providing powerful role models. (pp. 339–40)

Given the observation above that failing schools tend to be dysfunctional and so different from other schools, it might have been thought that some more animated, dynamic approach might be needed here. But experience of the ninety failing schools so far monitored by OFSTED suggests that this is not so: the calmer, organizational approach works in both contexts, and the catalogue of successful leadership characteristics outlined by the National Commission (1995) — excellent judgment, an 'omnipresent' personal style, shared leadership, building a team, and team development — is the same for both types of school.

Leadership: Governing Bodies

The evidence shows that governing bodies at failing schools are often weak. In some cases the senior management have exploited the weakness to keep them away from too active involvement. The declaration that the school is failing often has a galvanizing effect on them. It is quite common for the chairmanship of the governing body to change. In around half of cases, authorities or dioceses have used their powers to strengthen the governing bodies by appointing additional governors.

Meanwhile the inspection report will have provided the governors, usually for the first time, with a full audit of the school's activities, highlighting strengths and weaknesses. Many governing bodies have found it a powerful tool for grappling with a strategic role, especially at schools where the head, for whatever reason, has previously shut them out. Governors at some failing schools have told the DfEE and OFSTED that, after the initial shock of discovery, they found the outcome of the inspection process helpful and liberating.

Governing bodies often feel unqualified to get involved in the most crucial area for their school's recovery: classroom teaching. Lay governors who show this awareness of their limitations are only being realistic, although the appointment of former headteachers to governing bodies of failing schools is quite common and usually a great benefit.

Nonetheless, there are three particular ways in which governors can usefully get involved in turning around a failing school. The first is in *preparing the action plan*: while all governing bodies rely heavily on the head and LEA advisers in preparing this, there is often a high level of governor involvement as well. Second, in many cases governors are involved in the *appointment of new staff*, often a new headteacher; and occasionally, as an unwelcome prelude to this, they are involved in formal competency proceedings. Third, governors have played a particularly useful role in *monitoring* the implementation of the action plan and *evaluating* the outcomes. To all of these roles the governors can bring the perspective which a governing body should always bring to a school: the view of the friendly outsider and sympathetic critic.

In a few cases, LEAs have used very extensively their powers to appoint additional governors: inner London, in particular, has seen several examples of a mass transfusion of new blood into the governing body, by the recruitment of a new cadre of governors with impressive experience. In one case, the Director of

Education described the new phalanx of governors appointed as a 'mini-education association'.

The Role of LEAs

In this and other ways, the role of LEAs is being redefined. The nature and ethos of local authority and inspection and advisory services have been profoundly altered by the need to adapt to OFSTED's Framework of Inspection. The ethos and dynamics of the system have changed: there could not now be a return to the sort of relationship between schools and LEA advisers that existed in the 1980s.

Beyond this, however, a new two-fold role is developing for LEAs, in setting targets and supporting improved teaching and learning. First, in all the schools they have a responsibility for encouraging the setting of standards. Each school must take primary responsibility for its own performance, but good LEAs are helping schools to do this more effectively. This includes helping schools to use 'benchmark' performance data, and to set challenging targets built into a systematic planning and improvement cycle.

Second, in the specific case of failing schools, they have played a key role over the past three years in providing intensive support. This has often been crucial to the recovery of schools, particularly in the early stages, when the school has lost the capacity to regenerate itself. Most LEAs have shown that they are aware of the risk of schools becoming dependent on this support, and their action plans seem generally to envisage the gradual diminution of support to failing schools, after the initial intensive phase. Failing schools have usually lost their capacity to renew themselves, and after the first shock of failure, the core purpose of the renewal of leadership and preparation of an action plan is to rebuild the school's capacity to regenerate itself.

Conclusion

The experience in England and Wales is unusual because it combines systematic inspection of schools with a thorough regime of improvement and possible intervention. Radical experiments have been undertaken in other countries — including in certain school districts in the USA — but in the absence of a system of inspection of the processes as well as the outcomes of teaching, large-scale intervention in weak schools is less easily undertaken. This is a growing area of international concern, reflected in the programme of study the Organisation for Economic Cooperation and Development (OECD) has under way on 'combating failure at school' [see Kovacs in this volume], and the decision of the Republic of Ireland to make failure at school one of the twin themes of their six-month presidency of the European Union in the second half of 1996. An international seminar co-hosted in 1995 by the Institute of Education, OFSTED, the TTA, and the DfEE, under the auspices of the OECD, showed that overseas countries are very interested in the

British experience; many are beginning to take tentative steps down the same path, and there is a growing tendency for industrialized countries to hold schools to account for their performance.

The work in this country has been undertaken in close collaboration between agencies. The working relationships between schools, LEAs and dioceses at the local level are reflected at a national level by the work of the DfEE-led consultative group on improving schools, which brings together representatives of academic life, LEAs, headteachers and commerce to advise on the shaping of this policy. The DfEE has made a point of gathering the opinions of those with practical experience of special measures, including several seminars for schools under special measures and a conference hosted by the Institute of Education in 1996. There is also a close and developing relationship with the academic world, who have generally proved very constructive in their criticism and analysis, of which this book is an encouraging example.

In summary, most schools have not been destroyed by special measures: in most cases they have been revived by them. It is not necessary to wait for a decade to see substantial improvement in a school: recovery, or in some cases substantial progress towards it, within two years or so seems to be the general rule. This is a very encouraging first set of experiences.

References

NATIONAL COMMISSION ON EDUCATION (1995) *Success Against the Odds: Effective Schools in Disadvantaged Areas*, London: Routledge.

NORTH EAST LONDON EDUCATION ASSOCIATION (1995) *Report to the Secretary of State for Education and Employment: The Future of Hackney Downs School*, London: DfEE.

Part 2

LEAs

Confusing messages are being given and received about the LEA's role in school improvement. On one hand, various acts of parliament over the last few years have reduced the LEAs' power, and subsequently their influence, over the schools in their territory. At the same time, the case of The Ridings School has demonstrated that LEAs are deemed responsible when things go wrong. It is ironic that, under legislation passed by the last Conservative government, once schools are judged to be 'requiring special measures', GEST money is released and LEAs are able to intervene in ways they are unable to do prior to the inspection, when, in some cases, earlier intervention may have prevented the 'failing' label.

Both the chapters in this section focus on the role of the LEA in connection with schools in difficulty. The first is an external perspective of LEAs. It is written by Rob Watling, David Hopkins, Alma Harris and John Beresford from the University of Nottingham. The authors describe what happened in the London borough of Waltham Forest when it was identified by OFSTED as being one of the first two LEAs subjected to the Accelerated Inspection Programme (AIP). Over 40 per cent of the schools in both these boroughs had been identified as either 'failing' or as having 'serious weaknesses' in inspection reports. (The other LEA was Lambeth — see, also, Chapter 3 for Michael Stark's view on this procedure.)

The chapter has been written before completion of their research, consequently here they concentrate on the early stages of the AIP and hazard tentative conclusions about the process. Issues are raised concerning the haste with which the programme was implemented and the quality assurance of the process. The writers describe the trinity of emotions that teachers, advisers and officers undergo during inspection — *anticipation, elation*, and *disillusion* — and suggest that the prime purpose should be to help professionals finish the cycle with development rather than disillusion. They conclude the chapter by suggesting strategies for improving LEAs and schools in difficulty.

The second chapter is an insider's perspective, written by Christine Whatford, director of education in Hammersmith and Fulham. She tells the story of what happened to The Hammersmith School from the establishment of the new LEA, including when it was deemed as requiring special measures and the subsequent painful process leading to the rebirth of the school, renamed as The Phoenix School.

Anyone who believes there are quick fixes should read this chapter with care. The author charts the problems facing an LEA meticulously and explains that defining the problem and knowing what to do is not the main difficulty in these situations. For her the issue is about finding and recruiting people who can undertake the necessary changes. She suggests that LEAs have a key role to play in trying to prevent decline and dealing with failure and advocates more power for LEAs so that they can intervene at an earlier stage. She concludes the chapter with a discussion about how to turn the hype of improvement into reality:

> ... this is almost boringly simple. It is about setting up routines and procedures that work, consistency, following everything up ... about expectations, monitoring and sheer hard work. (p. 84)

Chapter 4

Between the Devil and the Deep Blue Sea? Implications for School and LEA Development Following an Accelerated Inspection Programme

Rob Watling, David Hopkins,
Alma Harris and John Beresford

Introduction

In this chapter we look at some of the implications for schools and a Local Education Authority (LEA) who have recently been the subject of an OFSTED Accelerated Inspection Programme (AIP). We explore the background to the schools in this particular part of London, and the processes by which the AIP was initiated and conducted. We look specifically at the way that the schools and the LEA have reacted to the Programme, as identified during an evaluation funded by the London borough of Waltham Forest and undertaken by the Centre for Teacher and School Development at the University of Nottingham. We argue that those working in the fields of school effectiveness and school improvement who are committed to action in such circumstances would be well advised to focus their considerable research, conceptual, strategic and practical experience on issues connected to school development, and offer a range of strategies that we consider appropriate for schools and LEAs in difficult contexts.

Context

The implementation of the 1992 Education Act radically altered the arrangements for the inspection of schools in England and Wales (DES, 1992). It had a major impact upon LEAs in terms of increased responsibility for monitoring and evaluating the operation of schools. Previously, LEAs had the statutory right to inspect schools but it was apparent that different authorities were giving different degrees of emphasis to this function with many preferring to work in an advisory capacity (Maychell and Keys, 1993). The 1992 Act unequivocally located the delivery of inspection within the domain of the LEA.

Most accounts of inspection would argue that it serves two main purposes in an educational system. The first set of claims relates to accountability and providing both a national and local picture about the state of the system through identifying aspects of quality and standards as well as some gaps. The second set of claims concerns the influence of school inspection upon school improvement. Millett (1993) points out that OFSTED adopted the phrase 'improvement through inspection' to sum up its corporate hopes.

The crucial question, of course, is whether inspection really does bring about improvement. Regrettably this is a question that is easier to pose than to answer with any certainty. Perry (1995) underlines OFSTED's explicit assertion that it does represent a departure from the previous practice of HMI, although not, it should be said, from LEAs. It would seem that LEAs have been instrumental in initiating and collaborating in school improvement work. They have taken a lead in planning appropriate training for their schools, regulating the provision of data, offering advice and providing an audit service (Audit Commission, 1989; Kennedy, 1990; McGee, 1991; Gray, Jesson and Sime, 1991).

LEAs are now expected to set the context for the improvement of their schools. Government expects them to provide help to the 10 per cent of schools that are likely to be identified as having serious weaknesses, and LEAs are permitted to put aside 20 per cent of their centrally held GEST funds to assist them with this (DFE, 1994). It has been suggested that LEAs could help schools by promoting discussions about good practice, and by disseminating examples (Birmingham Schools Advisory Service, 1995). Also, it has been posited that they could act as the critical friend of their schools, 'able to challenge and support any of [their] functioning' (Mortimore, 1995), through the provision of data to assess that functioning.

In particular, the development of 'validated self-review' and the relationship it requires between LEAs and their schools would, it is suggested, enable LEAs to concentrate their resources and efforts on 'failing schools' (Barber, 1996). Such resource allocation, however, is premised on there being a small proportion of schools in any LEA in the category of 'failing' or 'in difficulty'. Clearly, if this were not the case, the prognosis for LEA expenditure would look rather bleak and the requirement for external help would be an emergency rather than a necessity.

The LEA

The London borough of Waltham Forest is situated in the north eastern corner of England's capital. It was formed in 1965 during one of Britain's periodic reorganizations of local government and is made up of three former authorities — Walthamstow, Chingford and Leyton. As such it serves a wide variety of people ranging from affluent households in the fringes of Epping Forest (an expansive ancient woodland) to areas of dense inner-city housing in the south, which have developed unequally over the last 100 years and now contain large areas of significant deprivation. According to the borough council (who in turn cite the Department of the Environment's index of local conditions), Waltham Forest is the twentieth most deprived district in England. Two of its council wards (both in the south of the borough) are among the fifty most deprived wards in London.

At the time of writing, the LEA maintains fourteen secondary and sixty-two primary schools. It also has five special schools, and four nurseries. There are four grant-maintained schools in the borough (one primary, two secondary and one special school) for which the LEA has no direct responsibility. The borough's services to these schools are managed by its Education and Advisory Service (EAS) which has been slimmed down over the last ten years and now consists of just twelve posts (four of which were vacant at one point of our research). Ninety-five per cent of the LEA's budget is devolved directly to schools, and this has resulted in the EAS having to raise around £250,000 a year from consultancy work outside of the borough — most notably through inspection work for OFSTED in other parts of England.

The Announcement of the AIP

In 1993 the Office for Standards in Education (OFSTED) began its four-yearly cycle of inspecting all the secondary schools in England and Wales. This was followed, in 1994, by a similar process for primary schools. By 1995, therefore, OFSTED had the first opportunity to look at a substantial number of inspections from across the education system. All the existing inspection reports were analysed early in autumn 1995 to see patterns emerging from the data. Data from all LEAs were reviewed in terms of:

- the number of schools in each authority;
- the number of schools in each phase (primary, secondary, special);
- the number of schools in each authority that had outstanding reports;
- the number of schools in each authority where inspectors had identified serious weaknesses (these schools were not, at that time, identified to LEAs); and
- the number of schools in each authority that inspectors had identified to the LEA as 'failing' and requiring 'special measures'. This is the most severe category of need, and such schools are required to produce an action plan and be inspected again before they can be removed from this category.

The overall picture presented by OFSTED at that time was one that inspections had found many LEAs in England and Wales with no schools falling into any of the last three categories. There were some LEAs that had at least one school that was failing, or had some serious weaknesses. But two LEAs, in OFSTED's opinion, stood out as being significantly different. The London boroughs of Waltham Forest and Lambeth both had over 40 per cent of their schools identified as having 'serious weaknesses' or as 'failing' [see Stark's chapter].

Three of the first ten primary schools inspected in Waltham Forest (but none of the first eight secondary schools) were deemed to require 'special measures'.

This represented nearly 17 per cent of the sample, compared with a national average of 10 per cent. Two more primaries, and three secondary schools in the borough had 'serious weaknesses' according to the inspectors. This meant that eight of the first eighteen schools inspected (44 per cent) were in OFSTED's two main categories for concern. Figures for Lambeth were broadly the same.

OFSTED responded to this analysis in October 1995 by announcing an Accelerated Inspection Programme (AIP) for these two LEAs whereby all schools in these boroughs would be inspected by the end of 1996. The intention of this process, as outlined to OFSTED, was to check whether this rate of failure was consistent across all schools in Waltham Forest and Lambeth. In addition, they wanted to ensure that an appropriate level of education was being provided for all children in each borough. Hence, there was some justification to do so more urgently than the normal inspection cycle would allow.

The Commissioning of the Research

The LEA in Waltham Forest had reservations about the AIP process and in particular was concerned that the AIP was misguided and inappropriate (Lockart, 1996). It argued that OFSTED's analysis was made too early in the inspection cycle, was based on too small a sample (eighteen out of eighty-three schools) and was not representative of the full range of schools, or performance in the borough. The LEA also suspected that there was some political motivation behind the AIP, although OFSTED consistently denied this.

In view of these concerns, the LEA commissioned an independent evaluation of the AIP focusing on two central issues:

- What has been the effect of HMCI's decision on schools and the LEA?
- How effectively have schools and the LEA responded?

While both these evaluation questions were undoubtedly legitimate, they tended to focus upon the net effect of the accelerated inspection process rather than any consideration of underlying causal factors. In addition, there was little opportunity within the scope of these two questions to focus down on the critical question of school improvement. If, as Frost (1995) advocates, 'inspection is encouraging schools to focus on their core functions in a systematic way and through that action and development planning schools are gradually improving' (p. 4), there was a unique opportunity to explore this within the evaluation. Hargreaves (1995) points to the lack of research demonstrating the effectiveness of inspection as a route to school improvement. He notes 'the writings of distinguished researchers . . . provide little support for mass inspection as a sound (school improvement) strategy' (p. 119).

Hence, the evaluation provided an important and somewhat unique opportunity to explore the proposed relationship between inspection and improvement in more depth. Consequently, the research team added four other issues to those identified by the LEA. These were:

- How valid were HMCI's reasons for requiring an accelerated programme of inspection in Waltham Forest?
- What are the schools' perceptions of the level of support provided by Waltham Forest prior to the accelerated programme?
- What is the impact of the OFSTED inspections on the individual schools' improvement efforts?
- What is the impact of Waltham Forest's level of post-OFSTED support and its impact on school improvement?

The Research

Research Design

The commissioned evaluation consisted of five main strands:

- postal questionnaires to all schools covered by the AIP at three stages:

    one week before their inspection;
    the week following their inspection; and
    when the school's action plan has been completed;

- face-to-face interviews with staff at fifteen selected schools at the same three stages;
- face-to-face interviews with staff from OFSTED and the LEA;
- independent analysis of the data generated by OFSTED and LEA on schools in the borough; and
- an independent rating of schools' own approach to improvement.

Current Progress of the Research

At the time of writing this chapter (February 1997) the AIP process is almost complete. One confidential interim report has been presented to the LEA by OFSTED who are now completing their analysis of inspection data and the progress of the AIP. We understand that they will be using this in three main ways:

- to compile an overall picture of education in the borough as measured by the OFSTED inspection process;
- to prepare AIPs for other LEAs where OFSTED believe there to be similar levels of underachieving schools; and
- to prepare OFSTED for the forthcoming inspection of LEAs.

The research team, meanwhile, have made a preliminary analysis of all questionnaires received to date; completed the first two stages of interviews with schools, the LEA and OFSTED; attended a range of meetings with LEA staff; and produced interim reports for the LEA on the perceptions of OFSTED, the schools, and borough officers. What follows is based on an initial analysis of that data, the reactions of various stakeholders to our reports, and our expectations of the next stages of the process. It also links these observations to the wider issues related to the LEA role in school improvement and, in particular, to the types of interventions required for 'ineffective' or 'failing' schools.

Reactions to the Announcement of the AIP

Certain LEA staff (including teachers and advisers) first heard about the AIP through rather unusual channels. Some heard when they were attending a weekend education seminar and others (including the local community) learnt about it through the media, whose coverage went through several distinct stages. At the time of the announcement, some national papers labelled the AIP as 'a crackdown', and 'a blitz on poor teaching'. The local press also ran 'bottom of the class' stories, but soon began to explore the complexities of the issue in response to local views. National coverage has waned as the local debate has become more sophisticated.

The initial media references to 'failing schools' and to a 'failing local education authority' heightened teachers' first impressions that they were about to face a harsh, critical and politically motivated inspection process. Headteachers and teachers in the borough alike were upset and angered by the media coverage of the AIP's announcement. The initial feelings of indignation at being picked out were followed by low morale and a sense of hurt. There was a general feeling that criticism would be inevitable, and that no credit would be given for any contribution by teachers in what were generally felt to be very challenging circumstances in Waltham Forest's schools.

Many teachers and a significant proportion of the LEA officers suspected that there was a political dimension to the decision to launch the AIP. They criticized the lack of clarity of OFSTED's announcements and believe they may not have been entirely honest. This perception, that OFSTED were effectively inspecting the LEA (as well as the schools), raised the stakes concerning AIP for those involved. Much importance was placed on each aspect of the inspection. Each judgment, each report and every aggregation of data was emotionally charged.

The Impact of the AIP on Schools

Among the LEA staff there was some disagreement concerning the effect of the AIP on schools. Some people voiced concern that the inspections were 'traumatic' for schools and (although they accepted that was the case with all inspections) the scale and speed of the AIP gave these an added dimension and added pressure. Other advisers were less sympathetic, pointing out that all the secondary schools (and most of the primaries) in the borough should have reasonably expected an inspection during the year anyway.

Many advisers believed that schools were much more focused on important educational issues as a direct result of the AIP. It was felt that some schools were finally facing up to problems which had been in evidence for some time. In addition, there was a more positive response to inservice courses run by the LEA than previously experienced. Advisers genuinely felt that they were now able to revive their lapsed relationships with schools, and that these were now established on the basis of 'critical friendship' rather than accountability.

The Impact of the AIP on the LEA

The AIP had undoubtedly caused increases in the workload of the EAS, but several officers shared the view there were major benefits from this process. Relationships between officers were described as being more cooperative and effective as a result of the need to get through the extra work much more quickly. New processes were required to check on the status of schools, colleagues talked and shared information in a more formal way, and joint meetings were established between advisers and other council officers. Such effort ensured that the service presented a reassuring and confident stance to schools.

Despite these benefits, some reservations remained. There was a concern that long-standing problems in the LEA (as well as in the schools) were not being systematically addressed. Several headteachers agreed with this latter point. They voiced concern over whether the AIP would lead to anything other than a temporary improvement in their relationship with the LEA. This point was sharply underlined by the fact that many schools used services from outside the borough because they considered them better than those provided by Waltham Forest. Many headteachers stated that this would remain the position even after the conclusion of the AIP.

Role of the LEA during the AIP

After the announcement of the AIP, one of the first tasks undertaken by the LEA was to conduct a 'health check' of all the schools that were to be inspected. Using the OFSTED Framework for Inspection as their template, advisers conducted in-depth interviews with headteachers to assess the levels of support that schools needed in fourteen different areas of their work. These ranged from curriculum planning to pupil behaviour; from levels of achievement to the quality of the accommodation; and were used as the basis for an overall judgment of high, medium or low level of need. They formed the basis on which advisers' time (and in some cases additional resources) were allocated to schools in the run up to inspection. The LEA also ran an extensive series of inservice training courses for heads and teachers which in total numbered over 2,000 participants.

The LEA was aware that such a health check was an imperfect exercise. It was described by them as a 'blunt instrument' and an unsophisticated one, drawn up in unreasonable haste, and implemented with inadequate piloting. But it was, nonetheless, a tool which was perceived as valuable in its concept and application. It had provided a long-lost opportunity for the LEA to get into their schools, talk to headteachers, listen to the problems of schools, and most importantly to encourage heads to ask a series of very important questions about their school's performance, the quality of its teachers and teaching, and the role of management in moving things forward. It also proved to be a good predictor of OFSTED's judgment of schools.

Many schools believe that the LEA-led health check and training sessions offered important opportunities for them to take stock of their position and prepare for their OFSTED inspection. A few found them less useful, and were concerned that the LEA had been panicked into actions that were underprepared. Several advisers noted that the health check suffered from being linked too closely to the OFSTED Framework, and that it consequently missed the opportunity to assess other, equally important features of education within the borough. In particular, there was concern that the health check had ignored certain non-curricular elements of education and failed to explore longer-term, developmental initiatives in the schools.

The LEA interventions were characterized by different teachers as either 'too little too late' or 'too much too late'. Both phrases suggest that the LEA had been relatively slow to react to the problems in Waltham Forest, and that the interventions were either possibly misplaced (too little) or misjudged (too much) for the circumstances of their school and the time available. There was also some suspicion that, even where the changes in LEA support were appreciated, they were in danger of not being sustained beyond the period of the AIP.

Criticisms of the AIP

Apart from the concerns about the way that the AIP was announced, the evaluation work in Waltham Forest raised a number of criticisms about the way the AIP had been conducted. These issues among others will inform the final stages of the project and will be accommodated in the final report. However, some of the issues and criticisms that have emerged from the project are worth exploring in this chapter: in particular, issues arising directly from the haste of the implementation of AIP and the quality assurance of the AIP process.

First, teachers in Waltham Forest reported the same feelings of stress, pressure and rush that schools in the normal cycle of inspections frequently report (Brimblecombe, Ormston and Shaw, 1995). However, because the announcements of inspection dates for individual schools were often quite late (in one case only three weeks before the actual inspection was due to take place), it is conceivable that teachers in Waltham Forest schools experienced far more concentrated stress and pressure than teachers undergoing inspections as part of the normal cycle. Some teachers stated that they felt deprived of the right to prepare mentally for the inspection.

Second, the pressure on time during the preparations in schools for the AIP meant that a number of the customary activities in schools had to be temporarily postponed. Staff meetings which were used for staff development were taken up with preparations for OFSTED. For a similar reason one school abandoned its school-based inservice training. Some extra-curricular activities were abandoned, as were events in the community. Similarly the rush to prepare for the inspections meant that school development planning was badly affected in nearly all the schools. Heads felt they spent less time with children in the build-up to the inspection. This is confirmed by teachers who reported seeing the head less in evidence around the school.

Third, there was a proliferation of paperwork in the form of school policies, which once again is a recognized feature of most OFSTED inspections. However, Waltham Forest schools had much less time than other schools to fill any perceived policy gaps. Schools felt obliged to produce schemes of work that they knew to be inadequate, and they were identified as such by OFSTED. Most schools reported less consultation taking place with staff before policies were put into place, although one school claimed to increase the amount of consultation with parents over school policies during this period.

Finally, in addition to the general strain upon staff and the school as a result of AIP, some major concerns about the quality assurance of the AIP were in evidence. There was some suspicion within the LEA that OFSTED had found it difficult to recruit sufficient Additional Inspectors (AIs) to conduct this work. Many teams were thought to be under-prepared and some had not followed the normal course of an OFSTED inspection. Others were perceived as 'soft' on schools, or gullible since they did not have the in-depth knowledge of schools that local advisers had build up through their work.

There were many criticisms of the slippage in OFSTED teams' production of the final reports which, according to OFSTED guidelines, should be ready in forty days. LEA records indicate that several reports took two to three months to arrive and we were told of schools having to wait eighteen, even twenty, weeks for their report. This was seen as having an intolerable effect on the individual schools, but also on the Education Advisory Service (EAS) who had timetabled their support visits to schools to coincide with the reports and the production of the action plans.

Essentially, criticisms of Additional Inspectors' conclusions focused upon three main areas:

- advisers were much less satisfied with the consistency of reports being produced by AI teams;
- advisers believed that inspectors on the AIP relied too strongly on discussions with teachers, and especially headteachers, rather than their own observations; and
- advisers felt that some AI teams were too ready to include heads' opinions in the inspection report without subjecting these to any independent or objective analysis.

If these concerns are well founded, they have serious repercussions for OFSTED in ensuring the reliability and consistency of its inspection reports. But they also have major implications for the LEA. As funding and support tends to follow OFSTED recommendations, if such recommendations prove unreliable or inconsistent then the LEA may misdirect its energies, even where it claims to know more about the school than OFSTED does. The worst outcome (and some advisers believe this is happening) would be if weak schools were to be sheltered by the reports coming out of the AIP — protected from the sorts of interventions that others believe are needed to bring about genuine, far-reaching improvements.

Two Strategic Interventions

Apart from its immediate responses to the AIP, Waltham Forest invested time and effort into the development and implementation of two strategic interventions. The first became known as Waltham Forest Improvement Network (WIN) which developed a school improvement programme. The second involved a 'Towards Employability' bid for the Single Regeneration Budget (SRB) programme.

WIN funded the secondment of two headteachers (one primary, one secondary), with contributions from an adviser and administrative support, to develop frameworks to raise standards by:

- raising pupils' achievement;
- enabling schools to manage change successfully;
- improving the LEA support to schools;
- strengthening school and LEA links and mutual accountability;
- providing a forum for celebrating and disseminating good practice; and
- coordinating current and future school and LEA improvement initiatives.

Initial funding was for one year, during which time the management team developed strategic frameworks for achieving these improvement goals. The future of the WIN project, however, is at present in the balance, not least because the authority has been successful in attracting £6.4m over seven years from its SRB bid. This has a different (but equally admirable) focus that could alter the impetus and direction of the LEA's improvement work. The SRB money will fund a partnership between schools, the LEA, government, the community and the private sector. It is designed to equip the young people of Waltham Forest with the skills necessary to secure employment. The money will fund major new initiatives, including: extensions of the borough's literacy scheme; more after-school provision; improved training for managers and governors; recruitment, retention and retraining of good quality teaching staff; and an improved IT network for all schools in the borough.

Evidently, it is too early to say how these two initiatives will affect the future of educational provision within Waltham Forest or how they link to the judgments of OFSTED and their Accelerated Inspection. The LEA have put a lot of effort into both strategies, but there is an extent to which the SRB bid in particular is constrained by the programme's emphasis on employment and training. The LEA is aware that these crucial issues are not the only ones that need attention in Waltham Forest, and that it will sometimes be difficult to reconcile the impetus of such a large, well-financed project and the broader educational needs of the borough.

Indeed the borough, like the schools themselves, has now been faced with a series of government-led initiatives, which are designed to 'improve' the quality of educational delivery. Local government reorganization, educational reform, local management of schools, the National Curriculum, OFSTED, accelerated inspection programmes, City Challenge and Single Regeneration Budget — each comes with their own agenda and momentum. These can, on the one hand, offer attractive solutions to the educational problems in Waltham Forest. But they are not panaceas and professionals are frequently ambivalent about them. Each time a new initiative is launched the teachers, heads, advisers and officers in Waltham Forest (and every LEA like it) feel caught between the devil and the deep blue sea.

In our experience professionals (teachers, advisers, officers) undergo a characteristic trinity of emotions during inspection and, we suspect, during all these centralized solutions to educational improvement. These emotions come in cycles — some that last the whole length of the initiative, and others that are smaller and shorter in duration. The initial reaction is frequently one of *anticipation* (often linked, as with the AIP, to suspicion and apprehension about the motives of such interventions). During, and particularly after the process, there is a feeling of *elation* (either because the inspection is over, or because the new processes are in place, the documentation is finally up to date, and everyone is 'focused'). Then shortly afterwards there is a pervading sense of *disillusion* — a feeling that the results were far less dramatic, the exercise less worthwhile, and the improvements far less permanent.

One of the prime purposes of research must be to help professionals find opportunities for development rather than disillusion at the end of each of these cycles. Our experience in Waltham Forest (and in other LEAs with which we are working) is that a number of strategies can be useful in ensuring development rather than disillusion. In presenting strategies it is important to remember two things. The first is that we are not yet at the stage of writing the final report on this particular project, so these are general observations rather than specific conclusions for Waltham Forest. The second is that, when analysing educational culture, different LEAs (and different schools within them) require different strategies for development. These strategies need to fit the 'growth state', or culture of the particular LEA or school. There are few universal quality management strategies that are applicable across all stages of any organization's development, and strategies such as those detailed below must always be implemented with due regard to the individual context of each authority and school.

Strategies for Improving an LEA in Difficulty

There are a number of ways in which LEAs can strengthen their position with schools and the local community. While some of these strategies need to be internally driven, there are a number of external forces which can move LEAs in a more positive direction. We suggest some of these general forces, or stimuli, can be readily harnessed into strategies for improvement and development at LEA level, and offer some suggested ways forward.

The Centrality of School Improvement

School improvement should be at the core of all advisory and inspection work. Many LEAs are already moving in this direction by appointing specialist advisers for school improvement. We believe this strategy is not far reaching enough because school improvement work should necessarily be the concern of all advisers and LEA personnel. In this respect, school improvement should be the driving force behind all LEA structuring and development.

Links to Inspection

While the criteria for successfully negotiating an OFSTED inspection are clearly laid out (OFSTED, 1994), many schools have found it difficult to translate these criteria into effective action. Much advisory activity, therefore, should inevitably be taken up with advice about planning for and after inspection. The analysis of OFSTED inspection data should be used more effectively in LEAs to inform planning and provision of future services. This analysis of inspection data should be a core function of any advisory service.

The Importance of LEA Data and Measuring Value-Added in the Local Context

LEAs remain the main collectors of data about their schools, and even schools keen to go their own way have been grateful for access to the LEA database for use in their own improvement efforts. LEAs, therefore, should look towards providing more sophisticated data sets for schools and should assist schools in using their specific data for in-school improvement purposes (for example, Birmingham Schools Advisory Service, 1995). More proactive LEAs are setting up their own measures of value-added by their schools, unhappy that raw examination data give an incomplete picture of their schools' achievements. All LEAs should evaluate whether the existing value-added measures are appropriate and useful to the needs of their schools.

Different Solutions in Different Contexts

LEAs need to create their own type of school improvement partnership, or alliance, with schools rather than replicate others. Loose collaboration rather than formal structures provide the pattern for the organization of most urban education partnerships, but LEAs remain the most important driving force within partnerships. Most importantly, the scope and range of the school improvement partnership needs to reflect the immediate educational needs of the local area. There needs to be clarity of purpose and success criteria at the start of any partnership and continuous monitoring and evaluation to ensure real rather than perceived needs are being met.

Strategies for Improving Schools in Difficulty

As we have shown, there are specific strategies that LEAs can adopt to improve and to increase their effectiveness. Similarly, at the individual school level, discrete strategies exist which can energize and improve school performance. Yet, it is unreasonable to expect schools to improve themselves. As the research literature shows, many ineffective schools are 'stuck' and need a high level of external support. The LEA has an important role to play in assisting schools in their improvement efforts. The LEA should be instrumental in introducing, implementing and developing improvement strategies with schools. While it is acknowledged that the local context will dictate the particular strategies adopted, it is our view that certain strategies are effective for improving schools in difficulty. Moreover, such strategies are likely to be most effective when instigated and supported by the LEA.

Change at Leadership Level

It is too sweeping to say that the headteachers of ineffective schools do not have the capacity to be effective school leaders. It is, however, unlikely that they will have the capacity to resurrect such schools and therefore are potentially a part of the problem. It is usually the case that poor management and leadership is endemic within the ineffective school. This means the overall style of leadership at all levels might need to be changed in that particular context. The LEA has a central interventionist role to play in diagnosing poor leadership within a school. It can be instrumental in creating appropriate opportunities for new appointments and staff re-organization, and can mobilize resources to assist schools in regaining effective management and leadership.

Provision of Early, Intensive, Outside Support

Ineffective schools are likely to be isolated and in a state of cultural stasis. They are unlikely to have the potential for constructive self-analysis, or evaluation and will need support from outside to provide knowledge about school improvement strategies and models of ways of working. The LEA has an important role to play in assisting schools with the intensive support and encouragement they need to engage in self-evaluation and planning for improvement. While other forms of external support may be available, the LEA should seek to be the main partner in the improvement process.

Disaggregate Data on Student Achievement

Most ineffective schools will need to collect data to find out why they are unsuccessful and where to direct their efforts for greatest improvement. LEA data (see above) is an important source of evidence for schools in this position. Using locally collected data to illuminate potential problems is a first, but very important, step towards school improvement. LEA-led data analysis has the potential to give the school community ownership of the improvement agenda and to locate the problem away from individuals to a whole school focus.

A Short-Term Focus on Things that are Relatively Easy to Change

Changes to the school environment, attendance and uniform, while short-term changes, can result in tangible gains. Following a period of low morale, visible changes demonstrate that things are to be different in the school. These changes should reflect the core values that the leadership is articulating and should be endorsed by the LEA as meaningful and valuable indicators of a climate change. Evidence suggests that such early indicators of a climate change in the school are important in sustaining further improvement. They have a symbolic and real function, in that they show that change is taking place and a new and different school culture is emerging.

A Focus on Managing Learning Behaviour, not on Behaviour Management

Much of the evidence concerning the improvement of ineffective schools points towards an emphasis upon managing learning behaviour rather than behaviour management. This means creating the conditions within which learners can learn most effectively. Strategies for managing learning behaviour include a focus upon praise and positive reinforcement rather than punishment and discipline throughout the school. The LEA could act as a useful resource in this respect through providing inservice training and specialist advice and help. In fact, viewing the LEA as the main training and development resource is an important dimension of any partnership arrangement for school improvement.

Intensive Work on Re-skilling Teams of Teachers in a Limited but Specific Repertoire of Teaching/Learning Styles

There is evidence to suggest that staff development in ineffective schools should focus primarily upon effective teaching and learning. This should then be supported at LEA level through the provision of specialist training and development opportunities. Such training opportunities might include a focus upon seating arrangements;

classroom organization; the phasing of lessons; active use of resources; and different teaching and learning styles. Ideally, teachers should be encouraged to explore new skills in teams in order to create new partnerships to support the re-skilling process.

Progressive Restructuring to Generate New Opportunities for Leadership, Collaboration and Planning

Restructuring or planning must also be focused at the level of the classroom. Collaboration and planning must be predominantly about enhancing pupil achievement and developing the potential of all staff. Nothing should be more important in an ineffective school than timetabling staff together to engage in mutual learning and plan curriculum and school improvement. The LEA could offer advice and support concerning alternative ways of organizing this time and might also be able to provide various models or approaches that work best.

Withdraw External Pressure/Inspection in Order to Remove Fear and Give Space to Grow

As we have highlighted in our overview of Waltham Forest AIP, ineffective schools can become paralysed by the fear of imminent inspection. They dare not take the risks required to produce long-term improvement, which means seeking help from external agencies and, in particular, the LEA. Consequently, LEAs have to be proactive to the needs of ineffective schools rather than just reactive. They need to encourage schools to plan ahead on the basis of a realistic view of the school's current position. The school development plan and an inspection action plan need to be shared with LEA advisers so everyone is secure that the structures and processes are in place for improvement. Following this, the pressure of inspection needs to be withdrawn (in the short term) with the LEA acting as a critical friend providing an appropriate balance between support and challenge.

Evidently, there is much more to be said about the role of the LEA than these preliminary findings reveal. We recognize these are initial thoughts on a very important theme and the final research findings should provide a more comprehensive and sophisticated analysis. However, the research has illuminated some important features of the process of school improvement. First, the school improvement strategies we have suggested are not homogeneous but holistic and eclectic. Thus the rhetoric of a single school improvement approach, or remedy, is at a glance exposed. It would appear that a range of strategies are needed for successful school improvement to take place and that these strategies will differ in emphasis from school to school. Second, any combination of strategies must harness external support for internal purposes. As we have shown, external challenge and support from the LEA is critical in the improvement process but requires internal development and change at the school level to be most effective. Consequently, any approach to school improvement needs to ensure there is a mix of externally and internally driven strategies for improvement. As our work progresses, we hope to be able to develop the strategies outlined here and to measure more accurately the differential growth rates of schools. Most importantly we hope to extend our work concerning the identification of strategies most suited to schools with different growth states (Hopkins, Harris and Jackson, 1997).

Conclusion

Even though this project is still incomplete and some of the above discussion still speculative, the issues raised in this chapter have the potential to give us a better grasp of the role of the LEA in school improvement. While the dynamics of the improvement process are highly sophisticated and complex, they are achievable if the right mix of strategies are applied. This means, among other things, taking seriously the school's 'internal conditions' or 'capacity for development', as well as its growth state in selecting the strategies for school development.

This view supports the argument that those working in the fields of school effectiveness and school improvement who are committed to action, would be better advised to focus their considerable research, conceptual, strategic and practical experience on issues connected to school development as a means of achieving integration between the two traditions. For it is a focus upon school development that holds the key to improving levels of student achievement and which can give schools and LEAs a choice between more than the devil and the deep blue sea.

References

AUDIT COMMISSION (1989) *Assuring Quality in Education*, London: HMSO.

BARBER, M. (1996) 'The eye of the storm', *Guardian Education*, 30 January, p. 2.

BIRMINGHAM SCHOOLS ADVISORY SERVICE (1995) *School Improvement Butterflies*, Birmingham: Birmingham City Council Education Department Schools Advisory Service.

BRIMBLECOMBE, N., ORMSTON, M. and SHAW, M. (1995) 'Teachers' perceptions of school inspection: A stressful experience', *Cambridge Journal of Education*, **25**, 1, pp. 53–61.

DES (1992) *Education (Schools Act)*, London: HMSO.

DFE (1994) *GEST 1995–6: Schools with Serious Weaknesses, Letter to LEAs*, 5 December.

FROST, R. (1995) *Improvement Through Inspection*, Briefing paper 9, London: National Commission on Education.

GRAY, J., JESSON, D. and SIME, N. (1991) 'Developing LEA frameworks for monitoring and evaluation from research on school effectiveness: Problems, progress and possibilities', in RIDDELL, S. and BROWN, S. (eds) *School Effectiveness Research: Its Messages for School Improvement*, Edinburgh: HMSO.

HARGREAVES, D. (1995) 'Inspection and school improvement', *Cambridge Journal of Education*, **25**, 1, pp. 117–25.

HOPKINS, D., HARRIS, A. and JACKSON, D. (1997) 'Improving the ineffective school: Strategies for development', *Education Management and Administration* (forthcoming).

KENNEDY, J. (1990) 'Inspection and advice within the wider local education authority', *Head Teachers Review*, Spring, p. 24.

LOCKHART, A. (1996) 'Week by week', *Education*, **187**, 4, p. 7; and **187**, 5, pp. 7 and 12.

MAYCHELL, K. and KEYS, W. (1993) *LEA Evaluation and Monitoring*, Slough: NFER.

MCGEE, P. (1991) 'The quality contract: Role of the LEA in maintaining standards in school monitoring', *Education*, 27 September, p. 250.

MILLETT, A. (1993) 'How inspectors can actually help', *Times Educational Supplement*, 25 June, p. 6.

MORTIMORE, P. (1995) 'Your local critical friend', *Education*, 7 July, p. 12.

OFSTED (1994) *Framework for the Inspection of Schools*, London: OFSTED.

PERRY, P. (1995) 'The formation of OFSTED', in BRIGHOUSE, T. and MOON, B. (eds) *School Inspection*, London: Pitman.

Chapter 5

Rising From the Ashes

Christine Whatford

Introduction

Hammersmith School was formed from a very large-scale amalgamation consisting of three schools, Hammersmith County, a mixed comprehensive, Hammersmith Girls, a girls school and Christopher Wren, a boys school. This took place long before Hammersmith and Fulham became a local education authority (LEA) and I had no direct involvement in or knowledge of it. Hammersmith and Fulham became an LEA in April 1990. I knew that we were to inherit a school with major problems. In fact, we were to set up an LEA where the majority of schools in the secondary sector were problematic.

Long before OFSTED or schools requiring special measures were invented, Her Majesty's Inspectorate (HMI) kept their own list of 'failing' schools. There were two differences between that system and the current one. First, the list was not public and second the route by which a school arrived on the list was less systematic. It might be there as a result of a full HMI Inspection but, given the infrequency of those, it was more likely to be there as a result of individual HMI visits for various reasons, whether associated with a subject, part of a dipstick or part of monitoring Section 11. This meant that the local HMI would have more information and evidence about some schools than others. However, as far as Hammersmith and Fulham's eight secondary schools were concerned, the HMI had enough evidence to alert the incoming authority that six were problematic and of those six, three were seriously problematic to the extent they were what would now be called failing and requiring special measures. Hammersmith School — the focus of this chapter — was one of those three.

We have on file an overview report written about this school by the ILEA inspector during the last year of ILEA following 'a substantial visit'. I was struck that it is written in the worst kind of 'Inspector Speak': if you dig deep enough and know the codes, all the issues and problems are in there, but they are buried very deep and surrounded by much praise and congratulation to and of the management and the staff. It was written in such a way that people could read what they wanted to into it. Furthermore, the report was not copied to the chair of governors and was confidential to the head.

Prior to the LEA Being Set Up

Many Inner London Education Authority (ILEA) heads took early retirement/ voluntary severance when the ILEA was abolished. It was offered on a widespread basis with generous terms which the boroughs were unlikely to be able to repeat. Hammersmith School's head availed herself of this opportunity. Although I am counting her in saying that the school has had four headteachers in six years, I did not have the experience of working with her. Her presentation to me of the school, its issues and problems did not differ very much from the picture painted by HMI, except what HMI was saying was that something dramatic needed to be done to improve the state of affairs, whereas the head's presentation was more fatalistic: presenting the problems with pupils and teachers as a fact of life, unlikely to change. The head had given long service and was tired: it was not surprising she took early retirement. She had suffered personal, physical injury during her period as head. At the same time she was experienced and confident. Her personal presentation to the outside world, given there was very little public information in those days, probably meant many people did not realize the depth and extent of the school's problems. However, the opportunity to appoint a new head is always a time of optimism and that was the situation the term before Hammersmith and Fulham took over.

Headship Recruitment for Difficult Schools

When we took over, the recruitment process was standard across the board. No-one would have dreamed of doing anything different for individual appointments. This meant that jobs were advertised, there was no canvassing of potential candidates to encourage them to apply, no informal briefing or assessment beyond what all candidates got on the visit and no checking out of candidates, informally or formally, beyond taking up references. In Hammersmith and Fulham, references were only taken up after interview which meant people were offered jobs without having any corroborative evidence beyond their application form and interview. I now believe it is not on its own an adequate process for headship appointment. I have also learned that it does not matter how clearly you spell out the difficulties of a particular job to try to dissuade people who may not be up to it; it does not always put them off. Finally, without breaking the confidentiality of any headship appointment interview, there are additional issues when professional advice offered relative to a candidate is not accepted by the appointment panel.

Defining the Problem Is Not the Issue

At the first opportunity in the first term of the authority's life (summer term 1990), we did our own overview of the state of the school to offer the incoming new head in September 1990 something with which to work immediately. That brings me to my second general point. Defining the problem is not the issue for failing schools. It was all there deep in the ILEA inspector's report, and was certainly all there in the report we did in that first term. As the story unfolds we will find that, although the degree of detail gets greater when you get into both the formal LEA inspection two years later, and the OFSTED inspection three years later, the fundamental issues are still the same. So knowing there is a problem and what it is, in some ways is the easy bit.

Supporting the New Head

The new head took up post in September 1990. The authority did not have a formal induction scheme at that time but because of the school's difficulties it was made a priority to give the head maximum support. Local management of schools was deferred for two years in the new inner London education authorities, therefore the LEA was able to provide support without depending on the school deciding to buy into it. The school had a link inspector who, during the course of one academic year, spent the equivalent of seventeen full days in the school, on forty-six separate visits, attended forty exclusions meetings, observed eighteen teachers in the classroom and met with the head and members of the senior management team. In addition, the full range of subject inspectors was made available to the school and they spent an average of two days each working with individual departments.

During the first year the LEA's concerns about the school increased. The new head was not having the kind of impact we had hoped. We could not see signs of improvement in any of the concern areas; indeed in some areas there was slippage backwards. The school began to experience industrial relations problems. I was informed that over the years that had always been an issue. There was a very active NUT branch who, fairly typically for some London secondary schools, had been at the forefront of any industrial action in the 1970s and 1980s. We felt we had to give the new head a year giving nothing but support and advice. At the end of that year he agreed that things were not going well and progress was not being made. Given this lack of progress, the head himself asked the LEA to do an in-depth review of the school's four major subject departments in autumn term 1991. The results were presented to the governing body in spring term 1992. The report included thirty-four points for action. The LEA reported to governors formally that there had been very little improvement in the school since the head came into post eighteen months before. This report was followed by a three-day conference for all senior and middle managers supported by LEA inspectorate. Targets were set for all heads of department and all heads of year. In spite of this, examination results in summer 1992 were poor. In autumn term 1992, the LEA responded with a thorough analysis of the results and called in the chair of governors and headteacher to go through the results and agree on action to be taken to improve them.

Inspection Evidence

I have already noted that identifying the problem is relatively easy. I would now go as far as to say that knowing what should be done to put things right is also not difficult. If you were to look in detail at the inspectorate memoranda, thirty-four action points, proposed action to improve examination results, and targets set for department and year heads, you could put together a list of practical and sensible measures that needed to be taken by the staff, individually and collectively. Indeed, these have proved to be the strategies which have turned the school around now they are being done: for example, such mundane things as a consistently implemented behaviour policy; following up all absences and lateness; systematically making sure all work is properly marked; checking all lessons are properly prepared and schemes of work exist; communicating efficiently with parents; teachers getting to lessons on time with a senior staff back-up system to clear corridors and get pupils into class on time; teacher awareness of the ability profile of each pupil and setting individual targets for achievement, including in external exams. The issue then is not just knowing what needs to be done to solve the problem. The issue is doing this regularly *and* consistently.

In the term following the headteacher's and chair of governors' meeting with myself and the chief inspector, the head attempted to implement the necessary identified measures, but the subsequent LEA inspection in spring term 1993 showed he had not been successful in this. The inspection report was devastating. As a new authority in 1990, the LEA had set up its own formal inspection system, before OFSTED was invented. In many ways it is similar to the subsequent OFSTED inspection regime except it was carried out by the authority's own inspectors. The framework covered the same areas as OFSTED's, although not quite as prescriptively, and each inspection resulted in a detailed written report, which was made public. Anyone who reads the LEA inspection report on Hammersmith School could not argue that LEAs doing their own inspections are likely to pull punches or cover things up.

The conclusion of this report was that poor management at all levels was the major cause of the school's failures. Given that research shows that leadership of the head and senior management team is key to any school's success, it is not surprising that the inspection report should focus on these areas. What it did do, however, was to enable the teachers to claim that the failures of the school were unrelated to them, and were all the fault of management, and the nature of the children. This was not so, but perhaps the report encouraged too much polarization along these lines. The authority published the report in summer term 1993 and the education committee responded by setting time limited formal targets for the head and SMT. The authority also paid for an experienced ex-head to be in the school for three days a week to monitor progress and work with the head and staff. The education committee called for a further progress report in January 1994. However, by January 1994 the head had finally asked to be released from his contract, as the term following the publication of the report had not seen any improvements.

Removing Headteachers

When it is necessary to remove the head of a failing school it very seldom happens through the normal competency processes, even if those exist. It tends to be done on an individual basis by negotiation. By now Hammersmith and Fulham and other London boroughs were under local management and therefore, in theory, this was a matter for the governing body and, in particular, the chair of governors. It would not be unreasonable, however, to assume that in most failing schools there is an element of failure in the governing body too, and therefore it is quite likely that they will be unwilling or unable to undertake this time consuming and, in many ways, unpleasant task. In Hammersmith's case I undertook the negotiations with the heads' union representative and the head left on the last day of autumn term 1993. By now it was known that there would be an OFSTED inspection in February 1994. Neither the deputy head or any other member of the senior management team was capable of acting as head from the beginning of the following term.

Finding Replacements

The leaving date and arrangements for the head were only finalized in the last week of the Christmas term 1993, which left only a few days plus the Christmas holidays to find a replacement. This meant it had to be someone available at ridiculously short notice, prepared to take over the school without seeing it in action and willing to face an OFSTED inspection within two months, which would certainly deem the school to be failing. Thus began my experience of headhunting, a method of recruitment I once considered politically incorrect but now very much favour in certain circumstances. I discovered none of the professional headhunters offered the service of finding suitable heads for failing schools. I therefore had to rely on my own contacts, and made many phone calls, knowing almost certainly they would not be successful, in the hope that just one would produce a result. In these particular circumstances, availability was a big problem. On the whole, people who are available are retired and the size of the task at Hammersmith did not really lend itself to someone who had retired. If you are going to find someone, at that sort of notice, it has to be someone with a reason for dropping everything and coming, and they need to work for an employer who is prepared to release them. In the event we were fortunate that this time coincided with major upheavals and reorganization within Her Majesty's Inspectorate and I found a person who wanted to do it, who resigned, and for whom I was able to negotiate release during Christmas week. I accompanied her to the school on the first day of term and introduced her to the staff having informed them of the previous head's sudden departure. This was the first of many such beginning of term visits when there was news to impart, usually related to a further problem or dramatic development.

The OFSTED Inspection and Its Aftermath

The OFSTED inspection took place in February 1994 in spite of a request by me, as director, to have it postponed. The report was very similar to the authority's own report except there was more emphasis on unsatisfactory teaching. The main findings, which deemed the school to be requiring special measures, related to inconsistent management of pupil behaviour, lack of coherent management and support systems, low standards of achievement and the long standing nature of these and other issues. Immediately following the inspection the governors agreed to the authority setting up a task force to support the new head, to prepare the action plan, sort out the school's budget and restructure the staff. As well as prioritizing the use of senior officer time the authority paid for the recently retired chief inspector to be employed two days a week solely to work with the school on drawing up the action plan. The authority gave an early indication it intended to exercise its powers under special measures as soon as it could to appoint extra governors and withdraw delegation. The governing body had been criticized in the report.

Three features of the Hammersmith School inspection are worth mentioning because I suspect they do not apply, or at least not in the same degree, to most failing schools. First, the report was leaked to the national press before the school or authority had received their copies. The source of the leak was never established, but the registered inspector, OFSTED and the Failing Schools Team in the DFE were found not to have been responsible. The effect of the leak was devastating: *The Mail On Sunday* ran a double page spread headed 'Is this the worst school in Britain?' (Brace, 1994).

The second difference relates to the political context in which the school was found to be failing. The chair of the school's governors at the time of the OFSTED inspection was a Labour councillor who had been chair of the education committee, and one governor was an opposition councillor. In some parts of the country where education authorities have been long established, there is an unwritten rule that the political parties confine criticism to each other and do not drag individual schools into the political arena. This was not the case in Hammersmith and Fulham. Conservative councillors blamed the administration of the council for the school's failures. The council's administration rejected that accusation on the grounds it had done everything it could since taking over the school in the state it was to support and improve it — including bringing about a change of leadership while it still had powers to do so — but that under local management those powers were limited. While it would seem to me that those two positions represent a proper political interchange, the problem was that the exchange was not conducted separately from additional comments and criticisms being made of the school. Right from the beginning when *The Mail On Sunday* article appeared, it contained quotations from the local opposition spokesperson on education. They were not confined to political comments about the administration, for example, one of the quotes in the Mail on Sunday article was 'they (the female teachers) are backed into a corner and the youngsters thrust their groins into them'.

Thirdly, the report was published at the time of local government elections in London in May 1994. The Secretary of State for Education, John Patten, was invited to a meeting in the borough. The public were excluded but press were invited and at the meeting, even at this early stage after the report's publication, he threatened the first use of an Education Association. The local Labour MP was not allowed into the meeting and was accused of trying to prevent the minister from getting into a taxi outside. This and other aspects, including circulation of a political leaflet about the school around the local council estate, meant that the story kept running almost weekly in the locals and occasionally in the nationals. It was at the beginning of the OFSTED process and so a failing school was itself much more of a novelty to the media and therefore much more susceptible to becoming a political football.

The Disadvantages of Freedom of Information

So, what is the correct balance between information being available publicly, and to parents, in the interests of open government and accountability, and the extreme position of the kind of highly damaging public scrutiny to which the Hammersmith School was subjected? This kind of lurid public exposure must worsen the situation in the school, and make it much more difficult to improve. While all failing schools must expect some adverse local coverage, most do not hit the nationals and with the exception of Stratford Grant Maintained School in Newham, I think no other has had the coverage which Hammersmith did until the case of the Ridings School. The awful thing about the coverage was that if you were a pupil at Hammersmith or a parent of a pupil at the school, much of the vilification must have appeared as if it was a direct personal criticism of you, your friends, and the local community on the estate where you lived.

School-based Union Activities

This kind of media coverage is probably not in itself unusual but its extremity certainly exacerbated the situation at Hammersmith. I have mentioned a very active trade union branch at the school. This in itself had not been unusual in ILEA secondary schools. It is also not surprising that if a situation in a school deteriorates and part of this is due to lack of leadership by the school's management, the power vacuum may be filled if there is a capable and active union representation. While not doubting that individually the teachers wanted the school to improve and be better, if only because it would make their own job of teaching much easier and more pleasant, collectively if what they needed to do to bring about improvement clashed with the position they wanted to take in relation to the rights of trade unionists, it was always the latter which they prioritized. For example, they went on strike over the issue of an independent appeals panel overturning a governing body decision on an excluded pupil, even though a school in the state of Hammersmith

School could ill afford the bad publicity and loss of confidence of parents that can follow from teacher action of this sort. They made an issue about the heads' and senior managers' rights to come in and observe their lessons unless they volunteered for such observation, even though it is an integral part of turning round a failing school that this kind of close monitoring must occur.

When any institution or organization reaches rock bottom one of the pre-requisites for getting out of it has to be that everyone works together to a common end. While individually union members, including the union representative herself, who played a very positive part in the drawing up of the action plan, have done that, in the background there has always been the wider collective political scenario which as far as the school is concerned has been counterproductive.

Appointing a Head — Again

In March 1994, one month after the OFSTED inspection, interviews were held for the substantive position of headteacher. The acting head applied but was not appointed. A non-appointment to a headship, in a school that desperately needs strong leadership, is always a difficult decision. The temptation is always to appoint rather than face the problems of non appointment but the right decision is almost always not to do so unless one is sure that there is a candidate who is up to the job. The interview took place after the OFSTED inspection outcome was known intern-ally, but before it was public and therefore the non-appointment did not attract publicity in the way that it would have done had it occurred at a later date.

The post was readvertised and the subsequent interviews took place in summer term 1994, after the report had been made public, after the national publicity, and just before the Secretary of State was due to consider whether to accept the gov-ernors' action plan or whether to move in an Education Association. As one of the factors that the Secretary of State would certainly be considering was the viability or otherwise of the school, and if two attempts at recruitment had failed to produce someone capable and willing to take the school over, it made an appointment almost essential. This was particularly true referring back to the political statements of the Secretary of State about wanting to have the first Education Association in Hammersmith and Fulham. That theme had been picked up by the press, particu-larly *The Evening Standard* who from time to time made it clear they were expect-ing the first EA to be in one of the London boroughs and intimated that the Secretary of State was hungry to get one in as soon as possible.

In summer term 1994, at the second round of interviews, the acting head was appointed to the substantive headship of the school.

The Action Plan

In the meantime, work on the action plan continued. The authority's ex-chief inspector, on behalf of the authority, led the exercise which was overseen by a small group of governors. A high degree of external assistance is needed because very often part of a failing school's failure has been the inability in the first place to have a proper school development plan, subsequently implemented. In some ways it is therefore unrealistic to expect such a school to be able to produce a very competent action plan without external assistance. Added to which, in a school like Hammersmith, the head and SMT's priorities really needed to be on sorting out the school on a day-to-day basis. They did, however, have to be involved at some level in order to agree on an action plan that they were able and willing to implement.

The action plan forms part of the evidence on which the Secretary of State makes their decision on whether to set up an Education Association, so we were very pleased that the then HMCI took the decision to make HMI's comments available to the LEA. Hammersmith's action plan was praised by HMI. With hindsight I now believe that, while being a very good theoretical document, it was too ambitious and demanded progress on too many fronts to be realistic. This was because of the way the legislation is framed and the system is set up. When the authority had originally inspected the school our criticisms covered the same range of issues as OFSTED, however, our recommendation to the governing body and head was to prioritize and select within the areas of concern and tackle and move forward on a restricted number of fronts. This approach was criticized by OFSTED because any action plan in response to an OFSTED report has to respond in detail to every finding. In order to meet that requirement, action plans may well prove to be over-ambitious.

Appointing Additional Governors

The authority's statement of action has to accompany the governors' action plan. We made it clear we were going to ask to be allowed to withdraw delegation and appoint an unusually large number of extra governors. The reason for this was the need to be sure the authority could control the election of the chair and vice chair of the governing body as those positions are key and we felt that the school needed to have those posts filled by new authority governors rather than existing governors.

There is nothing in the legislation and guidance about how an authority decides who will be extra governors. The normal process for LEA governors' appointment is a political one. The political parties nominate on an agreed proportional basis. The administration councillors decided not to follow that process because what the school would most benefit from would be people chosen for their particular expertise and the contribution they could make, rather than on the basis of party allegiance. As they were not to be political appointments, I was asked to find the extra governors, which I did by personal contact, telephone calls and letting it be known we needed people. While I cannot be certain, I believe that the strong authority team of governors put into the school to strengthen the governing body may well have been a factor in the decision of the Secretary of State to allow the school and authority the opportunity to sort things out themselves. The new chair of governors was a senior business executive of international repute. The vice chair had worked in the local community, was a magistrate and a specialist in the teaching of literacy. Other governors included the director of education of a neighbouring LEA, who was also a resident in the borough, an ex-HMI and a child psychologist as well as one of my assistant directors who was responsible for finance.

At the end of July the Secretary of State accepted the governors' action plan and authority's action plan. I suspect the decision was a very close run thing. We were very pleased it had gone in that direction. We felt strongly that the authority had done everything it possibly could both to support the school and deal with the situation when things did not improve as they should. Had the decision gone the other way, and had we sought to challenge it through judicial review as was our intention, we would have argued there was nothing that an Education Association could do which we were not already doing.

No Immediate Results

Having received that good news at the end of July 1994, I hoped to look forward to a new start and better things to come with the new academic year. This was not to be. The term did not get off to a good start. Timetables and class lists were not properly completed. The new Year 7's induction did not go smoothly. Even before half term it was clear that the implementation of the action plan was slipping. The amount of input the authority had made into the school had already been massive. Between 1990 and 1993 there had been 171 monitoring and support days from the inspectorate including twice the average amount of time for a secondary school from the link inspector. There had been a large amount of financial advice, personnel advice, information technology support, a buildings redevelopment scheme and resources support from the youth section of the community education service. This was on top of the revenue and capital resources that all our secondary schools had received through our school improvement project *Schools Make a Difference* (Myers, 1996).

My sixth general point learnt from this experience is that you can pour resources and support into a failing school but they find it very difficult to use it effectively until there is strong management and leadership, to ensure that general resources are not just dissipated. The support we had put in had been regularly monitored, and we found it was not being used effectively. It appears that when schools pass a particular point they find it very difficult to use support effectively. However, in spite of all this support, when things did not get better in the autumn term the authority stepped up a gear and produced a support package which I suspect is unique.

Bringing in Extra Staff

A major part of the latest support package in autumn 1994 was strengthening the senior management of the school by adding five experienced senior managers from other schools. To take a senior teacher or deputy head out of an existing school at extremely short notice and put them into a failing school, a certain number of criteria have to met. First, one has to be sure that they are extremely able and strong practitioners: it would be a disaster to put someone in who themselves could not cope. Second, they have to have a reason to be prepared to do it. The most positive reason is that they are deputy heads or senior teachers ready for promotion for whom such a temporary transfer would broaden their own experience and, therefore, help them secure their next appointment. Third, the school they are currently in must be able and willing to release them. Fourth, both the receiving school and the people themselves have to be clear about exactly what role they will play in the school and how they will fit in with existing structures and personnel.

It is difficult to find people around for whom all those circumstances come together. Indeed, in a small authority like Hammersmith and Fulham, it proved impossible to find any of them within our own secondary schools. It is not because there were no good people working in our secondary schools; it is because wherever they were, other circumstances did not come together in that the school was not in a position to release or the person themselves did not want to do it. I, therefore, had to obtain all five from schools and authorities outside Hammersmith and Fulham. This makes it even more difficult because you are not even negotiating with people who you know. You have to approach them completely cold usually because their names have been given to you by a third or fourth party. While not saying that no-one else could have undertaken the negotiations, I felt it was appropriate for me as director to do it: it was very intense and time consuming, with the pressure of having only three or four weeks between taking the decision it was necessary to do it, and actually signing, sealing and delivering the total deal. Only one of the five was known to me personally; the other four all came as a result of such negotiations.

They all started in the school at the beginning of the second half of autumn term 1994, introduced personally by me to the staff along with the rest of the support 'package'. The experienced ex-head who had been acting as a mentor to the head now changed role. He went into the school full time and acted as the link between the five extra members of staff who also joined the senior management team. This had to be done in a careful and sensitive way to avoid the pitfall of setting up an alternative management that undermined the existing management team. By this time all but one of the original SMT had left, but the new team was still struggling. It was largely due to the quality and sensitivities of the individuals concerned, and of the headteacher, which enabled the support to operate in such a way that it was not on the whole resented. The team had to operate at various different levels. In some ways they were simply five extra pairs of hands, five extra people to be around. In other ways they were direct role models picking up misbehaviour incidents, not letting them pass, and following things up. They also directly gave the benefit of their advice and experience in instituting proper systems across the board, for example, for following up lateness and attendance where those systems either did not exist or had broken down.

Other Staffing Resources

The rest of the support package introduced from autumn half term 1994 consisted of the authority putting one of its own staff members in the school office to support the school's administration; extra money made available to pay for more meal time supervision; and a team of youth workers who knew many of the students, particularly the more problematic ones, in a different context outside the school and who now set up groups at lunchtime to work in the school. This support was extended beyond the lunchtime groups and youth workers helped patrolling in the corridors, at the gate and outside school. In some instances they were effective in intervening in support of teachers who were obviously struggling. A temporary additional deputy head post was created and filled by an experienced ex-head and inspector. A subject adviser was put into the school two days a week to support one of the weakest departments. This new level of support was put together, agreed with the head and then presented to the staff by me personally in October 1994. I also met with all the newly appointed extra LEA governors, and during that term the new governing body met and elected a new chair and vice chair.

Still No Results — Should the School Be Closed?

In December 1994, the next OFSTED monitoring visit took place and indicated that in spite of all the extra measures there had been limited progress. In February 1995, the headteacher indicated she did not feel the school could be turned round with the existing staff, even though many of the original staff that had been in the school in the previous year when the inspection took place had either voluntarily left or had gone as a result of the summer's restructure. The headteacher herself began to suffer from stress-related illness which, following discussions during the second half of term with the LEA, finally resulted in her resignation in March 1995. One of the team of five LEA senior members of staff in the school acted as headteacher for the rest of spring term 1995.

At this point the situation was looking grim. The school had had three headteachers or acting headteachers in four years and neither of the substantive heads had succeeded in lifting the school clear of the position of failure that it had been in for such a long period of time. In addition, the authority was coming under pressure because at the same time during 1994–95 it was consulting on the closure of a second failing secondary school in the south of the borough. Understandably that raised the issue of why the Hammersmith School was not being closed. It is interesting to note that in the letter from the DfEE in relation to Hammersmith, one of the first failing schools, the issue of the authority considering closure had not been raised. I understand that it is now standard practice for the DfEE to raise it in the letter it initially sends to the LEAs about any failing schools.

Of course the LEA had considered closure very seriously. When things get as bad as they did at the Hammersmith School one has to consider whether there isn't a point of no return beyond which a school can go when it has sunk so far it is impossible to revive it. The overwhelming argument against closing the school was that it was needed in two senses. The number of surplus places in the borough justified closing only one school. The reason why Hammersmith School was not the one to be closed was partly because the pupil numbers were in that area rather than in the south and partly because the school was physically situated in, and should in practice have been a real focus for, the community in the White City. Councillors felt strongly that the most deprived and disadvantaged area of the borough should not be stripped of its secondary school with the result that children would have to be bussed out into other areas for their education.

If the reason for keeping the school, then, was that a school was needed on that site, did it have to be this school? This led to the idea of whether it was possible to close the school and open a new school on the same site. This had been a possibility that officers had explored throughout the whole of the preceding year when it was clear that under the new school management things were not progressing as quickly as they should. The difficulty is that there is only one piece of legislation which covers school closure and that was the 1980 Act under which ordinary school reorganizations — closures or amalgamations — take place. Even at its quickest, this procedure takes a year from beginning to end as it quite rightly includes periods for consultation and objections. This is appropriate in normal circumstances, but for a school at risk the very act of saying you were consulting on closing it and opening a new school on the site would have caused the school to collapse completely. While this would not have prevented the opening of a new school, it would have meant there were no children to start in it.

The LEA took Counsel's opinion on whether there was any other way. In his view there was not, apart from the emergency powers that exist under what was then Section 28 of the Education (No. 2) Act 1986, which would have enabled me to intervene on the grounds of breakdown of discipline and shut the school if the children had taken over complete control from the adults. This would have allowed only a temporary closure to give breathing space, and would hardly have formed the basis for reopening a successful school.

An interesting question arising from these discussions concerned the position of the staff if there was a closure and reopening, which raises the issue of Transfer of Undertaking and Protection of Earnings (TUPE). It was interesting to find out that if the LEA closed the school and opened another one, TUPE would not apply on the grounds that there would be no transfer of undertaking as the undertaking was originally with, and would remain with, the LEA. However, if an Education Association was moved in and they closed the school and opened a new one, all staff employed in the school would transfer to the Education Association under the Education Act 1993. Ironically this means that an LEA *could* get rid of poor staff through a process of closure and reopening, whereas an Education Association would be forced to use competency procedures.

Appointing a Head — Again

So what were we to do? There seemed no way out. We knew the school needed a fresh start but in law there did not seem a way round it. The answer evolved during the process of headhunting for the next head. When I started the process in March 1995 I assumed that the earliest I could hope to get a new head was September and possibly not until January given resignation dates of existing heads. By then I had concluded that only an experienced head could succeed in the school. On the whole, I still believe that for failing schools. For the previous two heads it was their first headship which meant they had to learn the ropes of headship as well as coping with one of the most extreme situations possible. To do both at once is too much to ask.

The method of headhunting the new head remained exactly the same, through many phone calls. What kind of person would be prepared to take on such a job, particularly someone who was already a successful head? The attraction one could hold out when bringing in the team of deputies and senior teachers (that it would help their career development), is hardly applicable to someone who is already a successful head. Possibly money? We had already decided not to bother with the national salary scales and to pay more or less whatever it took to get the right person. However, even on the very high salary which we ended up paying, one could not possibly argue that money would be a sufficient incentive to get the right person for the job. Indeed, it could be entirely the wrong incentive if we ended up with someone not up to it who was doing it just for the money. What we needed was someone who shared our passionate anger at the deal these young people were getting in that school. If a middle-class school goes through a bad patch one way or another there are safety nets. These children had no such safety nets and the longer the problem went on, the more permanent the damage became. They also needed to share our complete conviction that it was possible to run not just a good school but an excellent school in the White City, where children from the locality could achieve with no limit.

Endless telephone calls led me to such a person. He was an existing head of an extremely successful and very large community school in a neighbouring authority. He had himself been educated in an inner London school not dissimilar from Hammersmith. He was prepared to consider applying for the job but had a number of terms he wanted to set before agreeing to do so. He needed to be sure not only that the authority would give him its absolute support but that he would define what he found supportive and what he did not. One condition was the germ of the way we eventually found to close and reopen the school. He would only apply if he were able to start immediately on the first day of the summer term. His coming at that sort of notice was to be connected with making the maximum impact and the way to make the maximum impact would be to say that not only was it a new head but it was a new school. We could not do that in law but there was nothing to stop us just saying it. Most people do not understand the complexities of the legal process of a school closure anyway, unless they have been through it and so just announcing that Hammersmith School was closing on the last day of spring term 1995 and that Phoenix School was opening on the first day of summer term 1995 was simple but effective.

New Start — New Name

Yes, I agree Phoenix was a 'naff' name but interestingly enough it came up separately as a suggestion from a number of different people including the new head and the chair of the education committee — so Phoenix it was. An advert was placed with a week's closing date and the interviews for headship were held on the last day of term. Only one candidate was shortlisted as only one met all the selection criteria. The Easter holiday was one of intense activity on everybody's part. I remember with amusement the faxing backwards and forwards of various people's efforts to draw a Phoenix that did not on the one hand look like the Liberal Democrat's headed note paper, or on the other hand look like a design from some Nazi banner; the unhappiness from some members to discover that the new sign with the new name was purple not the council regulation yellow like everyone else's signs and me having to say that that was what the new head wanted and our role was to support what he wanted; the express delivery order we had to place to purchase a complete new school uniform based around a maroon sweatshirt with a gold Phoenix emblazoned on it; the painting, refurbishing, mending, patching up, glossing that went on in a frantic two-week Easter holiday which reminded me more of something out of *Challenge Anneka* than the normal activity of the council's building, decorating and maintenance service; the complete reversal of our policy in relation to press and the school — having spent the best part of the year trying to avoid publicity and keep the press at bay, we now had a head who could handle the press in a way that had them writing up positive stories about the future prospects of the school before he hardly got his feet across the threshold; the assembly on the first day of term where he first encountered the children and held their absolute and complete attention without a single exception (and he made a pretty good impression on the staff too!).

By the first day of summer term the aim was that every single person would be hit between the eyes that this was not the school that they left when they broke up on the last day of the previous term. Within the first week of the new head being there I knew I could sleep at night and not have to worry constantly about what was going to happen at the school.

The New Head

I no longer felt I was actually trying to be head of a school from a distance. There was now a head of the school and the authority could revert to its proper role of giving support and even sometimes risking giving advice; not that the new head was always easy to support or advise in that for a while there was no end to what he requested for the school. It was not always possible to say yes, and difficult to say no. He was right to make the demands and was realistic enough to know that some of them just were not deliverable, at least in the short term. Officer time we gave him in plenty whenever he wanted it and removed it if there were particular inputs he did not judge helpful. He had a knack of getting most of what he asked for and a good sense of humour which made it fun to work with him — and fun and enjoyment were words that it had not been possible to associate with any aspect of working with the school for a very long time. Before long everyone was absolutely convinced that this was a new school, even to the point that when the examination results came out at the end of summer term, and were dreadful, he managed to dispose of them with the least possible fuss and publicity by simply announcing that they were previous school's examination results and nothing to do with the current school!

The priority for the new head in his first term was to settle the school and sort out the behaviour problems. People tend to think that in a school where behaviour has been out of control that getting the children to behave differently will be extremely problematic. While not wishing to minimize the effort that has to go into it, it is one of the easier tasks to undertake. Children do not like being in an out of control situation. They want boundaries and parameters and to know with certainty that everyone will be kept within them. The children responded extremely well to the new head whose style was to be out and about everywhere as is absolutely necessary in the circumstances he inherited. Even the local shopkeepers were speaking in glowing terms within a very short time, as he patrolled the neighbourhood as well as the school, thus cutting down on truancy and preventing the kind of ugly incidents in the local streets and parks that had been a regular occurrence.

During that term, to give him a free hand to do that, the authority led on driving through a restructure of the staff. In these circumstances it was essential we had the personnel powers and it was greatly assisted by the assistant director with overall responsibility for that area also being on the governing body, thus providing the link. Our attitude throughout had been that although we had taken over the powers, we wished to act in a way that totally involved the governing body, as the aim was to restore delegation to them as soon as we could and therefore they needed involving and training so they would be in a position to take up those responsibilities again.

Appointing Effective Teachers in Failing Schools

Autumn term 1995 therefore started with a considerable number of staff having left and new staff taking up post. At this point it is appropriate to make a further general observation. Clearly, in a secondary school deemed to be failing, it is likely that the teaching will be at least part of the problem and probably a major part. Having achieved a considerable change in the teaching staff, it was tempting to think that from that autumn term, as far as having capable teachers were concerned, that the work had been successfully done. However, what I discovered was that the fact that a weak teacher had left did not necessarily mean that it was a stronger teacher who replaced them. In other words, being able to attract and recruit staff to a school in special measures was very difficult. Some posts were on to their second and sometimes third postholder in two years and individual teachers were still proving not up to it. In some cases this was because they would not have been up to it anywhere. In other cases it genuinely was the difficulties of working in that particular school which proved too much for people who either would be, or indeed in some cases had been, successful elsewhere. During 1995–96 the head came to the conclusion, and I supported him, that he was going to appoint temporary staff knowing it would be problematic rather than appoint permanent contract staff who in the event might not be up to the job.

Catch 22

The effect of this was that when HMI made their monitoring visits, the proportion of satisfactory lessons proved stubbornly hard to increase and by July 1996 was still only around two thirds. This meant that HMI were reluctant to take the school off the list even though they agreed that in every other respect it was now meeting the criteria to come off. It is my view that this exposes a weakness in the current system. The school was in a catch 22 situation. It was not going to be able to recruit staff satisfactorily while still in special measures. This was equally true of its ability to recruit a balanced intake of pupils. I would ask every reader whether, if their local school was deemed to be failing and requiring special measures, they would send their 11-year old to it. However, it was that very lack of ability to recruit successful staff and the difficulties that staff were having and the difficulties staff continued to have because of the untypical nature of the intake, that was in itself being put forward by HMI as the reason not to take it off.

The system was very much a 'tick in boxes' one. Unless you could get a tick in all the relevant boxes you might be found to be failing by a subsequent OFSTED team, which would of course prove embarrassing if it happened soon after HMI had recommended that the school comes off special measures. No-one is able within the system to stick their neck out and make a good old fashioned judgment that the school had turned the corner and would be alright, even if it hadn't yet got to the point where a tick could be put in every box. The head, the LEA and the governing body were convinced that the school should come off in autumn term 1996. HMI were not, and at the end of the day it is their opinion which prevails. What we did agree with was their opinion that the worst of all outcomes would be for HMI to do a major visit to the school with a view to taking it out of special measures and then publish a report finding it still to be failing. It was therefore agreed that the major visit with a view to taking the school out of special measures be put off until spring term 1997, three years after the original inspection.

Financial Implications

There is no doubt that any attempt to turn round a failing school must involve additional resources. This is because once an analysis has been made of what needs to be done to get the school off special measures, whatever has to be done has to be achieved regardless of the cost. What those resources may be will vary from school to school, although some of the features will probably occur across the board. At Phoenix, the head felt strongly that he needed money to improve the appearance of the school and upgrade some facilities so that it could be presented as a physically attractive place to attend. This was necessary even though the site itself was basically in reasonable condition. Certainly if one follows the route of closing and reopening, there needs to be some kind of physical facelift associated with the new school.

The main extra revenue resource relates to staffing and this occurs in various ways. If management is weak it may not be possible to wait until you can get rid of the weak links. You may have to create extra posts over and above the structure to bring in good people including an extra deputy head post. Under the local management formula if the roll has fallen in a school, staffing should fall proportionately. You cannot afford to allow that to happen in a failing school, which means you have to run for a period with a more generous staffing ratio and smaller classes than a school of that size would normally have. The same is true for the overall salary bill. You need experienced teachers that cost more. They will need to be paid scale points on a structure that a small school would not normally have. In a school like the Hammersmith School, stress levels of teaching there were very high which means that there is likely to be a lot of absence. This needs covering and so the supply bill is much higher than in an ordinary school. As well as the roll falling, it is likely that during the period the school is failing the intake will not be a balanced one, as at the Hammersmith School. In 1994, the authority ability balance aimed at was 25 per cent above average, 50 per cent average, 25 per cent below average ability entering secondary schools at 11. The entry to the Hammersmith was 75 per cent below average ability. The skewing of the intake will inevitably mean that more resources for additional educational needs and special educational needs will be required.

On the revenue side it is possible to do a profile over a three- to five-year period based on projections of how long it will take for the roll to pick up and the budget to reach a point where the normal delegated budget will be able to sustain the curriculum and staffing. This immediately highlights another problem of the special measures system because that period of time is likely to be much longer than the time it takes to come off special measures. It is obviously a nonsense to think that one can reduce the resources of the school the day after it comes off special measures, and yet once it has, the authority's legal ability to resource a school over and above the local management formula is extremely constrained. In the case of the Hammersmith School we have been able to supplement their resources by writing into our local management scheme that we can use the contingency to do so for failing schools. It is likely that we will now have to consult about changing our scheme otherwise we will not be able to continue to supplement the school's resources once it does come out of special measures. This is yet another area of the legislation that could benefit from being looked at again.

The Role of the LEA

Finally, what about the role of the local education authority in all of this? My observation about the way the failing schools issue has developed nationally in the three years since Hammersmith School failed is that the LEA invariably gets the blame for the failure and very little credit for the improvement. I particularly remember an article in one of the Sunday newspapers at the time that the Ridings School in Halifax was in the news. It was a double-page spread on the problems at that school which focused very much on the failure of the LEA and indeed personally on the chair of the education committee to the point of describing the fact that he wore two earrings and was unemployed! Inset into the double page was an article about Phoenix High School putting it forward as an example of what can be done to improve schools such as the Ridings. It was a very positive article and I was very happy for it to be there. I know that when the head was interviewed by the journalist, he made a very strong point of emphasizing the role of the LEA and partnership between himself, governing body and local authority as being essential to the school being turned round. The whole of that section was cut out and there was not one reference to the LEA. I hope it will be clear from the story told in this chapter that the role of the education authority in Hammersmith and subsequently Phoenix School has been a key one both in trying to prevent the decline, dealing with the failure when it happens in a formal sense, and lifting the school out of failure and special measures into success. Clearly, we failed to prevent the decline of Hammersmith School. It was not in a good state when we took over in April 1990 but it was in a worse state when OFSTED inspected it in 1994. Could we have done any more and would it have made any difference? Clearly, the last question is impossible to answer. I can honestly answer no, not as the current legislation stands, to the first. However, everything we did do, all the support we put in, all the monitoring that took place did not prevent the school from going downhill.

There are a growing number of people now, and I am one of them, who would wish to see a change in the law so that local authorities could intervene sooner in more than an advisory role. We currently have a falling off the cliffs system. Once a school has fallen and failed, not only can the LEA intervene directly, but it becomes the LEA's responsibility so to do. However, if the school is inexorably moving towards the edge of the cliff and perhaps could be stopped from falling over by more direct intervention by the LEA, it does not have the powers so to do.

Experience has shown that the quality of the headteacher is the single most important factor in both contributing to failure and bringing about improvement and it is not uncommon for there to be a change of head either just before or just after a school fails its OFSTED inspection. In the case of Hammersmith School, two heads tried and did not succeed. In one case the change of head had to be brought about when the power was in the hands of the governing body and in the second case, the change had to be brought about after that power was withdrawn and was in the hands of the LEA. In the former case it took over three years, in the latter less than a year.

Overall, then, the authority's role is to ensure that the head's leadership of the school is strong and capable of bringing about improvement. Its role then is to provide support to the head of the school that is flexible and tailored, not just to the needs of the school, but to the way the head wants to work and prioritize. There are many ways of being a successful head and my experience is that the kind of support that they want and require and the way that they want to work with the LEA will vary. The LEA should be prepared to allow the head to be in the driving seat once they are confident that there is a head in post who is going to be able to turn the school round.

There is no doubt that the LEA will need to provide support in terms of resources in a number of different ways. At a very simple level, the roll of the failing school will almost certainly have dropped to the point where a roll-related local management formula budget will be insufficient to enable the school to recover. There will need to be an element of protection of class sizes and staffing levels which would not be possible without supplementation from the LEA. There will also certainly need to be some kind of physical facelift to go with the new approach and new image even if only at a symbolic level. Staff will need to be paid over the odds to attract them to work in the school. Supply cover costs will be higher because of the stress resulting in teacher absence. I have not even costed the officer and inspector time that will need to be given to the school. However, resources alone will not do the trick. You can pour resources and support into a school but it needs to be able to use them effectively and that is an issue of leadership and management.

Finally, the LEA has the responsibility to make the biggest decision of all which is whether the school *can* be turned round and whether it *should* be turned round, because the LEA has the power to propose a school's closure. That decision by the LEA in the case of Hammersmith School was complex because our view was that the school *had* passed the point of no return and yet at the same time straightforward closure was not the answer because the community needed and was entitled to a secondary school for its children. The answer when those two circumstances come together was, as I have described, to shut one school and reopen another, albeit with no legislative basis for doing so. If it does become generally accepted that this is an effective way of proceeding in those circumstances, then perhaps that too should be considered as a future legislative change so that there is a formal process of doing what Hammersmith and Fulham did on an informal basis.

Conclusion

In conclusion, what is it that has actually happened between April 1995 and September 1996 which has moved me from despair to optimism about the future of the former Hammersmith and current Phoenix School? Clearly, the major part of that answer relates to the quality of the new head. If you could bottle what it takes to make a successful head in such circumstances I suspect there would be a lot of money to be made from the formula. Different people have different leadership styles and certainly there are not many people, if any, who would exactly replicate the personality and approach of the current postholder. An element of uniqueness is perhaps itself one of the factors that you need. Certainly you need to be a physical presence everywhere in the school and outside it. You need to lead from the front by example, and to inspire respect from pupils, staff and parents alike. You need to be good at public relations and talk a good story. At the same time you need to be able to turn the hype into reality. The how of how you do all of this is almost boringly simple. It is about setting up routines and procedures that work, consistency, following everything up, and about pupils and teachers knowing that you are going to follow everything up. It is about expectations, monitoring and sheer hard work. The head has not done anything that any head would not have to do going into a new school. It is just that it has been more difficult to do it in Hammersmith because the basis of the systems and routines and practices really were not there, and the number of staff who were not performing or not able to perform to the level required was higher than you would find in a successful school. The pupils, however, were crying out for it, and have responded enthusiastically and positively. At last they are now beginning to get the education to which they are entitled.

Postscript

The Phoenix School came off special measures in March 1997.

References

BRACE, A. (1994) 'Is this the worst school in Britain?' *The Mail On Sunday*, March 20.
MYERS, K. (1996) *School Improvement in Practice: Schools Make a Difference Project*, London, Falmer Press.

Part 3

Schools

The next three chapters have been written by heads of secondary, special and primary schools that were deemed requiring special measures or regarded as having serious weaknesses following their OFSTED inspections. None of the authors were in post during the initial inspection. Two were in the LEA advisory service and asked to cover following the judgment; the third, a substantive head of an improving school in a different LEA, responded to a second national advertisement for the job.

The qualities necessary to lead a school in this situation are raised in Christine Whatford's contribution in the previous section. The personal cost of being involved in such an undertaking is explored by all three heads in this section and discussed in particular detail with humour and humility by Steven Pugh. Two of the authors comment on the response of the staff to the school being labelled as failing. Steven Pugh compares it to a bereavement. Linda Turner is concerned about 'giving her staff back the sense of capability and professional ability that the OFSTED judgment took away'.

External support, particularly from the LEA, is deemed as vital. Headship under any circumstances can be lonely, isolating and stressful. These are clearly exacerbated in these circumstances. Support from governors is welcomed but, as Vivien Cutler explains, not always forthcoming. Not everyone wants to support the head and some people have their own agenda.

All the heads were faced with an exhaustive list of tasks that needed doing and could not merely concentrate on doing one or two well and putting others on the back-burner, as often seems to be the advice of management gurus.

None of the authors dispute that the schools were in much need of improvement when inspected. They all believe that their schools have made considerable headway since but they are not all convinced that the OFSTED way was the right or only way to achieve change.

Chapter 6

Highbury Grove — From Deconstruction to Reconstruction

Vivien Cutler

It is surely a measure of the paucity of the education debate in this country that the name of an underperforming inner-city boys school should continue to elicit widespread recognition when the achievements on which its reputation was based occurred over twenty years ago, in a socioeconomic and educational climate far removed from that of today.

The Legacy

All schools have a history. Few, however, have attained the iconic status of Highbury Grove, associated forever in the media's eye with its first head, Rhodes Boyson, who launched a national political career during his final year at the school. Boyson's model, with its reverence for the minutiae of public school organization, was never that of a school focused primarily on achievement or quality of teaching and learning. With its semi-autonomous houses, this was a school much more interested in the pastoral than the curricular. When the ex-grammar school boys who had comprised a significant proportion of the original intake left, at about the time of Boyson's election to Parliament, they and their academic achievements were never entirely replicated.

The inflexibility of the streamed system and the continuing pre-eminence of the house structure gradually became inadequate to deal with the changing nature of the intake and the 1981 HMI report was a clear indictment of their shortcomings. In the days before accountability, it was never publicized. The mythology was allowed to persist, nourished in a well-established and politicized climate of antagonism between the school and the Inner London Education Authority (ILEA).

In 1988, Rhodes Boyson's successor retired. This gave the ILEA the opportunity of appointing someone with rather different educational priorities. However, in a school whose leadership had traditionally charted a line from the Black Papers to the Hillgate Group, any challenge to the existing hegemony was bound to encounter some opposition. Within three years, although a number of significant changes had been introduced, there were widespread problems which were causing a seepage of confidence in the school. Two HMI reports were highly critical and the headteacher was dismissed. A very experienced ex-ILEA headteacher, who had once before carried out a similar 'holding and turning round' exercise, was brought in during the period of uncertainty whilst the substantive headteacher was preparing to go to an industrial tribunal.

What was initially expected to be a short tenure eventually extended to eighteen months, including seeing through an OFSTED inspection. The substantive headteacher's tribunal was lost and the post advertised. Unsurprisingly, this was not the most coveted headship in London and it took a second advertisement, with a rather better package of salary and conditions, to attract a suitably experienced field.

Why would anyone want to take on this poisoned chalice? Any headteacher contemplating a second school expects to be able to build on the experiences of the first venture — and to make a better job of it. As my first headship had been in a very run-down and unpopular mixed school with a preponderance of boys, and visible progress had been made over six years, I naively thought that I would be reasonably well poised to take up the challenge of Highbury Grove. Furthermore, I had known the school from a period I had spent as a deputy head in its consortium partner and had been involved in some sixth-form teaching there. Whether it was actually possible to create a good, inner-city, non-selective school out of such an institution was an intriguing proposition. The jury is still out . . . and will be for quite some time.

The Early Days

The above gallop through twenty-six years of the school's history, however truncated and open to contradiction, will give some idea of the complex context any new headteacher would confront over and above the conventional scenario of an underachieving school. This was, of course, a school in a media goldfish bowl and the arrival of a woman headteacher added yet another dimension. In the spectrum of stereotypes, I occupied either the Iron Lady territory (liberal broadsheets) or the diminutive and undemonstrative (right-wing press). In the latter, the ubiquitous Dr Boyson made several appearances by way of comparison.

No school in Highbury Grove's position provides a new headteacher with the luxury of a period of observation and reflection. On arrival immediately after Whitsun 1994, there was a post-OFSTED action plan to be completed by the end of my first half-term; a staff and pupils to get to know (and I was their third head in two-and-a-half years); and a senior management team with whom I had to build a working relationship. In addition, a huge image problem had resulted in the smallest ever September intake to the school and one which had extensive literacy difficulties.

That was in July. By August, there was a growing realization that I was on a collision course with a governor. Most problematic of all, perhaps, a newly appointed school finance officer had uncovered structural defects in the budgetary process and a pattern of spend which indicated that a supposedly manageable deficit was in fact heading for a sum five times that amount.

The Challenge

Climate setting? The environmental aspect at least had already been set in train. A brief encounter with the 'reception area' — a dingy, oppressive corridor — was all that was needed to embolden me at the end of my interview to insist that radical alterations would have to be made if I were to agree to take the job. In a recent study of women teachers in boys schools carried out by a colleague from a nearby boys school (Danischewsky, 1996), it is noted that most women cannot understand why no-one who works in boys schools seems to notice that the environment is so appalling. Highbury Grove more than fitted the bill.

Most of the school effectiveness and improvement literature gives little comfort to those confronted with a critical mass of problems. For a start, you search in vain to find one inner-city, non-selective and maintained boys school. Then there are those taxonomies of the characteristics of the successful, none of which your school appears to possess. They can be daunting: the advice to concentrate on only one or two key aspects to improve at a time is an impossible imposition when there are so many areas to address. And in the classic ineffective school, nearly all the priorities involve the longer term — and the seemingly intractable.

Thankfully, there were many practicalities to deal with in the short term, with literacy as a priority. Literacy levels had in fact been falling for a number of years, and the percentage of bilingual pupils had simultaneously been rising. (It is not unusual in inner-city boys schools to encounter over 80 per cent of new intake pupils with a reading age well below their chronological age.) However, there was little by way of a systematic approach to improving literacy other than from the English as a Second Language (ESL) team. We introduced a corrective reading scheme and tutor group book boxes. An enthusiastic librarian started to promote literacy and, later in the year, was joined in this by an equally committed English teacher. The library was given a higher profile through improved stock, poster campaigns, 'author of the month' displays, competitions and lunchtime sessions staffed by the librarian and another English teacher. Perhaps the biggest attractions were the new computers and interactive CD-Roms, but, no matter, they achieved the aim of enticing boys in.

There is now an active Bookworms club for lower school pupils, and going to the library and reading are regarded as quite acceptable activities, even for boys. There are also many opportunities to celebrate achievements in assemblies and through school-wide display.

As part of a new language and literacy policy developed in 1995, we introduced a language diary for all Key Stage 3 pupils; a mix of personal dictionary, subject glossary and aide memoire for grammar and punctuation. A good idea undoubtedly, this has been but one of a range of whole school policies dependent on consistency of usage by teachers and a commitment by pupils to bring the correct equipment. A relaunch took place in September 1996 to heighten its profile and embed an important whole school policy.

The mechanics of improving reading skills are being further refined by an enlarged and more effective special needs department whose resources will shortly include the American basic skills software programme, Successmaker. Whatever its potential for raising achievement, the need to provide half an hour's access per day per pupil is bound to create tension between the priority of radically improving literacy and numeracy levels and National Curriculum requirements.

With a view to better diagnosis of need and baseline data against which to measure performance, this year's Year 7 pupils are being tested — almost to destruction, I fear — with a veritable barrage of cognitive, literacy and numeracy tests. Again a conflict: the tests are important but the time taken to administer, and in some cases mark them, greatly reduces the possibility for early intervention by the special needs department for all but those who already have a statement. Let us hope that having identified the most needy, we can fight our way through the Special Needs Code of Practice to support them adequately. With around 300 on the special needs register, as much time can be expended on processing the paper as teaching basic skills. Fortunately for him, the headteacher quoted in the OFSTED and DfEE booklet *Setting Targets to Raise Standards* (1996) could, from the outset on appointment, devote himself to improving the quality of teaching and learning. Did he have no marketing, budgetary, or behaviour management issues to address? Certainly, he seems unlikely to have had to engage in power battles with a group of governors intent on his — and possibly the school's — downfall.

Working with Governors

The legislation underpinning the governance of schools and OFSTED inspections is designed, one would suppose, to enable underachieving schools to improve within a strong, supportive framework. Yet the pages of the education press are filled each week with horror stories of the relationship between heads and governors resulting from the ambiguities of the legislation and the effect on schools of the process of inspection.

When applying for the headship, I was aware of the part that some members of the governing body — and indeed staff — had played in the previous head's dismissal. There was also a history of governing body meetings almost totally preoccupied with parochial politics, to the exclusion of the role of policy making. In more troubled times, perhaps, this was to be expected. That these times were set to continue was presaged by the leak of my appointment to the London *Evening Standard* by one of the governors — leaked without other governors' knowledge or agreement and leaked even before I had told my then staff that I was going. The legislation does not compel governors to be discreet or to consult fully, as I was soon to discover.

Some governors do not understand (or perhaps choose not to do so) that there is a separation of the strategic and the operational in the running of schools. This can result in a perception that they have *carte blanche* to come on site without prior warning or clear purpose and to attempt to involve themselves in certain matters which are palpably the province of the head.

Fuelled by disagreements about these boundaries, certain governors decided, over a period of time, to complain to the LEA, the Chair of Education, OFSTED and HMCI (to the latter, just before an HMI review visit and without any reference to the Chair). On no occasion was I given forewarning that a complaint was going to be made nor was I copied into the correspondence. Indeed, I was never called to account by these governors for any of the specific actions that were supposed to have generated such concern. Allegations made by some members of staff who were opposed to my approach were taken at face value and used as the basis for such complaints. In the drive to maintain total direction of the school and to embarrass and undermine me, this alliance did not reflect for a second on the possible consequences for a school which had only just started to get back on its feet.

With the lapsing of all the key members of this clique from the governing body, and the retirement or resignation of the group of oppositional staff over the past two years, much of the energy directed into marginalizing and disempowering those factions has been channelled into more fulfilling tasks. But without joining battle at that stage, there might have been no school at all to engage with.

Changing the Culture

Penetrating the culture of a school is always a voyage of discovery. Here was a palimpsest; layers of values and practices — even some visible manifestations — from bygone ages. I could discern strong traditions which were undoubtedly worth preserving alongside the more negative aspects of the old-fashioned boys school. There seemed to be no reason to hold on to the more recondite elements of, say, a house system which had been dismantled some years before, yet such was the fragility of staff and student confidence that it took some time to gain agreement to abandon them.

If we were to move forward into the next century, the symbolic had to be addressed as forcibly as the harder indicators. The school badge, an angular and vaguely priapic creation emblematic of the 1960s tied us inexorably to the school — and expectations — of those times. If ever there was a school that exemplified Stoll and Fink's (1996) 'good school if this were 1965', this was it. Giving pupils the opportunity to design a logo, which was then refined by a professional graphic artist, produced a clear statement of contemporary design celebrating our pride in our richly diverse school community and an equally explicit break with the past.

Behaviour Management

You can almost identify to the day that point around week three of the school year when the 'cussing season' starts. We struggle to develop and refine listening and communication skills and experiment with a variety of groupings to support cooperation in the learning process. One carefully interjected 'cuss' can destroy that work in a trice, and the reluctance of many boys to expose themselves in discussion is proving a difficult barrier to overcome in the short term. Stereotypical constructs of masculinity held by a majority of boys, and reflected in disruptive power play or undermining of staff who do not fit their image of the authoritative teacher, undoubtedly undermine achievement.

For many boys schools, behaviour management is the key issue. In the early 1990s, Highbury Grove gained the reputation of being something of a blackboard jungle. Whereas Boyson's self-styled 'Eton of the comprehensives' could hide behind discipline enforced by corporal punishment and attitudes to exclusion and attendance which would not bear scrutiny today, we try to balance the need for an unequivocal stance on disruption and violence with the recognition that the causes are often complex and require longer term solutions. Thus my immediate predecessor introduced a positive discipline scheme which started to alter the prevailing culture. This is being continually refined and re-presented but is recognized as fundamental to our approach.

Last year, in response to the overrepresentation of black pupils in our exclusion statistics, we introduced a pupil support project for some very disaffected Year 11 pupils run by a former teacher at the school. That everyone who was able to avoid permanent exclusion after the first half-term managed to stay the course, and achieve at least one A–G at GCSE, gives hope that we can achieve even more with this year's project which will address the problem with younger pupils.

In tandem, we have now embarked on a rolling programme of conflict resolution and behaviour management strategies which should lead to a whole school community anti-bullying policy. These projects — and one which supports a part-time attendance officer and an electronic registration system — are funded by a borough Grants for Education Support and Training (GEST) bid. Their success depends on the continuity of that funding and serves to underline the OFSTED urban schools research which highlights the value-added effect of centrally funded short-term projects on underachieving schools (Barber, Denning, Gough and Johnson, 1996).

Teaching and Learning

So what of the core activities, teaching and learning? Going into classes in my first half term, the abiding impression was that of close-set ranks of desks, writing as a control mechanism and reams of copying. As a school which had undergone three inspections in three years and which had been criticized by HMI for a lack of discipline, this was hardly surprising. In addition, undersubscribed schools are a hostage to fortune in terms of being forced to take everyone else's expellees and a definable minority of pupils were undoubtedly extremely disruptive. (It is a vicious circle. Unpopularity, often starting as a result of a particularly difficult group of pupils, starts to have a pervasive effect. Numbers go down, as does income. To maintain your budget, and because you have spaces, you are encouraged by the LEA to take the displaced. At this point, all your resources are consumed by support for these casual admissions and your few remaining pupils who do not manifest severe problems leave.) Finally, many classrooms were inadequately sized and it was difficult to shoe-horn pupils into the space, let alone embark on flexible groupings once inside.

During the pre-OFSTED period and over the past two years, with two HMI review visits, colleagues have participated in a wide range of training. Whilst the prospect of inspection can concentrate the mind wonderfully, the cumulative effects of so many of them — five in six years! — and of adverse press coverage, can constrain even the most creative person. The most successful approach appears to have been the sharing of good practice, both formal and informal, with colleagues from our sixth-form consortium partner and at borough subject panels. This has been enhanced by the appointment of new staff unencumbered by the baggage of past failure. Strong language and learning support departments have also helped this process through their regular inputs on differentiation.

Complementing this work has been a borough Improving Pupil Achievement (IPA) initiative designed to increase the percentage of five A–C passes at GCSE. This scheme has combined the development of management skills among our core and foundation subject heads of department with a more sophisticated use of statistics and target setting to improve subject performance. Each school has tended to adopt its own approach to identifying and supporting pupils in this venture. At Highbury Grove last year, we targeted a cohort of approximately sixty Year 11 boys who then received fortnightly study skills lessons and additional mentoring from their director of studies and three members of senior management. They were further encouraged to attend after-school and holiday revision clubs, and a group joined with their counterparts in our consortium school to attend a residential weekend in March.

It is doubtful whether Miss Buss (the renowned first head of the North London Collegiate girls school) would have found it necessary, as did I, to struggle up a climbing wall and abseil down the other side 'pour encourager les autres', but this weekend of core study skills and team-building activities was both enjoyable and motivating. The whole IPA programme has been acknowledged by the students themselves to have kept more of them on track than we could possibly have hoped for.

Financial Constraints

This programme took place in a year of austerity that had seen the budget deficit almost halved, whilst class sizes had risen to unacceptable levels, capitation had dwindled and subsidies for trips and inter-school fixtures had all but disappeared. Schools that have lost popularity and intake soon begin to suffer diminished resources. Their deteriorating image then militates against the likelihood of sponsorship. If, as in the case of Highbury Grove, you additionally uncover poor budgetary management, the chances of lifting morale or supporting those initiatives which provide a little value-added, are reduced to a minimum.

It has been a very steep learning curve for many staff used to the enhanced resourcing levels of yore. They have understandably questioned the point of coming through OFSTED and HMI reviews to face such stringency. Pupils, the majority of whose families are on income support, have complained bitterly about the lack of cheap trips or new equipment, such as computers or for sports. They query why we cannot afford textbooks for everyone in many subjects and why the swimming pool walls continue to flake.

The negative effects of the environment have already been mentioned. Not only is the school building an unbelievably drab and unattractive place to work, it was actually built as two schools — a grammar and a secondary modern — which were umbilically linked but never structurally altered to take account of their unification as a comprehensive some three years later. Rooms were either wastefully large or woefully inadequate and, by the mid-1990s, there were more offices than postholders to fill them. This was a true gem of 1960s architecture whose crowning glory was the creation of science laboratories on the top floors of both buildings which could only be accessed by the technicians via a hike over the roof.

Over the summer of 1995, we were able to rationalize the accommodation of a number of key departments, but pleasure at the ability to group teaching rooms together in suites gave way to despair that some tiny classrooms could not be expanded without extensive demolition work and money which neither ourselves nor the LEA, on a minimal annual capital grant, could afford.

Persistent banging at the door of the LEA, and a report from HMI which expressed concern about class size and accommodation, has released a small pot of money to refurbish two science laboratories and the inclusion of the school in a larger bid focused on a nearby estate for significant reorganization. Even if unsuccessful this time round, participation offers crumbs of optimism that the right vehicle for generating the money will eventually appear. Any past sniffiness about having to expend energy on bidding for resources has long since evaporated. Recent bids have yielded improvements to our information technology and special needs facilities and we continue to enjoy a fruitful relationship as a British Petroleum link school.

Parental Involvement

Unlike many successful schools in more salubrious areas, we cannot count on legions of volunteer parents to augment our resources. However, our parent body, in addition to being fairly poor, is also extremely disparate. The richness of the ethnic and religious diversity is a tremendous learning resource but is more difficult to harness as a cohesive community, especially as it is spread over a wide geographical area encompassing a number of boroughs. Living in some squalid and difficult estates, our parents do not always share our educational preoccupations. Although attendance at parents' evenings is improving significantly in most years, it is in the area of parental support for the learning process that we still have much to do.

Team Building

Whatever the nature of the parent body, a new head has to be able to harness the staff to move a school forward. Colleagues at Highbury Grove, despite some of the more unusual occurrences of the previous few years, proved little different to those working in many inner-city schools. Some had undoubtedly been in the same milieu for too long, some had simply given up and others had never really got started. A significant number, however, provided such a positive model of commitment, skill and good humour that it would have been criminal had their efforts over the most difficult times been in vain and the school collapsed.

A more benign media gaze and an improving image in the local community have helped to restore self-confidence, as well as increasing our intake. Celebratory events such as a staff-student pantomime, concerts and a Euroweek which brought in national figures, could have been criticized by some as unnecessary diversions from the task of raising achievement. Without them, however, the rehabilitation of the school would be taking so much longer, and would not be half as much fun. (And who can survive the challenges of some schools without regular injections of celebration and laughter?)

Although changes in organizational culture tend to be incremental, Highbury Grove staff have moved a long way to embrace, however tentatively on occasion, the responsibilities of formulating new aims, an exhaustive school development plan and systems of self-review which previously would have seemed overly threatening. (Over two decades, management styles had been autocratic or over-democratic, with little in between.) Now that a largely new and supportive governing body is involved in the process of whole school review, we are even daring to look over the parapet to articulate our vision for the school of the twenty-first century.

Most studies of school effectiveness see leadership as key to school improvement. But this underestimates the importance of the senior management team in facilitating coherence and supporting middle managers in a range of roles. Whilst some colleagues would prefer to renounce all personal responsibility to the 'superhero' model of leadership, the complexity of the medium-sized enterprise that is the present day, large secondary school demands a more collegial and participative approach.

In the events of the past five years, the senior team at Highbury Grove has experienced the dismissal of a well-liked and respected colleague, the appointment of two other very different headteachers and more inspections than most people encounter in a lifetime of teaching. For such a group, possibly even more than the rest of the staff, it was understandably difficult to view new leadership and the change imperative with anything other than caution.

Conclusion

Contemplating the past two years, I recognize that embarking on such a wide-ranging programme of change was probably suicidal. Much better, as with that fortunate headteacher (q.v.), to have concentrated on one or two developments only. We could have focused solely on teaching and learning and improving literacy levels. But how could we have ignored a massive budget deficit, a poor public image and dreadful buildings — to name but a few of the worst problems? We could have confronted those staff clearly exhibiting shortcomings in the early stages. But what effect would this have had when self-confidence and esteem amongst the whole complement was so low?

There has been progress in almost all areas, though it has proved more marginal in some than others. New appointments to the staff and the governing body have challenged many of the old orthodoxies and brought a wider perspective to both. The mantra of raising achievement, drip-fed at regular intervals and supported by well-conceived inservice training, has effected a notable shift in culture. We are able to look at ourselves critically and constructively.

Some headteachers have taken to selling their prescription of improvement measures as a panacea for all schools from the depressed rural to the deprived urban. As we scuttle, crab-like, across the shores of school improvement, we can take some comfort from Gray and Wilcox (1995): 'How an "ineffective school" improves, may well differ from the ways in which more effective schools maintain their effectiveness' (p. 242). And to think that I always imagined we were just going backwards!

References

Barber, M., Denning, T., Gough, G. and Johnson, M. (1996) 'Urban education initiatives: Three case studies', in Barber, M. and Dann, R. (eds) *Raising Educational Standards in the Inner Cities*, London: Cassell.

Danischewsky, J. (1996) 'Are there Gender Specific Issues for Women Managers in All-boys Schools?' Unpublished MBA thesis, South Bank University.

Gray, J. and Wilcox, B. (1994) 'The challenge of turning round ineffective schools', in Gray, J. and Wilcox, B. (eds) *Good School, Bad School: Evaluating Performance and Encouraging Improvement*, Buckingham: Open University Press.

OFSTED and DfEE (1996) *Setting Targets To Raise Standards: A Survey Of Good Practice*, London: DfEE.

Stoll, L. and Fink, D. (1996) *Changing Our Schools: Linking School Effectiveness and School Improvement*, Buckingham: Open University Press.

Chapter 7

Turning Around a Struggling School: A Case Study

Linda Turner

The School in Context

Roundthorn County Primary School is housed in spacious and well-maintained but very old buildings on the edge of Oldham borough close to the open countryside. It has hard-surfaced playing areas and it benefits from shared use of the nearby comprehensive school playing fields. The school is one-form entry and has classes in two buildings on the same site. There are usually about 240 pupils on role with little variation on this number. The additional forty-place nursery is located in a nearby separate building. Most of the pupils at Roundthorn School come from the surrounding district which is comprised of mainly good quality terraced housing. Forty-two per cent of the children come from homes where parents originate from Pakistan.

Towards the end of June 1994 the school was inspected through one of the OFSTED training inspections knowing that the results of the inspection would be published, even though this was a pilot inspection. The school and LEA believed that the inspection would be successfully completed, even though, just prior to the inspection, the then headteacher was off school seriously ill, and the deputy headteacher was absent from school on secondment to the local authority. The school was carried through the inspection by the acting deputy headteacher who had very little management experience. Temporary and supply teachers covered two of the classes. One (good) teacher was at the LEA outdoor education centre and was not included in the inspection. Following the inspection, the school was put in the category of 'likely to fail'. The staff were devastated. In the fullness of time we learned that the term 'likely to fail' meant that the school would be accorded the same measures as schools which fail their inspection. These are termed 'special measures' in OFSTED-speak.

I was at that time on secondment from headship to the local authority as an adviser and was asked if I would take over the management of the school for a term. I agreed and began working with the school in late July 1994, just before the summer break.

In the Beginning

It is true that the school had inadequate, and often an absence of, necessary systems and structures. It is also true that roles and responsibilities were unclear and in some cases very inappropriately allocated. The OFSTED report, in its key issues for action, pointed the finger very clearly to what needed to be improved in the school.

An action plan must be written following an OFSTED inspection. The LEA guided me on how to proceed and I had the informal help of an LEA inspector in the actual writing of the draft document. This draft then went to both the staff and the school's governing body for their comments. The governing body was, and still is, very supportive of the school but had little knowledge of, or involvement in the day-to-day running of the school. They had not experienced consultation on school issues at this level of importance before but were very anxious to develop their roles and responsibilities and readily accepted guidance and training from both myself and the LEA. They set up a committee to monitor progress on the issues highlighted by the OFSTED inspection and by the end of my first year at Roundthorn they were ready to draw up their own governing body development plan. The action plan set out in detail how all the key issues for improvement would be addressed. It included success criteria; how the targets in the plan would be monitored and by whom; the time-scale for improvements, and an indication of the costs involved.

Drawing up the plan was most useful as it enabled me to think through and prioritize the issues in the report. It helped me to clarify in my own mind the way forward for the school. The school had two years in which to demonstrate that it was becoming effective, which would indicate that some 'quick fixes', such as introducing formats for whole school planning, were required to move the school on swiftly. After all, two years is not long to turn a school from 'failing' to becoming at least satisfactory in the quality of education it is offering its children.

The issue for me was, and still is, how to make those so-called 'quick fixes' stick and become embedded in good practice, for what OFSTED inspections do not take account of is what the label 'FAILED' does to teachers' morale and self-confidence. In my experience this is an area which also has to be addressed. I believe that unless the staff have the self-confidence and professionalism to take on board the areas for improvement, the action plan has no chance of succeeding or of having the desired long-term effect of improving teaching and learning.

The Way Forward

I have divided up the approaches and actions that I took during the two years I have spent at Roundthorn Primary School into three sections. The first I have called the 'highly visible'; these are the systems and structures which were introduced within the first year following the inspection. For the most part it could be said that these are the 'quick fixes'. Certainly they are obvious and measurable in that they are evidenced in writing and can be scrutinized by inspectors, HMI and anyone else who chooses to look at them.

The more obvious systems and structures are supported by the second section which is concerned with the approaches I have described as the 'visible'. These developments are concerned with the areas of staff roles and responsibilities. Work began immediately on raising expectations of and from the staff and some changes were made. The progress in areas of staff development can usually be observed. They are usually evident even if the changes and improvements are not always documented. It is inevitable that the successful implementation of the systems and structures very much depends on enabling the staff to take on board new initiatives. The professional development of teachers and support staff alike would never be seen as a 'quick fix' but is hopefully an ongoing career-long process.

I think it is quite possible to turn around a struggling school by putting in place effective systems and structures coupled with a complementary programme for staff development. It is my belief, however, that for school improvement to have maximum effect and lasting impact there needs to be a third set of actions, which I am sure will be self evident but which, nevertheless, I feel to be worth exploring particularly with the label of 'failed' in mind.

The third section is concerned with approaches that are more intangible and frequently difficult to measure. These are the actions concerned with interpersonal relationships and the recognition of skills or, inevitably, the lack of them. This section addresses the area of self-esteem and my view that people will be more effective if they feel good about themselves and the job they are doing. By giving back the sense of capability and professional ability that the OFSTED judgment took away, the staff are able to take on the tremendous pressure and work-load that accompanies a school on 'special measures'. It is very necessary to arm the staff on a personal level because they have to withstand negative publicity and the relentless pressure of constant monitoring visits by HMI, in addition to the taxing workload. Not all staff withstand the pressure.

Highly Visible — Systems and Structures

When a school has 'failed' its OFSTED inspection there are some measures that can be taken immediately to make improvements. In Roundthorn's case I worked with the staff and school governors to put in place an effective and comprehensive whole school development plan in addition to the OFSTED action plan. I produced a whole school plan in the belief that, not only did Roundthorn need to get out of 'special measures' as soon as possible, but the school needed to feel that it was functioning and developing as any other school would.

Staffing issues

Immediately on taking up the post of acting head of Roundthorn, I took the opportunity to improve staffing and staff allocations to classes. The teachers who had worked on a supply basis were no longer needed and in their place the acting deputy resumed a class teacher role and a new appointment was made. The new person appointed was fully aware of the situation of the school. Over the two years I negotiated the movement of some teachers into different age groups so that stronger teams were established for curriculum planning and delivery. Staff were not pushed into teaching year groups outside their teaching range or abilities. The proposed changes were always talked through, and support from within the teaching teams and from management was always made available. The majority of the staff began to build new teaching strengths but one member of staff recognized that the school would benefit if she retired and one is still absent on long-term sick leave. As the staff became more confident and successful in their teaching they were anxious that no one person should let the school down. I am sure that this feeling would have imparted itself to the staff who are no longer with Roundthorn even though the overriding atmosphere was one of mutual and often structured support.

Some of the classroom support assistant posts were temporary, therefore I had the opportunity to advertise, appoint and reallocate the support team which took account of their areas of expertise and the needs of the school as a whole. I established a senior management team and a management team with regularly planned meetings, but there was the issue of the deputy headteacher who had been out of the school on secondment to the LEA for two years. I chose not to request her return until I felt the school was settled under my leadership. There had evidently been some tension between the former headteacher and deputy headteacher and I needed to have an understanding of the causes of that tension to be in a position to handle any staff concerns. I also wanted time to establish a working relationship with the deputy and to have a clear picture of the role the returning deputy would have in the school. In the meantime, the member of staff who had been acting head would resume her previous role as acting deputy.

Planning meetings

There was a pattern of two staff meetings each week which were now to be used for focused staff development but with a mutually agreed start and stop time. The meetings were very necessary because the school had such a deficit to catch up on: for example, there was no whole school format for the planning of the curriculum. I imposed the format for short-term planning so that all staff had a common framework to work from and from which to build a shared understanding of good planning and planning into practice. Development of long-term and medium-term planning followed closely, and alongside the work on planning we organized inservice training on its component parts for example on developing skills in children, offering differentiated activities and building in assessment opportunities.

Record keeping

The OFSTED report had indicated that the staff lacked sound knowledge of the National Curriculum levels and Sir Ron Dearing had just begun to review the

National Curriculum. I gave the staff a clear record-keeping system so that they could plot the levels at which their children were working. This, in turn, would make their planning and differentiated activities more appropriate to the needs of the children. The staff also reported that they found the records useful when having discussions with the teachers who were to receive their children at the end of the school year. Following the advice of HMI, the staff worked in pairs to develop a curriculum matrix. This weighty document matched old National Curriculum with new National Curriculum in levels. Through this activity, the staff produced a reference document which enabled them to check whether their planning was appropriate. It also formed the basis for the development of schemes of work. A consequence of this activity was that all staff most certainly improved their knowledge of National Curriculum levels.

Assessment

Systems for assessing children were not in place. The staff were introduced to the statutory requirements for assessment under Dearing, and a policy and ways of working were agreed. Children were to be assessed on a regular basis and this would be indicated on the short-term planning. The procedure for collecting and levelling children's work for the school portfolio was reviewed and regular meetings were planned to ensure that this happened.

Special needs

There was a need to bring the staff up to date on special needs issues and to introduce them to the Code of Practice in the area of special needs. Over the first year of 'special measures', the staff became knowledgable on issues to do with special needs through inservice training and by using the expertise of the school's special needs coordinator. The coordinator met with teachers in the LEA's Special Needs Service to access information on how to move children onto the Special Needs Register. The staff were then able to adopt clear procedures for identifying special needs children and could provide effective evidence of why those children should receive extra funded help. The detail of help given to special needs children also began to be indicated in the teachers' planning.

Classroom observation

The plans produced by staff were scrutinized on a regular basis and one-to-one advice for improvement given where necessary. But of course, there is little point in having an efficient planning system if this does not impact on the children's learning in the classroom. To that end, regular observation of teachers teaching was a necessary system to have in place. Observations began in the second term following the OFSTED inspection. This gave the staff some time to take on board OFSTED criteria for the quality of teaching and the quality of learning and to regain some of their confidence as class teachers. Classroom observations have continued to be carried out on a termly basis with the involvement of an external inspector and the school's liaison inspector. When a school is in 'special measures', HMI make return visits approximately every term, and it is important therefore that the teachers are well prepared for the monitoring visits. They need to be accustomed to regular, quite formal, classroom observations. Teachers need an understanding of how OFSTED inspectors operate and what they are looking for, to be able to cope with the reality and stress of inspection. The staff wanted to know the areas in which they were improving against OFSTED criteria and they wanted to be given regular feedback on how they could further develop their teaching skills and classroom management.

Governors

The governors lent their support by each agreeing to adopt a class and a teacher. They did their best to visit or keep in written contact with the children in their class and began to develop their monitoring role by looking at the children's work. They invited staff to governing body meetings to describe classroom organization and management, and governors listened to key members of staff as they explained their responsibilities and how these were carried out.

External support

I invited into the school a relatively high number of outside expert advisers to deliver inservice training in important areas of development such as assessment, quality teaching and quality learning, classroom organization, special needs, evaluating planning into practice and subject specific INSET in the humanities. Religious education policies were developed when appropriate and others were reviewed and updated. The school also took part in the LEA's programme of school improvement projects which had, and continues to have, a significant effect on the quality of teaching and learning and on the professional development of teachers as subject coordinators.

I brought in an inspector from outside the local authority to assist me in observing teachers in their classrooms and to give them supportive advice and targets to work on in order to raise standards in their teaching skills. The observations and targets were recorded and copies given to the individual teachers. I requested that the LEA provide me with an inspection team so that when the climate was right and significant progress had been made, an OFSTED-style inspection could be carried out to prepare the staff and myself for HMI monitoring visits. Through this kind of pressure I was enabled to keep the school on the right track and also ensured that the staff received tangible feedback on the progress they were making, particularly in their increased percentages of sound, good and, by this time, some very good lessons.

Not all was rosy of course. Not every member of staff was able to take the pressure. One teacher has been absent for many, many weeks suffering from stress and sickness. The class suffered a series of supply teachers until I could stabilize the situation by securing a teacher on secondment. Some parents, understandably, took their children out of that class — the first children to leave the school in spite of the 'failure' label. There were grave concerns and a great deal of worry in the school that this single situation would have a detrimental effect on the school's chances of coming out of 'special measures' within the allotted two years.

Alongside the programme of staff development it soon became apparent that the governing body, too, needed development, for example in having effective committees, in understanding the work of teachers, in how to identify school improvements, and in having an active role in drawing up a school development plan. Once the development planning process had been worked through by governors, they were then encouraged to draw up their own development plan, which proved to be the most effective tool for increasing the effectiveness of Roundthorn's governing body.

This section has given a flavour of some of the changes and developments that the school underwent. A few were 'quick fixes' but for the most part the systems and structures introduced will need to be revisited and reviewed time and again as they become embedded in good school practice. The work was hard, but rewarding, and the pressures tremendous.

Visible — Roles and Responsibilities

It was important that the staff were empowered to work through all our key issues for action successfully, and to this end the extent of staff responsibilities needed to be clear and their roles developed. Actions taken under the headings of roles and responsibilities or staff development are usually recorded and are a part of either the whole school development plan, the school's action plan or the school improvement project plan.

Development and action plans

The whole school development plan spans three to four years in planning for developments in curriculum, teaching and learning, management, school environment and the community. It is written up in a detailed form annually and incorporates the issues for development identified through the OFSTED inspection. The school's action plan, written in response to the OFSTED inspection, concentrates solely on the key issues that the school must address and has very detailed information on precise objectives and strategies for school improvement. The school improvement project plan has grown out of a local authority initiative concerned with improving schools and raising achievement across the borough of Oldham. I wanted Roundthorn School to be part of this initiative because it would give the school the opportunity to work with other schools in the authority. We had to take one aspect for improvement as identified in the action plan and refine it still further to show how we would make use of training and target setting to demonstrate and measure school improvements. The school's achievements against the improvement plan are monitored and evaluated with the help of the school's liaison adviser. All the plans show where staff carry a particular responsibility. These responsibilities are more explicit in the action plan and the improvement plan.

Staff development

Planned staff development needed to mature alongside the developments of the systems and structures so that both could be increasingly effective. The earliest inservice training sessions for staff development were concerned with raising awareness of what constitutes quality teaching and quality learning particularly in OFSTED terms. The teachers themselves produced statements which set down what could be described as the school's code of practice in relation both to teaching and learning, based on teachers' responsibilities and children's entitlements. I wanted to give the staff the opportunity to judge for themselves, in a reflective way, how they felt their teaching compared with the common characteristics of a well-managed class.

This individual exercise contributed to the first of a programme of regular one-to-one meetings with me. In these meetings we discussed how each individual member of staff was performing, using data from OFSTED and other inspections and including information from classroom observations. The staff were encouraged to discuss their successes and their failures and to set personal targets for improvement. The one-to-one meetings took place each term while the school was in 'special measures' and constituted a form of appraisal in addition to the statutory two-year appraisal cycle. Differences between the termly meetings and formal appraisal included the opportunity for the staff to engage in a two-way exchange of views. Their comments were invited on the progress of the school and also the performance of the senior management team — not least the headteacher — so that I then had a picture of how the staff perceived we were developing as a whole school and I could act accordingly.

The needs of the school, the interviews with staff and the views of inspectors all helped me to target whole school inservice training or individual training as appropriate. Staff development has included in-house training, staff attending inservice training at the local Centre for Professional Development, staff visiting other schools and staff liaising with advisers and inspectors in their subject areas and in aspects of school development. As with most schools, staff uptake for centrally run courses varies considerably and research shows that one-off INSET sessions make little impact on raising achievement in schools. It has been vital that staff training effectively improves teaching and learning in the school, therefore other avenues for training have been explored and adopted. With financial assistance from the local authority I have funded an annual residential conference attended by all staff, both teaching and non-teaching. All staff participate in the training devised through the local authority's school improvement project. Both of these initiatives in their separate ways have made significant impact on the work of the school. The residentials have enabled concentrated efforts to be made on focused improvements in an atmosphere of hard work combined with team building through working and socializing together.

School improvement initiative

The 'school improvement' initiative, which began in September 1995, had significant impact on the staff and followed a tightly focused action plan with clear and measurable targets. Through the project every member of staff developed in their role as a coordinator. The process enabled them to become more professional in outlook and more confident in monitoring the achievements in their curriculum area, particularly in relation to the planning process. They have also gained in confidence in advising other members of staff through an activity that involves carefully planned paired interviews to discuss planning in depth in the specific curriculum areas. This cooperative process is now a regular feature of the planning cycle. Through the project each coordinator has produced a document indicating the vocabulary development and skills needed to foster the development of that vocabulary as children progress through the school.

The message carried by us all throughout the 'school improvement' tasks was that if one person is taking part, everyone is taking part and so everyone had 'homework' to do (including myself), everyone fed back at staff meetings, everyone produced written copies of their work, and then saw these produced in a reference document for the school.

It became part of the thinking of the staff that everyone had responsibility for making Roundthorn a better school. Although each teacher's efforts were accepted with the minimum of alteration, there was always the notable impact of the stronger and more able members of staff on the weaker staff, again reinforcing pressure to 'perform' to the best of one's ability in order to avoid letting 'the team' down.

The descriptions so far of the methods used to take the school out of 'special measures' demonstrate the high level of pressure the staff were under.

I believe that for the improvements to make a lasting difference to the education of the children of Roundthorn School there has to be a level of development which is about the esteem of the staff in the school and so I move to the third section which is concerned with relationships in the school.

Observable — Interpersonal Relationships and Self-esteem

An inspection that tells a school that it has failed appears to tell all of its staff that they also have failed. They all feel like failures even where it is evident in the OFSTED report that in particular areas of the school and curriculum, the teaching was not contributory to the overall judgment. It is my belief that to do a job well people need to feel competent and to be empowered. It was distressing to hear good teachers questioning their basic capabilities. It was of paramount importance to raise the self-esteem of the staff, and for me to let the staff know that whatever we had to work through, I would be doing it with them and not just to them. They had to know that their efforts were valued and appreciated. Their successes had to be praised and they had to feel that someone cared about them on a personal level as well as a professional level.

All of these comments may seem to be stating the obvious, but picking a staff up from the floor is no easy task. Strategies for this need as much thought as systems and structures, and the person in charge of such a school needs to be committed to the staff; they will see through any other approach. This is why I believe sending someone into a school as a 'quick fix' measure is doomed to fail and also why an 'education agency' taking over a school will not of itself improve the school. Genuine improvement will occur only with the commitment of the staff, so commitment must be encouraged and nurtured. The staff at Roundthorn experienced plenty of positive feedback from myself and from others outside the school. Their efforts were thanked sometimes overtly and sometimes covertly. There was the quiet personal word, the messages given through assemblies, positive feedback on planning, displays and good work achieved by the children. In working on positive reinforcement with the staff, notable strides were made with one member of staff in particular who had previously been very unhappy in the job and bordered on disaffection. This member of staff is now achieving very satisfactory results in the classroom and is noticeably happy with life in school.

The staff have met with and worked with the governing body, pleased that they are able to report their achievements to the governors, and to help the governors in carrying out their responsibilities in monitoring the work of the school. Most staff at some time have liaised with other staffs, inspectors and advisers and know by such contacts that the work they are doing compares well with other schools.

The staff have been given genuine responsibility. They are given release time and staff meeting time so that they feel valued in their efforts, knowing that they and their tasks are seen as worth being given time. They have gained a real sense of achievement in getting things done both as a staff together and as individuals. I showed that I had confidence in their abilities as teachers and coordinators and in the additional activities and responsibilities they carry out. I chose to handle staff problems and difficulties in a private way, offering personal help and advice and, when necessary, dealing with issues firmly but in a fair and supportive manner. I have tried to be available to staff and operate a genuine 'open-door' policy for them.

Most important, the staff I now manage have developed into a genuine team with no divisions between individuals or teaching teams. They will go on operating as professionals with the self belief they need to be quality teachers and quality support staff.

A Metaphor

For me, the turning around of this school has been rather like a circus where the head has to be both ringmaster and juggler: the ringmaster controlling the 'acts' and the timing — and on occasion cracking the whip; the juggler keeping all the balls in the air. Every headteacher is familiar with the scenario!

The staff, however, are rather like the tightrope walker who has not only to get to the other end of the wire but also has to turn somersaults along the way. It is the responsibility of the ringmaster to provide the safety net for the staff so that they will take risks with and for the ringmaster knowing that she or he has provided the underlying security which will 'save' them: the systems, the roles, the knowledge, and the self-esteem.

I am sure that it is possible to turn a school around by introducing sound systems and structures accompanied by a programme of staff development, but I feel that it is the third level of development which empowers staff to make the improvements that are lasting. The management of the process is vital. It seems to me that this is the difference between being the 'manager-leader' and the 'leader-manager' — one who is committed to carrying out all three aspects of the process I have outlined.

Conclusion

It may be true to say that the school would have continued to fail to provide a satisfactory standard of education for its children if it were not for the OFSTED inspection. In that sense I believe that the inspection was a positive force for improvement and has been a learning experience not just for Roundthorn School but for other schools and the education authority. On the other hand, the negative effects on staff are considerable. How this is handled when the teachers themselves shoulder the judgment of failing can make the difference between becoming successful as a school and driving deeper into negative feelings and responses through lack of direction and self-belief. I have hopes that the new OFSTED framework, coupled with monitoring visits by HMI giving clear guidance and further advice, will mean that the staffs of failing schools are managed sensitively and receive the supportive help they need.

Chapter 8

Failing the Failures: The Conflict Between Care and the Curriculum

Steven Pugh

Brookside Special School was identified as 'failing to give its pupils an acceptable standard of education' in November 1993, tying with a primary school in another county for the doubtful honour of the first school to be failed under Section 3 of the Education (Schools) Act 1992.

The School and the Response to the Inspection

Brookside is a residential school for pupils aged 11–16 who have been statemented as Emotionally and Behaviourally Disturbed (EBD). At the time of its failing there were forty-seven pupils on roll. With something approaching 200 schools presently requiring 'special measures' (a phrase which has the sinister quality of a CIA euphemism), the processes and procedures have become all too horribly familiar to those involved in education to require rehearsing at length. More worthwhile, perhaps, is a brief examination of the responses that failing status elicited from other special schools' staff; responses which can best be summarized in the word 'unfair'. To fail an EBD school was unfair because many of the pupils were too emotionally disturbed to be educable; unfair because the pupils required therapy and understanding rather than education in the National Curriculum; unfair because it was impossible to recruit staff who could teach their subject to examination standard and also be capable of forming the right kind of relationship with their pupils; and unfair because EBD schools are volatile establishments which manage to operate at all only because of a carefully constructed set of balances and compromises, too complicated to be understood during the 'snapshot' taken by an OFSTED inspection. Perhaps most unfair of all was the idea that a special school could be inspected within a framework that was designed to measure quality in mainstream schools, establishments which are intended to have quite different expectations and purposes.

My Role

In early December 1993 I was the head of the secondary behaviour support service for Derby City. My role was essentially geared to maintaining difficult pupils in the mainstream setting. Although I had worked in several off-site units and had acted as head of a special school for one term, I was not notably well equipped to undertake a leading part in the drama to come. As it happened I was — by virtue of being the only headteacher without pupils — the only headteacher who could be made available.

When I took up this responsibility the school staff, were in what might fashionably be described as the 'denial' stage of bereavement. A number took refuge in recounting the perceived follies of the system which had exposed the school to tabloid ridicule — 'School For Dunces' read one memorable headline — and professional censure. Moreover, many of the staff were anxious to express support for the departing headteacher for whom the entire business must have felt like a personal and professional pillory. Unfair or not, it is certain that the school was unfortunate to be caught in the highly public vanguard of a new system, one that had been unequivocally designed to judge rather than support or advise.

The Report

The report that OFSTED produced certainly contained judgments. There were nine key issues that touched on virtually every aspect of the school, most particularly the curriculum, the length of the school day, the preparation and implementation of policies, and the establishment of financial procedures. It must, in justice, be emphasized that the school was damned not for dramatic failure in any one area — quality of learning was, for instance, recorded as satisfactory in 50 per cent of lessons and better than satisfactory in a further 20 per cent — but rather for an accrual of failings in a number of areas. On the plus side, the report conceded that: 'Staff work hard in establishing good relationships with pupils and seek to foster their self-esteem and create a sense of community' (OFSTED, 1993, paragraph 133). For many, including the great majority of parents, this was approbation enough; after all, it was this element of personal care in the school that made sense of the prefix 'special'. The willingness of staff to tolerate what had been intolerable to mainstream schools and continually to accept pupils whose behaviour had caused them to be rejected in the past was what set them apart from teachers in other kinds of school. Therefore, the *raison d'être* of the school was perceived by those in and around it not as delivery of the National Curriculum, but the less defined and more urgent task of remedying the emotional damage that society and so many other educational establishments had inflicted upon its pupils.

More than anything, this chapter is concerned with the personal and professional cost which was involved in beginning to move Brookside from this indistinctly conceived pastoral mission to undertaking the task of creating a school where the curriculum would become the therapy rather than an obstacle to it.

Making Changes

To pursue the metaphor of bereavement mentioned earlier, the process of making change at Brookside closely followed the recognized pattern of grieving: denial;

anger; depression; search for meaning; gradual acceptance; and internalization (Kubler-Ross, 1970). With hindsight, it is possible to see that the necessary pace of change helped to move the school and its staff through these stages with surprising rapidity.

December 1993–March 1994

The action plan which was eventually delivered to the DfEE just within the pre-scribed forty days (and nights — a timescale which pleads for biblical allusion) was comprehensive. The plan included major changes to the length of the school teaching day — increased by 30 per cent — revised schemes of work in every subject area, the establishment of individual education plans, new systems for financial manage-ment, and the development of seven new policies and plans to reduce physical restraint and the level of exclusion. In writing the plan, we (the LEA's special needs adviser and I), attempted to focus not simply on responding to the school's identified failings but rather upon the idealized outcome of what a good school should be.

Initially, the principal difficulty was to develop a vision of what a good special school should look like. Ultimately, the answer was that it would look rather like a good mainstream school — only different. The difference would lie partly in the solutions to the problem of providing a full National Curriculum with a teaching staff of eight among whom there was no modern language specialist, PE specialist or music specialist. It would also be partly in the development of the residential care facility. Many of the teachers were contracted to perform duties additional to teaching in the evenings. These duties involved working alongside the full-time residential care assistants. This commitment meant they had little time for lesson preparation during the week and, with the additional workload of developing new curriculum and schemes of work, they became more than ordinarily tired and jaded. Coupled with the strain of the inspection and its aftermath these factors contributed to a staff absence level through illness that rose alarmingly. Within the year, one member of staff would leave through ill health associated with stress.

The stresses were not caused merely by changes to the school system and the curriculum. The post-OFSTED effect was clearly evident in the behaviour of the pupils. There was a mutiny from the Year 11 group who said that the work they were doing was rubbish and so was the school — they had seen it so described on television and in the newspapers — and they were not going to do it. A dramatic increase in the number of pupils leaving lessons without permission was also seen, and there was an upsurge of vandalism (twelve broken windows in one memorable week). Most worrying, there was an increase in the number of assaults against staff and the level of physical restraints ran at a steady average of seventeen a month. To compound the disaster, all this resulted in a soaring rate of short-term exclusion.

By late February, about three months since I had assumed the acting headship, I began to lose my nerve. I felt that I had achieved nothing beyond a few room changes and an arbitrary extension to teaching time which had done no more than enrage pupils and further tire staff. I had an overwhelming sense that I was failing both staff and pupils and daily adding another nail to the coffin of what was once quite a promising career. I was also becoming slightly resentful about the position I found myself in. I had been asked to 'mind' the school until more permanent arrangements were made. Instead, I now found that I was leading it through the whole special measures process. This was a possibility I, foolishly, had never considered and for which I, frankly, felt quite unprepared. I was, after all, not a special headteacher. I did not, and do not, believe that grouping together pupils with behavioural difficulties provides a thoughtful solution to their problems. Had I been in less of a panicky sweat, I might have taken wry amusement from the irony of my position. Other difficulties included the fact that I had only a sketchy knowledge of financial management, limited understanding of the inspection process and only a theoretical knowledge of differentiating and delivering the full National Curriculum. These first months were a period of intensive learning.

Something like 70 per cent of failing schools are managed by an acting headteacher for some or all of the journey back to the fold. Here is some advice for those who may find themselves in a similar position: do not whine to anyone who gets paid more or less than you; neither group is sympathetic. Confine complaints to other headteachers, the school's adviser, and the person you sleep with. Other advice is more difficult to give as I suspect that the relatively small number of failing schools give rise to a broad range of situations. It is important to have an understanding of the process of change and I recommend the now venerable but still relevant paper by Georgiades and Philimore (1975) which charts the obstacles that any organization throws up to slow the pace and reduce the impact of even the simplest modification.

The school reached its low point in March with virtually every area identified as a key issue in a worse state than when the original inspection had been made. To the eternal credit of the staff, nobody ever made the comparison out loud; not to me, anyway.

What were the factors that kept the school going? Staff professionalism — and I would include both teaching and residential staff in this — and an innate knowledge that making change is always hard and this was a period that had to be got through. There was also a growing perception that although the behaviour of some pupils had got worse, there were others who were improving. The value of the support given by the LEA's advisory and inspection service was inestimable. In addition to straight curriculum support, particularly valuable for teachers working outside their subject specialisms, the adviser for Special Educational Needs provided a vital external outlet for my spiralling self-doubt. He also offered constant support for the view that the application of sound pedagogical principles, which made no concessions to behaviour but were rooted in expectations of achievement, would eventually yield the desired results.

April–July 1994

April marked the turning point in the school's progress. This improvement is attributable to a number of factors. The Easter holiday gave teaching staff an opportunity to improve schemes of work and produce good quality lessons for the coming term. Several of the most difficult Year 11 pupils left school and I took the diffi-cult decision to exclude two other pupils permanently, thus making the exclusion figures still worse in the short term. I think, also, that several key staff had begun to see that, notwithstanding the difficulties of the previous term, the pupil-centred approach to teaching had begun to pay dividends. For instance, a number of Year 11 pupils now asked if they could stay on until July.

Attendance had begun to improve and restraints had fallen by 50 per cent. HMI wrote to me in April to advise that the first monitoring inspection would be in June. Taking stock of what had been achieved revealed entries in both the balance and debit side of the account book. The school now taught slightly more than twenty-five hours a week of full National Curriculum. There was a scheme of work for every subject. The deputy head had resuscitated an idea he had once had for an individual education plan for every pupil and this was serving to focus attention on pupils' academic needs. There was an embryonic learning support department, each pupil's reading had been tested and a number were withdrawn for supportive reading. There were policies for behaviour, equal opportunities, anti-racism and sex education. There were clear schemes for marking, recording and assessment. In the residence, there were three independent living flats available to all pupils on a rota scheme. This allowed residential staff the opportunity to teach basic skills of self-management; cooking, cleaning and productive use of leisure time during the evenings. Every member of staff had a clear job description, all staff met for a weekly briefing, and senior staff met regularly following this briefing.

On the debit side, vandalism remained a significant problem, providing a con-stant drain on the school's slender financial reserves. Aggression between pupils was unacceptably high and the school still projected an atmosphere of unpredictability and tension. I consoled myself with the knowledge that significant change in an institution could take between five and seven years; that the modification of behavi-our relied on techniques of extinction that inevitably required interim periods of what is commonly referred to in small group work as 'storming before norming'. I still dreaded the morning journey to work. During the seven minute drive, I smoked two cigarettes and relished any traffic delays. A good day was one in which I did not exclude a pupil and there was no physical restraint of a pupil.

I have noted that staff were never openly hostile or antagonistic towards me, and this is true. It is also true that a number felt that the curriculum-based approach to working with emotionally and behaviourally disturbed pupils was wrong. They felt that it was only possible to educate academically after a rigorous programme of social education had soothed the savage beast, raised self-esteem and demon-strated the value of relationships based on respect and cooperation. The stock response to the observation that this strategy had not produced outstanding results in the past was that the school only had them for half their lives; the negative effects of family and friends were outside anybody's control. The sense of this conflict was most usually conveyed to me not in the context of a staff meeting or policy discussion but in the lacklustre way in which jointly agreed new practices were conducted. For example, from time to time I would enter a classroom and find pupils engaged in computer games rather than the timetable lesson to be told by the teacher that the class had had enough hard work for that day or that they were 'getting high' and it had been necessary to reduce the pressure to avoid an explosion. Although I felt angry at the time, with hindsight it is possible to see these lapses as an attempt to anticipate and manage behaviour rather than to allow an explosion and then resort to physical restraint, as might have happened a year before.

The Senior Management Team

Up to now I have written little of the role of the senior management team, creating the erroneous impression of a solipsist manipulating the fortunes of the school through the sea of troubles and navigating according to an internal chart. In practice, senior staff were the source of many developments and were able to put flesh on the bones of my skeletal ideas. One particular area, that of the whole school points system, is worth exploring in further detail as it demonstrates quite effectively the kind of processes the school went through during the course of special measures.

At the time of the original inspection, the school was operating a variation of a system known as assertive discipline which relies upon clearly delineated and consistently enforced boundaries to behaviour, supported by a strong reward system and an agreed hierarchy of sanctions. Pupils lost points according to the number of rules they infringed in the classroom. Within each lesson they could lose a maximum of five points. I was anxious to refine the system so that points were clearly earned rather than lost and so that rewarding good behaviour would take priority over punishing bad behaviour. Initially, the rewards attached to the highest points earners were small items of sweets or chocolate. This was fine for younger pupils but older students were not motivated by what they perceived as childish rewards. During the ensuing months we added good behaviour certificates and McDonalds meal vouchers, a weekly raffle with cash prizes and a termly visit to a theme park. Whilst all of this served to focus attention on the rewards of good behaviour, each innovation achieved only a brief effect on behaviour before the novelty wore thin and we were thrown back to punitive measures. Ultimately, it was the staff who devised a system that relied on the award of three points only for specified behaviours which were taken directly from each pupil's individual education plan. Rewards were varied to include small items of equipment that would be useful in school, for example, pencil cases and geometry sets; while the whole school was rewarded for good behaviour by the purchase of some bicycles to be used at breaks and lunchtimes. The most significant reward, however, was that each child was achieving his own target at his own level.

I use this example to illustrate how open staff were to change and development in areas where all could agree that change was necessary; and to applaud the willingness of senior staff to undertake the review of systems, to rewrite points sheets, daily to add the accumulated points of forty boys in order to accommodate my insistence on immediate feedback.

Senior staff were not the only group who were both open and forbearing. It was necessary to accommodate the increase in teaching hours, which would otherwise have resulted in a change to the times of the school's start and finish. This was impractical both because of the need for wide consultation and a year's notice of change, and also because of the need to remain within the contracted times of taxi drivers who brought and collected day pupils. The only option was to reduce the length of the lunch period from eighty to fifty minutes. This in turn ruled out the continuation of the traditional set meal service and entailed the introduction of a cafeteria style cuisine served on flight trays. There were a number of associated benefits to this change; a reduction in opportunities for bullying and a system that more closely resembled mainstream schools. Benefits notwithstanding, the changes involved a great deal of extra work and upheaval for the domestic staff who produced a perfectly functioning system, complete with revised menus, with less than three weeks' notice.

The Problem with Action Plans

Both the examples given above indicate one of the principal difficulties of implementing any action plan for school development. Although the plan addresses particular key issues, the changes wrought to meet them inevitably involve adjustments both small and large to other areas of the system. An action plan implemented within the prescribed two-year time-scale means that the school must for extended periods find itself in a condition of flux; uncertain about the long-term viability of any of its systems. The decision taken at Brookside was to implement as many changes as possible as quickly as possible, pre-empting the time-scale of our own action plan.

In June 1994, the first monitoring inspection of the school was conducted by HMI. Two inspectors spent two and a half days in the school. If that sounds like a 'light' team, it is worth pointing out that when there are only forty pupils taught in four groups, two observers seem to be everywhere at once.

Inspections and How to Cope with Them

The role of the headteacher in any inspection is a difficult one. There is a professional desire to demonstrate every confidence in the staff and its pupils and to stay in the office catching up on paperwork, unconcerned by any thoughts of failure. There is also an overwhelming urge restlessly to patrol the school, spying out signs of trouble and heading them off before they become an incident. I opted for the former approach, but was unable to project the necessary aplomb. The expression of intense anxiety that distorted my face elicited worried conjecture from staff that something terrible had gone wrong already and an inspector had been confronted by an uncontrollably hostile youth; for in an EBD school in the throes of inspection that is the great fear. I felt reasonably confident that the teaching was of a sound standard. I knew that paperwork was in order, and the steadily falling exclusion and restraint level and improving attendance supported an objective view of the school as improving. What was impossible to predict was that there would not be a major incident of misbehaviour and what reception it would receive if there was. In fact there was a major incident that involved a boy throwing a chair through five windows and eventually required a police escort off the premises. No other incident of such severity had occurred during my time at Brookside.

The report at the end of the inspection acknowledged that the school had made significant progress in addressing the key issues, but that the improvements were fragile and in need of consolidation. In other words, we were trying hard but it all looked a bit 'iffy' at the moment. As this accorded precisely with my assessment I could not complain. Nonetheless, I was disappointed. In my wildest imaginings I had hoped for an early release from special measures. At this time nobody had a clear idea of the average amount of time a school might spend on the failing list and I was willing for six months to be long enough. HMI were clear that there would be at least one and probably two more monitoring inspections.

Consolidation, as any manager knows, is a great deal harder than innovation, which has at least the charm of novelty. The revised action plan we put together recognized that the school was on the right path and that the task was now about doing things better and with a greater clarity of purpose. In mild contrast to my cautious optimism, the LEA had become positively 'bullish' about the school's prospects. I was asked to stay on as acting head for another two terms — what could I do but agree? — the freeze on new admissions was lifted, and plans for eventually closing and re-opening the school as an all age, co-educational residential EBD school were published. Recently, a school inspector shared with me the view that following any inspection, a school's performance is likely to deteriorate as a result of staff relaxing and recouping the energy that has been exhausted during the inspection period. From my own experience I would agree with this. The task of motivating staff to build on their successes was almost remarkably difficult.

On the whole, staff morale was bolstered by the report. There were few outright criticisms, such damning as there was being of the 'faint praise' variety. There were two less than satisfactory lessons but both of these were in areas where specialist teaching was lacking so the failing was understandable, if not excusable. What was important was that ideas such as managing behaviour rather than repressing it; working from the basis of individual needs rather than some generalized view of educational need; and, perhaps above all, conveying an expectation that all pupils could achieve academically, had clearly gained sufficient currency to be recognized by an objective eye.

It would be a travesty to assume that all staff accepted the desirability of this curriculum-focused approach at a uniform rate or that pupil achievement immediately accelerated in response to the changing pattern of teaching. The developments at Brookside have been about an attitudinal change that may take some years to translate into concrete achievements. Most of the pupils have had seriously disrupted educational histories; many have reading levels which at age 11 do not score on standard reading assessments. The A–C results at GCSE are unlikely to inspire a frenzied envy in other schools. Nobody, however, rules out the idea that success is a possibility and everything is done to achieve it.

Release

Brookside was inspected again in November 1994 and again in March 1995 when it was released from special measures. The final inspection was conducted by three of Her Majesty's Inspectors and, although still a notably tense occasion, there was, nonetheless, a sense of confidence among staff that the outcome would be positive. This confidence, I think, reflects the fact that everyone was aware that they could scarcely put any greater effort into doing the right things. As a consequence they were able to expect that the behaviour of one or two pupils would not undermine a sound professional judgment of overall competence. If misbehaviour occurred they knew how to manage it. Lessons were well planned and presented and teachers knew it. However, the most telling sign of their own confidence was to be found in the one-day monitoring inspection that was conducted in May 1996, a year after release from special measures. On this occasion only one inspector called. At the end of the successful visit, there were complaints from teaching staff that their lessons had not been observed, denying them the opportunity to show off!

There is, I think, always a danger that things look better looking back. It becomes too easy to minimize the difficulties, both personal and professional, of making change. For a number of individuals, the entire period of special measures was a time of long hours and extreme stress. There is, however, a risk of over-stating the importance of particular individuals in making beneficial change. The shift in the fortunes of Brookside was a relatively speedy affair; unquestionably that was the result of hard work and determination on the part of both the school staff and the LEA's support services. Without that joint approach, it is difficult to imagine that the outcome would have been the same. As I have indicated, there is even at this stage, three years on from the original inspection, no room for complacency. The need for a sustained joint approach in managing the institutional education of a group of pupils with complex difficulties continues to be as necessary as ever before.

I am sure that many would argue that reference to a conflict between care and curriculum is an unnecessary polarization; that it is more appropriate to assert that EBD pupils cannot live on the bread of education alone, and emotional needs which cannot be reached through the curriculum must also be nourished. While I would not take issue with the sentiment, the compromise position is ultimately unsustainable because the resources to do both are not available. The conflict is not about caring or not caring, or educating or not educating, but where the line is drawn in deciding when as much as possible has been done within existing resources. The staff at Brookside accepted the view that educational objectives are more attainable, more measurable and, most immediately, more inspectable. I would not say that this acceptance means that they have ceased to offer a caring environment to pupils. The object of caring has become the need to ensure that every individual is able to take advantage of the education offered. In this sense, the school has defined itself firmly within an educational context rather than as an auxiliary branch of social services or the Health Authority. In so doing, it contrives to work to its strengths. The purpose of the school is to educate, and without that clear direction and purpose, caring too easily becomes an object in itself and then a law unto itself. When this happens any external criticism appears churlish and may be scorned as bureaucratic meddling.

From my own perspective, I cannot say that I have been a teacher in a school that has failed, I have not had the daunting experience of sitting through a governors' meeting as a list of the school's shortcomings is recited. I have, though, been a teacher in a school that is failing. The pressure is different because, as an acting headteacher you have been brought in to, at the very least, prevent things getting worse, and, hopefully, help them get very much better. Expectations of your competence are high. In the early stages, consolation may be found in the thought, 'Well, it really isn't my problem. I'm only visiting'. However, once embarked on the recovery process, and implementing your action plan, there is no escaping the responsibility and the real possibility of failure. It is not an experience I would wish to repeat. Eventually, during the course of the several monitoring visits, staff at Brookside learned to trust the inspection process and, as confidence grew, one or two teachers even seemed to relish the opportunity to demonstrate progress. However, I recently received notice from OFSTED that the next inspection in the four-year cycle was due. The news was greeted with quite a marked silence . . .

References

GEORGIADES, N.J. and PHILIMORE, L. (1975) 'The myth of the hero innovator and alternative strategies for organizational change', in KIERNAN, C.C. and WOODFORD, F.P. (eds) *Behaviour Modification for the Severely Retarded*, Amsterdam: Associated Scientific.
KUBLER-ROSS, E. (1970) *On Death and Dying*, London: Tavistock.
OFSTED (1993) *Report on Brookside School*, Ref 416/93/SS, London, OFSTED.

Part 4

External Facilitators

The external change facilitator has been shown to play a key role in school improvement. In the two chapters that follow, the authors describe the complexities faced by the consultant, or 'critical friend', in John MacBeath's terms. This first chapter explores the nuances and tensions in the role between building trust as 'friend', and providing honest and necessary feedback in the capacity of critic, even when this is perceived as 'disturbing'. John MacBeath draws attention to different schools' varying capacities for learning and development, and highlights the necessity for a wide range of interpersonal, group and technical skills, many of which may not be possessed by those who offer support to schools. He also suggests that working with schools in difficulty can sometimes require specialist counselling skills, an issue also raised by David Reynolds.

In the second chapter James Learmonth, writing from his experience as a consultant to secondary schools and Kathy Lowers, from hers working with primary schools, identify several themes that occupy their attention. Notably, the emphasis on teaching and learning ('reinstating the individual lesson') is high on their agenda, and their work is driven by their desire to see improvement ultimately expressed in enhanced pupil outcomes.

In both chapters, the authors identify a long-term purpose for the school to be self-evaluating, and able independently to review its own process and manage change. They emphasize the power of collecting data or evidence, as James Learmonth and Kathy Lowers describe it, and using it for further development and dialogue. Bringing 'bad news' to a school, however, needs careful handling and, as John MacBeath notes, part of the skill of the consultant lies in her ability to convey feedback in a way that will not produce denial or rejection of the information or consultant.

The authors are all too aware that expectations of them are high. Each school in difficulty provides its own challenges and subtleties, which means that the consultant 'is only as good as their last assignment', to quote James Learmonth and Kathy Lowers. Nonetheless, one is struck by their optimism that schools can improve, with positive encouragement, support, honest feedback, and if they can be persuaded to believe and act on the fact that they do make an important difference.

Chapter 9

'I Didn't Know He Was Ill': The Role and Value of the Critical Friend

John MacBeath

Schools need friends. Much has been written about the self-managing and self-improving school but in reality there are few schools with the self-assurance and inner resources to reform themselves. Ineffective schools, which may be characterized as schools with learning difficulties, are likely to lack self-confidence, mistrust authority, and eschew risk. The more hostile and anti-educational the political environment, the greater the need for honest friends whose first impulse is to support and whose second impulse is to offer a constructively critical perspective.

The critical friend is a powerful idea, perhaps because it contains an inherent tension. Friends bring a high degree of unconditional positive regard. They are forgiving and tolerant of your failings. They sometimes even love you for your faults. Critics are, at first sight at least, conditional, negative and intolerant of failure. Perhaps the critical friend comes closest to what might be regarded as the 'true friendship' — a successful marrying of unconditional support and unconditional critique.

At an organizational level the tension between support and critique has often been resolved by separating the two functions. So one arm of the local authority service becomes 'Quality Assurance', taking the form of an external inspectorial process, while the other arm forms the friendly advisory service. It is a separation that has been seen, in many instances, as conspicuously unsuccessful. It has been accused of making the worst of both worlds — being neither friendly nor objective.

The separation of inspection and advice has been taken too literally, argue Gray and Wilcox (1995). Commenting on the OFSTED approach they observed that:

> Schools in trouble do seem to have greater difficulty in taking stock. For them a constructive analysis (preferably offered in a manner which enables them to retain a modicum of dignity) is essential. Unfortunately what they thought they got was just a 'bad report'. (p. 23)

Experience in different authorities and in different countries, suggests that the critical friend role is a complex and difficult one to get right. It is a role for which people have not had training and which authorities find hard to accommodate within conventional structures.

The following pages explore these issues in the context of a large research and development project currently underway in Scotland. The Improving School Effectiveness (ISE) project (MacBeath and Mortimore, 1994; Robertson and Sammons, 1996) has provided us with a useful testbed for developing our understanding of failing schools and the role of the critical friend. Hopefully by the time this chapter is published we will wish to rewrite it because our understanding will have moved on.

Improving School Effectiveness

The study involved eighty Scottish schools covering both a geographical range and the entire spectrum of cruising, moving, strolling, sinking and struggling schools (see Stoll and Fink, 1996). Twenty-four of these were designated 'case-study schools', with which we contracted to work over a period of two years in a research and development capacity.

Members of the project team were attached in pairs to each school, one in the role of researcher, the other in the role of the critical friend. The job of the researcher was to observe, interview and document, including (by the end of the project) a critical appraisal of the actions and impact of the critical friend. The role of the researcher was to be a credible commentator and faithful witness. The role of the 'friend' was to be both of these and in addition a listener and learner, a knowledgable broker and resilient critic.

The entry point to the school was via the headteacher and senior management team, through whose lens the critical friend had to get to know the school. It was important to spend time with them, establishing a mutual comfort zone before venturing out too far into the wider school community. There is a danger in the comfort zone becoming too familiar and too cosy a retreat, however, because of the different lenses through which the critical friend has to learn to view the school.

In the early stages we found ourselves being cautious and tentative about our role, and asking ourselves whose friend we really were, aware that the effect, or effectiveness, of the critical friend may ultimately depend on whose friend you are seen to be. In the first instance it is almost inevitable that the role will be exercised in relation to the headteacher or management team, since that is the entry point to the school and because change tends either to be top down or endorsed at top level. That may, however, be an obstacle to becoming accepted and trusted more widely. If there is a climate of mistrust between senior management and staff, being seen as the friend of management could be particularly counter-productive.

Our awareness of this made small considerations loom larger, at least in the early stages. There were micro-decisions to be made, some of which seemed to carry symbolic weight. Some conscious decisions made by critical friends were:

- to visit the upper (smokers') staffroom at the lunch break;
- to go to the pub at lunchtime with a mixed group of staff;
- to sit at the technicians' table in the lunchroom;
- not to take morning coffee in the head's office with the senior management team on every visit;

- to drink coffee out of beakers in the science base;
- to use the staffroom as a workbase; and
- to play football with a group of pupils.

In the early stages these symbolic acts may be important in confirming or confront-ing expectations, signalling an impartiality, or negotiating a role. These could be important contexts in terms of establishing relationships and forging alliances but also in terms of significant 'data sites', providing microcosms of the school cul-ture. The upper staffroom in one school gave us an early flavour of what the term 'balkanization' (Hargreaves, 1994) means:

> On our second day in the school we made the conscious decision to make an uninvited visit to the 'top staffroom'. The dead tea bags in the sink, the congealed sugar, and the archaeological layers of caffeine on the glass cups told their own story. One member of staff was asleep with his feet on the mantelpiece, apparently oblivious to our presence, but his occasional smiles betrayed his careful monitor-ing of the conversation. The conversation (no dialogue here) was the 'top staffroom' perspective on the school, on school effectiveness and on the value of researchers in particular. Making friends with this group of staff might, with a little ingratia-tion, have been easy, but attempting to engage in a productive critical dialogue might not have been so easy, nor the wisest investment of time and energy. The aphorism 'don't water the rocks' sprang simultaneously to the lips of researcher and critical friend. (researcher's fieldnotes)

Our brief visit to that staffroom was a data-rich, if not personally enriching, experience. Our suggestion to management to close the top staffroom was one tangible outcome of that visit, even if the benefits to the organization of such a move have still to be tested. The process by which that closure came about, how-ever, did have intrinsic merit.

The process is illustrative of the work of the critical friend. We agreed that school senior management would not raise the issue nor take executive action, but instead we planned to find a way to raise the issue at a staff development day, allowing it to emerge from the staff themselves. The theme of the day was 'making learning more effective', examining how staff could share and develop good prac-tice across the school. In the reporting-back session following a group exercise one of the groups raised the issue of staffroom talk, collegial relationships and the value of informal exchange of ideas and experience. They suggested that the staff look at the common staffroom issue as an important aspect of school culture. It was a suggestion which met with wide, if not unanimous, agreement among staff present. The subsequent move to a shared staffroom came to be seen as a positive staff-led development rather than an executive closing down of cynics' corner.

Who Invited You Anyway?

The critical friend, feeling her way in the early stages of a relationship with the school, can easily play into hidden agendas and power struggles. It is crucial, therefore, that she is aware of the development stage of the school. 'Readiness' may not be a whole school state of mind, however. Openness to learning and resistance to learning are typically to be found in different pockets within the school.

In all eighty schools in the project the contract with the senior management team was that our involvement should be negotiated with the teaching staff. We were to discover that in some schools consultation had, in fact, been minimal. In one school the deputy head's opening words of welcome to the staff development day were pre-empted by the union representative who wished it to be known that staff had *not* agreed — 'with all due respect' — to the presence of the critical friend.

Having weighed the options in the few available seconds — withdraw? seek clarification? negotiate? repent? pass the buck? plough on? — the decision to steer the latter course proved, in this instance, to be the right one. But it could just as easily have been the wrong one, a reminder of the ambiguous position of the critical friend and the indeterminate locus of that friendship. Following his introduction to the staff as 'the critical friend', a remark from the floor helped to relieve the tension. From the back row a voice called, 'I didn't know he was ill'.

It is all too easy for the critical friend to be seen as an ally of 'management' and we met different kinds of struggle between head and members of the management team to establish proprietorial priorities over the critical friend; sometimes to use her as an ally against groups of staff. In one school the locus of the problem was seen as the staff in general, with an attempt by one or more members of the management team to enlist the critical friend's support against them. Manoeuvring a way around, or directly confronting, those expectations requires a fairly high degree of tactical skills and political acumen. In another school the power lay at two poles — the deputy headteacher and the union representative. Staff clustered at these two poles, monitoring carefully the magnetic movements of the critical friend between them, testing the neutrality of the visitor but also engaging in tentative lobbying.

Judgments about when, where and how to move along the spectrum from friend to critic are often delicate and finely balanced. They require an empathic understanding of what it means to the recipient of critical feedback, of how challenge or advice is likely to be heard and contextualized. This aspect of the critical friend's role was put to the test early on in the project. The first task of the critical friend was to feed back data from the data-gathering exercise. This feedback usually took place in the first instance with the headteacher and/or senior management, helping them to make sense of the data and to explore some of its ambiguities and implications before sharing it more widely with staff, parents or pupils.

The handling of this discussion called for a high degree of 'emotional intelligence' (Goleman, 1996), as well as technical intelligence. It called for skills in dealing with data, explaining but demystifying, yet rigorous in attention to valid inference. On the other hand, it called for interpersonal and group work skills, many of which could be recognized as the province of 'counselling'. These included, for example, accurate listening, reflecting back, reformulating, accepting, working within the client's frame of reference, challenging and confronting, at times soothing and smoothing.

Therapeutic counselling, it might be argued, transgresses the boundaries of the critical friend's role. However, the ISE Project presented us with a number of occasions when person-centred counselling skills seemed both appropriate and necessary. Armed with foreknowledge that the head did not have, and which sometimes contained nasty surprises, we found ourselves having to prepare the ground, looking for ways of breaking the news, helping the head to deal with information whose explosive impact was, in his or her own language, 'shattering' or 'a bombshell'.

There were occasions when we had to advise the headteacher to spend some time alone with us before blithely sharing the data more widely with the whole staff or with the management team. On some occasions we had to deal with genuine personal distress. We were to discover within some headteachers a fragile ego.

The head was normally the only individual in the school to feel exposed and personally vulnerable in light of feedback. This may be, in part, because of the particularly close identification of the Scottish headteacher with the school, deeply imbedded in the language — 'my school', 'my staff'. In part it may be because some of the criticism of leadership, communication, and decision-making, was explicitly or implicitly directed at the head.

In these circumstances a human sympathetic response on the part of the critical friend is an appropriate one, but we had also to be careful to keep an eye on the long-term purpose, and on the other constituencies to whom we were accountable (ultimately pupils and parents). It is unlikely to be of help to collude with denial, rationalization or blaming others, all of which were not uncommon responses to unwelcome news. Nor was it helpful to promise that time *would* heal wounds and indeed improve general health in the long run. However, we were confident from our previous experience that it would prove to be a useful and enhancing learning experience in the longer term, perhaps even in a matter of days or weeks. And so it proved in virtually all cases. It is both a comfort and a challenge for headteachers to learn that the significant distance between perceptions of management and those of staff is not only an endemic feature of schools in our project but of organizations generally (Anders, 1996).

The balance between friend and critic shifts over time as the friend comes to be taken for granted and the role of critic becomes both comfortable and legitimate. This differs, however, with each set of relationships and, to some extent, within each transaction and within each new context. The balance has to be maintained, therefore, in the relationship with the school over time in relation to specific groups and individuals, and within each separate transaction. With the headteacher, for example, there are issues which may be looked at with cooler energy and with the benefit of critical distance. We might have to seek the right mature moment to raise the question 'Why did you have such a strong emotional reaction to negative feedback about decision-making and communication, but not about learning and teaching, or shared values?'

A Sequence of Events

We may distinguish a broad sequence of events and two parallel processes going on, one through the more formal agenda, the other through a more informal, pragmatic and intuitive process. Table 9.1 suggests a number of stages in the developing relationship with the school. It should be read as a starting point for thinking about the process rather than a definitive statement of 'how it is'. Some of the formal and informal processes may well be interchangeable and certainly less discrete than they appear in tabular form. The timescale will also vary from one context to the next. In our twenty-four project schools there were huge differences depending on the capacity for change and the ability to use the critical friend. Anders (1996), in his consultancy work with business organizations, uses the metaphor of the red, yellow and green companies. He finds that green-light companies (ready to go) can be taken on and move with new ideas in a matter of months. Red-light companies, at the opposite polarity, may take years.

Table 9.1   The formal and informal agenda

Formal	Informal
• *Introduction* clarifying roles, agreeing parameters	• *Background reading* documents, contextual information, getting to know the school
• *Gathering data* interviews, observation, group activities	• *Familiarization* making contacts with staff and pupils, building trust, confidence
• *Organizing data* making sense of and systematizing data	• *Negotiating a role* establishing style, listening mode
• *Feeding back data* selecting a mode of presentation, confirming, challenging	• *Building alliances* moving out of the comfort zone, beyond the management team
• *Making sense of data* helping the school to understand and define issues	• *Facilitating* entering into discussion, raising questions, offering suggestions
• *Considering the options* working within the school's agenda, planning priorities, target setting	• *Monitoring* reflecting on actions taken, evaluating self; record-keeping, reviewing
• *Supporting initiatives* sitting in on working groups, working alongside teachers (e.g., cooperative teaching)	• *Challenging* broadening and extending the school's self perception
• *Embedding* helping to develop structures and procedures to sustain long term growth	• *Maintaining momentum* encouraging, praising, clarifying, revisiting issues
• *Evaluating* identifying achievement	• *Disengaging* removing crutches

Critical Friend or Trojan Horse?

The invitation to the research team to be involved with the school came, in the final analysis, from the headteacher. However strong or weak the consultation with school staff, it rested on some interpretation of what we could, as a research team, help the school to achieve. The explicit 'contract' was that our intervention would support change, but the nature and process of change was not one we could easily spell out in advance. The full story of how change works could have been put on paper, and indeed there are many papers to draw on, but for the school it could not really be fully understood prior to it being experienced.

Parallels have been drawn between the process of client-centred counselling and the work of the critical friend (for example, Cockman, Evans and Reynolds, 1994). It is argued that, like the counsellor, the critical friend works within the clients' frame of reference. This is true only up to a point. The notion of the 'non-directive' counsellor is in fact a misnomer since he or she works from an implicit set of values and in an implicit direction for change. Client-centred counsellors believe, for example, that self-knowledge is better than self-deception, self-direction is better than direction by others, acceptance is preferable to denial, and adaptability is preferable to intransigence. The purpose of counselling is to help the client to move towards some preconceived notion of the 'healthy' or 'self-actualizing' individual. The same is true, in organizational terms, of the critical friend's role.

As critical friends we brought our own vision of the healthy or self-actualizing school. We had ideas about what a 'good', 'effective' or 'improving' school might look like, a body of values, a 'theory' of change, some practical experience of how it worked in other schools and principles which we believed would in some ways be transferable. It was of utmost importance to us to move away from 'the effective school' and the 'best practice' template, but however flexible and fluid our own model of 'improvement', it inevitably contained a number of articles of faith about the process and outcome, for example:

- *the reflective practitioner* — it is good for teachers to think critically about their own practice as a basis for improving it;
- *sharing good practice* — it is good to share ideas, to observe, critique and learn from one another;
- *ownership* — people are more likely to believe in and to follow procedures if they feel they have had a part in shaping them;
- *emphasizing the positive* — reward and encouragement work better than criticism and blame; and
- *the power of the self-fulfilling prophecy* — thoughts are things. What you believe influences your own and others' behaviour.

These are perhaps considerably more than 'articles of faith', since they are drawn from a substantial body of research evidence (for example, Little, 1988; Rosenthal and Jacobson, 1968; Schön, 1983) but none of these axioms are self-evidently true, and they have to be constantly tested in action. This is particularly important because they are likely to be seen in some quarters as the new orthodoxy, and

Figure 9.1   Achievement and the learning organization

indeed are essential tenets of faith for school improvers. Equally we came to this work with an implicit rejection of certain beliefs; for example, that people need to be directed and controlled to get the best out of them, or that the most efficient systems are those where there is a clear hierarchical authority.

In struggling schools there is a real sense in which the critical friend is a Trojan horse. The gift contains a subversive intent. He or she comes with the knowledge that change, especially bottom-up change, is likely to de-stabilize the existing order. It may engender tension and conflict, either in a collegial or hierarchical sense. For schools that are already demoralized, disturbance is something to be avoided rather than embraced.

But disturbance may be just as important in apparently 'successful' schools. The failing school is, after all, a matter of definition and perception [see Lodge's chapter in this volume]. How far is the school willing to accept an external source of reference as to its quality and effectiveness? To what extent are we, as critical friends, willing or able to challenge some of those assumptions? We have worked with schools that would be widely regarded as 'good schools' (even meriting mention in the *Sunday Times'* 'Good Schools Guides' for parents) but that we have seen as ineffective schools across a number of dimensions, primarily because they signally failed to exploit the learning capital of community and family and took credit for achievement which belonged rightly elsewhere [see also Stoll and Fink in this volume].

At the risk of propagating yet another two-dimensional model (see Figure 9.1) we may place schools on an axis from low achieving to high achieving (in measured attainment terms), but on the second intersecting axis they are located in terms of their capacity for learning and development (the 'learning organization'). This gives us a typology with four dimensions, encompassing a range of intermediate possibilities. In this model, ineffective or 'failing' schools fall to the right-hand side of the vertical axis, rather than, as they might more conventionally be seen, as falling below the horizontal axis.

The challenge for the critical friend lies not simply with the schools on the right-hand side of the vertical axis but with the schools in the bottom left-hand quadrant — the self-satisfied 'high achieving' schools. It is in these schools, perhaps, that there needs to be some of the fundamental challenges to the most deeply imbedded assumptions of achievement, effectiveness and the 'quick fix'. Schools may be seen as intrinsically quick-fix organizations in that they control, legitimate and package knowledge to satisfy the demands of a quick-fix assessment process. Ulrich Neisser (1976) argues that academic knowledge is typically assessed with arbitrary problems that a student has little intrinsic interest or motivation to answer, and that performances on such instruments have little predictive power for performances outside of a scholastic environment.

Some of the schools in our study have been eager to embrace the developing work on neuro-linguistic programming (Bandler and Grinder, 1979) accelerated learning (Lozanov, 1991), multiple intelligences (Gardner, 1983) and emotional intelligence (Goleman, 1996). In this respect, the role of the critical friend as knowledgable broker and informed critic is of paramount importance.

A Matter of Style?

'Disturbance' to a school's way of life, however tranquil or troubled the culture, may be caused simply by the style of the critical friend. It may not be helpful, particularly in the entry stages, to exemplify a style which is too far away from the school's behavioural norms. For example, in one staid and formal school with little history of participative management, one of the critical friend team became aware that his own open and collegial style might be undermining that of the head. Consequently he found himself toning down his own style, in a sense 'mirroring' the headteacher.

As invited guests in the school, even invited 'friends', there is a natural sense of accountability to the headteacher. The school would widely be seen as 'his' or 'her' school, and giving the head his or her place is important. However, it did become a trickier issue when it became clear that the headteacher was the source of the problem in the school and subversion, or indeed revolution, was the obvious solution. In some cases we came to the school with knowledge, prejudices or prior experience of that person. In one case we learned that we were in the school on sufferance by the head, the invitation having come from the staff, united in their disenchantment with their leader and hoping that we might be the instrument of his downfall. We have arrived at a school carrying the weight of our assumption that the most direct route to school improvement would probably be to replace the head.

If there is a mythology that researchers can approach each new school with untrammelled objectivity and a totally open mind, it is a mythology that should be immediately dispelled. But putting our own preconceptions and prejudices to the test has been a significant aspect of the project, and the more data and the better the instruments we have had to do that, the more we have learned. In other words, the critical friend, adviser, consultant or inspector — anyone who works in an evaluation and change capacity with the school — has to be an integral part of what is being examined. Is the OFSTED inspection team an integral ingredient in what is being 'seen' in the school? When the story of the school is written, are they featured as leading players? Supporting cast? Or are they silent ghosts who play no part in the unfolding of the drama? David Bohm (1983), the physicist, offers the compelling insight that even atoms change their behaviour when they are under observation!

The Change Process

In some schools there was an implicit message from the headteacher, 'don't call us, we'll call you'. In this situation should the critical friend be proactive or reactive, be accepting or assertive, or even devious? This proved to be the most contentious issue we had to deal with as a team. It was argued on the one hand that we were there on invitation and should respect that. A counter argument held that our accountability was not just to the headteacher but to others in the school and/or to the project funders. One strategy which did work in some instances was to enter the school by another door, not necessarily in a literal sense, but bearing a different kind of gift; for example, 'I have just come across this resource/book/wonderful idea which I thought was exactly what you were looking for'.

The 'other door' in some schools led us directly to a group of staff, or to an individual member of staff, who were eager to be involved and with an enthusiasm that eventually spilled out among their colleagues and proved a potent force for change. Joyce (1991) uses the metaphor of the interconnected doors to describe the process of school improvement, an apt metaphor for the critical friend's search for the key to a progressive unlocking of the doorways to change.

The metaphor of unlocking of doors is an apposite one, and finds echoes in Wardrop's (1996) phenomenon of 'lock-in'. This is where the institutionalization of ideas and practices become self-perpetuating and comfortable because those practices 'work'. He cites the example of the QWERTY keyboard (the ingenious device to prevent the jamming of metal typewriter keys by separating frequently used letters) as having become so powerfully locked-in economically that modern technology has learned to live with its patent inappropriateness. The triumph of the inferior VHS over Beta is another such example.

Argyris and Schön (1978) talk about the organization which cannot seem to learn what everyone knows. This is because the organization does not have the tools and expertise to unlock the experience of the individuals who comprise it. They do not have the collective intelligence or the synergy by which the whole becomes genuinely greater than the sum of its parts.

Covey (1989) uses the analogy of the man sawing the tree. When asked how he is progressing the man says that he has been sawing for the last five hours, and feels tired and decreasingly effective. When asked if he has stopped to sharpen the saw he says, 'No, I am too busy sawing'. It is a metaphor that often resonates with school staff who are too busy teaching to think about learning, and managers who are too busy managing the status quo to deal with change. People in schools are often too busy to share what they know, or perhaps even too afraid.

Using Data in the Information-rich School

Perhaps the most powerful and invidious form of lock-in is the deeply institutionalized belief that some children simply cannot achieve success. In one inner-city secondary school the teacher questionnaire produced the following result:

Item	strongly agree	agree	disagree	strongly disagree	uncertain
Teachers in this school believe that all children can be successful	0	8	42	31	19

What does it take to overturn such a belief system? How can the critical friend effectively challenge what is more than an aggregate of personal beliefs, more than an interlocking belief system with a distinguished history, but an operational system providing daily confirmation of children's inability to learn? Could this staff pessimism not only be understandable but right? To suggest that things could be radically different requires a confidence and conviction on the part of the critical friend — an arrogant assumption for an occasional visitor who does not have to work day in, day out in embattled classrooms.

We found that the data itself provided a useful starting point for opening up the issue (Stoll, 1996). The staff questionnaire had not only asked them for their view of current reality but also committed them to a view of what the effective school might look like (Stoll and Fink, 1996). They responded as follows:

Item	crucial	important	quite important	not very important	not at all important
Teachers in this school believe that all children can be successful	78	22	0	31	19

This allowed us to explore the gap between things as they 'are' and things as people would like them to be. Could they be convinced that closing the gap lay to a very large extent in their own hands? That it should not be viewed as a 'problem' but as an area of creative tension? Senge (1990) uses the metaphor of the rubber band stretched vertically between thumb and forefinger. Tension is only released by lowering from the top (aspirations) or raising from the bottom (current reality).

At its very least, the instrument allowed us to hold up a reflective mirror to a belief system, allowing a collegial exploration, explanation of words and meanings attached to words, moving towards the possibility of genuine dialogue. Bohm (1983) makes a distinction between discussion (the normal mode of operation in an organization) and dialogue (a lost but valuable art in most 'developed' cultures). In discussion, people typically work from within their own mental set, seeking to defend their position and to avoid shaking their most cherished assumptions and prejudices. In dialogue, people are able to separate their thinking from themselves and to view it with 'cool energy'; in other words, taking the heat out of hot issues. He offers three conditions for dialogue:

1   People leave their prior assumptions behind — there is a genuine free flow of ideas;
2   People treat one another as colleagues — status is irrelevant and positions are not defended; and
3   The facilitator (or critical friend) holds the context — the critical friend ensures that ground rules of dialogue are observed.

Figure 9.2 describes some of the blocks to genuine dialogue, or 'learning disabilities' which we encountered in the course of the project, and suggests some possible responses from critical friends. Helping people to recognize the inhibiting power of these is in itself a step to unlocking school improvement doors.

The End Goal

The end goal is for the critical friend to disengage with the school as it develops what Covey (1989) calls 'habits of effectiveness'. That is, knowledge of what to do, skills of how to do it, and attitudes of 'want to do it' are congruent and routine. One of those habits is that of 'interdependence' which he describes as a move from dependence (being reactive to change), through independence (becoming proactive as an individual), to interdependence (learning how to think collectively), because individual thought is destined to ricochet around in the confined space of one's own head whereas collective thought has many escape routes.

As the relationship with the school continues and develops, the main contribution of the critical friend lies in helping people move to a more reflective dialogic approach, with an openness to questioning and respect for evidence. The question 'how do you know?' eventually ceases to be put by the critical friend and becomes a routine way of thinking. In other words, the question itself can help schools to move from the right-hand side of the vertical axis to the left-hand side. It is, in our view, axiomatic that in a genuine learning, information-rich organization, pupil standards of achievement rise and broaden.

Conclusion

The critical friend is in some ways a lonely and exposed role because much is expected. In the ISE Project expectations came from a number of quarters — from staff, from school management, from within the research team itself, from the SOEID (Scottish Office Education and Industry Department), from the education authority, and from the researcher whose role it was to evaluate the impact of the critical

Figure 9.2   Eight learning difficulties

- **I am my position**
  The hierarchical secondary school provides a daily reconfirmation of people's status, which is the platform from which they speak. Primary schools without the same formal hierarchy can be equally, and often more, status conscious. It is important to help people see when status is counterproductive and how a different way of relating can release energy and creativity.

- **I am other people's position**
  Speaking on behalf of others — the union, the management team, the department — is often a convenient denial of one's view and can be difficult to challenge or confront. 'What is your own view on this?' is an important question to get an answer to, but it may be a long-term process.

- **You are our position**
  The critical friend may come to be seen as having some instrumental uses — an advocate, a mouthpiece for an interest group, or as a lever for action. While these may at times be legitimate expectations, to meet them makes it easy to be seduced into a role which simply reinforces a dishonest and dependency culture. Helping people to understand the limitations and possibilities of the critical friend's role can of itself model different kinds and qualities of relationship.

- **They are out to get us**
  'They' is a common feature in school language. Management use it to refer to staff, and staff to management. 'They' often refers to parents, the authority, the government, and to pupils. It is a language and a set of accompanying assumptions which needs to be confronted, however gently and skilfully.

- **Things are not what they used to be**
  It is transparently true that things are not what they used to be, but it can be helpful to find a forum in which people can openly examine some of the mythology a little more closely and identify what the real underlying concerns are.

- **You are the expert**
  It is not an unreasonable expectation that the critical friend is the expert and should be able to offer shortcuts to school improvement. Discovery learning is, after all, a slow and inefficient process. Deciding what can be told and what has to be discovered is as important in consultancy as it is in teaching. Helping people to recognize those distinctions may have many wider applications.

- **We need better systems (resources, structures, plans, etc.)**
  The solutions to organizational and communication problems are often seen in terms of more and better structures, more time and planning. While all of these may help, the contribution the critical friend can make is to help people look beneath these to deeper lying attitudes, values and expectations.

- **This is the first time we've spoken like this**
  When people say they have never had the chance to speak openly about matters of professional concern to them it is indicative of the school culture. The 'neutral' listening role may in itself hold up a mirror to that culture.

friend. In these circumstances it is vital to have opportunities to share issues and problems with a common reference group (other critical friends). It is important for that group to be able to share and make explicit:

- personal criteria for effectiveness or 'success';
- examples of 'success' — where those criteria have been met;

- instances of difficulty in meeting them — sense of frustration or failure;
- expectations others have of you — are they legitimate or not?;
- managing the boundaries — between friend and critic, adviser and facilitator; and
- advice or guidance on what to do, or what to do next time.

The group also serves to bring us back to the central purpose of the critical friend in the context of a school improvement project. It is to offer support and challenge to the school in a way that is empowering, that makes it more able to:

- understand itself;
- understand the process of change;
- become more open to critique and to conflicting views and values;
- engage in genuine dialogue;
- become more effective at managing differences and change;
- be more effective at self-evaluation and self-monitoring;
- be more thoughtful in defining and prioritizing targets;
- develop greater self-confidence at self-management and self-improvement;
- learn how to use outside critical friends, networking and other sources of support; and
- learn how to maintain and sustain habits of effectiveness.

There is one touchstone question for the critical friend, which is not too far away from what a teacher would, or should, ask in relation to the class or individual learner: 'Will this help to develop independence, the capacity to learn and to apply learning more effectively over time?'

References

ANDERS, T. (1996) *Customer-driven Leadership*, Atlanta: Anders Corporation.

ARGYRIS, C. and SCHÖN, D. (1978) *Organizational Learning: A Theory of Action Perspective*, Reading, Mass: Addison Wesley.

BANDLER, R. and GRINDER, J. (1979) *Frogs into Princes: Neuro-linguistic Programming*, UT: Real People's Press.

BOHM, D. (1983) *Wholeness and the Implicate Order*, New York: Ark Paperbacks.

COCKMAN, P., EVANS, B. and REYNOLDS, P. (1994) 'Consultants, clients and the consulting process', in BENNETT, N., GLASTTER, R. and LEVACIC, R. (eds) *Improving Educational Management: Through Research and Consultancy*, Buckingham: Open University Press.

COVEY, S. (1989) *The Seven Habits of Highly Effective People*, New York: Simon and Schuster.

GARDNER, H. (1983) *Frames of Mind*, New York: Basic Books.

GOLEMAN, D. (1996) *Emotional Intelligence: Why it Can Matter More Than IQ*, London: Bloomsbury.

GRAY, J. and WILCOX, B. (1995) 'Doctor the spin cycle', *Times Education Supplement*, 25 July, p. 23.

HARGREAVES, A. (1994) *Changing Teachers, Changing Times: Teachers' Work and Culture in the Postmodern Age*, London: Cassell.

JOYCE, B.R. (1991) 'The doors to school improvement', *Educational Leadership*, **48**, 8, pp. 59–62.

LITTLE, J.W. (1988) 'Assessing the prospects for teacher leadership', in LIEBERMAN, A. (ed.) *Building a Professional Culture in Schools*, New York: Teachers College Press.

LOZANOV, G. (1991) 'On some problems of the anatomy, physiology, and biochemistry of cerebral activities in the global-artistic approach', *Modern Suggestopedagogic Training, The Journal of the Society for Accelerative Learning and Teaching*, **16**, 2, pp. 101–16.

MACBEATH, J. and MORTIMORE, P. (1994) 'Improving School Effectiveness: A Scottish Approach'. Paper presented to the Annual Conference of the British Educational Research Association, Oxford University.

NIESSER, U. (1976) *Cognition and Reality*, San Francisco: Freeman.

ROBERTSON, P. and SAMMONS, P. (1996) 'Improving School Effectiveness: A Project in Progress'. Paper presented to the Annual Conference of the British Educational Research Association, Lancaster University.

ROSENTHAL, R. and JACOBSON, L. (1968) *Pygmalion in the Classroom*, New York: Holt, Rinehart and Winston.

SCHÖN, D. (1983) *The Reflective Practitioner: How Professionals Think in Action*, New York: Basic Books.

SENGE, P. (1990) *The Fifth Discipline: The Art and Practice of the Learning Organization*, New York: Doubleday.

STOLL, L. (1996) 'Asking the right questions', *Managing Schools Today*, **5**, 6, pp. 13–17.

STOLL, L. and FINK, D. (1996) *Changing Our Schools: Linking School Effectiveness and School Improvement*, Buckingham: Open University Press.

WARDROP, M. (1996) *Complexity: Order at the Edge of Chaos*, Harmondsworth: Penguin.

Chapter 10

'A Trouble-shooter Calls': The Role of the Independent Consultant

James Learmonth and Kathy Lowers

> What on earth can he offer? He hasn't taught for years. He doesn't know the kids in this area. Why isn't the head spending the money on something that would really help, like extra staff or more books? They're parasites, these consultants, peripatetic voyeurs . . .

Many staff in schools that are in difficulty or, in extreme cases, that have been judged by OFSTED to require special measures, are proud, hurt people. They feel that the commitment they have given to the education service has not been properly recognized. They feel that society and/or the government of the day does not value education sufficiently: if it did, it would provide more resources so that there could be smaller classes and more specialist help for those in need. They feel that if the catchment area of the school was different, it could be an excellent school. They feel that senior managers in the school do not fully understand the pressures of a full day's teaching, and do not provide enough support, particularly with young people whose behaviour is causing problems. There is often some real basis for these feelings, which makes it important that they are acknowledged. The basic characteristic of such groups of teachers is a loss of confidence in their own capacity to make a difference in pupils' levels of achievement, a belief that the most important variables in determining student outcomes are outside their control. How can someone from outside, unfamiliar with the school, understand the complexity, impossibility even, of the tasks they're required to undertake? If the school requires special measures, and if the OFSTED verdict was unexpected or disputed, these defensive feelings may be allied with the pain and despair of grieving.

So what can an external consultant offer to schools in difficulty? In this chapter we offer two separate perspectives — one drawn from experience in secondary schools, the other from primary school experience — and provide some common principles that might usefully underpin the approach external consultants take to work with schools in difficulty.

A Secondary School Perspective

The first tasks of an external consultant are to listen and to learn. Gradually during this process, possible advantages of involving someone from outside the school or

LEA community may become evident to the staff: she or he is not carrying the luggage of the school's management, or of the LEA's perceived lack of support; is not passing immediate judgments on their professional performance; and is not making statements which confirm the staff in their belief that nobody out there understands. It may be possible to put the school in touch with effective experience elsewhere, although no assumptions are made that what works elsewhere will necessarily work in *this* school. Each school is unique, and it is important for the consultant at this stage to learn as much as possible about the particular circumstances of the school.

It is likely, but not always feasible, that the general outline of the role will have been negotiated with the LEA or head before the consultant's first visit to the secondary school, and that some documentation about the school will have been made available. There are occasions, particularly post-OFSTED, when the school is still too shocked or demoralized to define clearly the role it wants or needs the external consultant to adopt. Even when the head passes on to the staff the clearest possible definition, there may well be suspicions of a hidden agenda or of a fifth column. It is also important for the staff to be clear as to who is employing the consultant: is it the head, or the governors, or the LEA? The consultant's reporting lines need to be understood and agreed: in those early stages of the vulnerable relationship between consultant and school, a misunderstanding in this area can be disastrous. The extent of confidentiality must be agreed, and the roles of agencies such as the governing body and LEA clarified.

It may make sense more quickly if the consultant's role reflects aspects of the school's development plan, or its post-OFSTED action plan. At least that provides evidence of a coherent approach to the school's difficulties. Difficulties or uncertainties related to management may involve a much wider range of contacts in secondary schools than in primary: heads of department and heads of year are certainly now perceived by OFSTED as important middle managers who have some responsibility for pupils' success within the area for which they are responsible. The greater the number of teachers the external consultant is working with, the more challenging is the task of sustaining open, clear and consistent communications. For example, training middle managers in monitoring and evaluating the areas of provision for which they are responsible is likely to have repercussions for the senior management team who need to be kept informed and consulted about issues which arise during such training.

It may be that initially different 'stakeholders' (for example, staff, parents, governors, LEA, pupils) have a different perspective on the school's difficulties. An external consultant may be able to take a more objective view of the school's circumstances and support the school in drawing up priorities and strategies for school improvement (see Figure 10.1). However, every school is different and external consultants must beware of the illusion that they bring with them the medicine that will cure a 'sick' school. It will be of the utmost importance to match the nature and pace of developments with agreed needs. Underlying the external consultant's approach to the school's developments, there are often three particular processes:

Figure 10.1   Towards identification of schools in difficulties

SYMPTOM	SEVERITY		
PUPILS	*MILD*	*PRONOUNCED*	*EXTREME*
Poor learning skills			
Academic underachivement			
Poor attendance			
High level of exclusions			
Poor behaviour			
High number of incidents			
Low pupil self-esteem			
Low pupil expectation			
High pupil mobility			
Number of exclusions from other schools			
Substantial imbalance of gender or class			
'Reasonable' results, but underachievement in relation to potential of pupil intake			
TEACHERS			
Poor quality of teaching overall			
Staff demoralization			
High staff absence — illness			
High staff absence — training			
Unduly high or low staff turnover			
Low staff expectations of pupils			
Lack of communication, cooperative working			
MANAGEMENT			
Lack of clear vision			
Weak leadership			
Erratic decision-making			
Role confusion			
Poor communication			
School trying to do too much, too fast			
Gap between paper (policies, brochure, etc.) and reality			
Low level of effective support from LEA			
Ineffective use of external support			
Poor environment for learning			
COMMUNITY			
School has low status			
Alternative peer culture			
Alternative local culture			
Racism			
High level of social instability			
High levels of unemployment			
Cultural insularity			
High incidence of vandalism			
High attaining, well-motivated pupils attending other local schools			
Poor resource levels			

1   Rebuilding the confidence and the development of skills in the teaching staff by *reaffirming the importance of each individual lesson.*

2   *The recourse to evidence* rather than anecdote, precedent or prejudice within the culture of the school.

3   *The composition of an 'alternative vision' of what the school might be like,* and of different levels of achievement reached by its pupils.

The external consultant has the opportunity to play a major part in each of these processes.

Reinstating the Individual Lesson

A key step in rebuilding the confidence of teachers, and encouraging the further development of their skills, is reinstating the individual lesson as the heart of the school organism. Most of the time and money spent on education over the last twenty years has gone into restructuring the school system or deciding the content of the curriculum, in neither of which the classroom teacher has a powerful voice or any responsibility. What happens in the classroom, where the teacher's responsibility for the quality of teaching and learning is crucial, has been relatively neglected. A consultant, coming fresh to work in partnership with teachers, may be able to encourage the classroom teacher to give an account of what she or he is doing in a lesson: what was planned, what actually took place, and what both teacher and pupils learnt from the experience. Such a process emphasizes the professional choices a teacher constantly is required to make, and the skills a teacher must have if those choices are to lead pupils to achieve success in their learning. The teacher is the person on whom the quality of teaching and learning depends, rather than a senior manager, OFSTED inspector, or government minister. This assumption of responsibility is not always comfortable — it is helpful to have scapegoats — and of course the teacher remains partly dependent on the context of resources within which he or she is working. Nonetheless, an external consultant, who is not part of the day-to-day school community with whom the individual teacher comes in contact, can often start the precarious process of professional self-review, and when appropriate can extend it to other members of the department and to senior managers. Pupils also have an important part to play in this process: their evidence about the sorts of teaching and learning approaches which help them make progress should be a vital influence on the choices teachers make in planning each lesson. In due course it will be an important task for the consultant to suggest that there are areas of the curriculum — the use of language, for example — where it will be useful for all staff to share their experience of individual lessons in the spirit of self-review.

Having concentrated on the importance of the individual lesson, the external consultant should be well placed to contribute to discussions about continuity between lessons: by 'tracking' a class through one or two full days, for example, the consultant is able to offer a view of the teaching and learning that pupils experience within that period of time. It may also be possible for the consultant to attend all the lessons in one week that a class has in a particular subject, and thus be in a position to comment on the coherence or discontinuities of provision during the week. Finally, the consultant is often able to identify teaching strengths within a department which, if shared, could be of considerable benefit to pupils: schools talk a lot about 'the dissemination of good practice', but rarely do much about it. For example, discussion of an example of effective teaching and learning could be a standing item on the agenda of departmental meetings.

The Recourse to Evidence

Many schools in difficulty have a culture built on anecdote, precedent and prejudice. It is often difficult for those in the school to recognize and challenge these elements, partly because they themselves are part of the culture, and partly because challenging the culture of those with whom you work on a daily basis is an unpleasant and stressful business. It is possible for an outsider to bring evidence from other schools or identify evidence within the school as yet unrecognized or inadequately used. Despite the promises and proposals of decades, teachers rarely get the opportunity to visit other schools, other LEAs, or other countries. Too often researchers of schools elsewhere cloak their findings in mantles of jargon or theory which make them impenetrable for classroom teachers. The external consultant's task is therefore to bring, modestly and disinterestedly, relevant evidence or research findings, from other schools, which may help the school grow.

The consultant should also advocate the collection and use of evidence, quantitative and otherwise, within the school which should be used to shape policy and practice: baseline scores on pupils' entry to secondary school and attendance figures are straightforward examples of quantitative evidence; pupils' and parents' views of the school's effectiveness are likely to be more qualitative. Very often such data exist in schools, but for a range of reasons are not used. Little frustrates or demoralizes teachers more than painstakingly collected information which is apparently unused. The consultant's previous experience in interpreting various types of evidence may be helpful to the school in difficulty, as well as the insistence that the most important evidence is that which relates to pupils progress as they go through the school, or that both quantitative and qualitative, which reflects their levels of attainment when they arrive at the school and when they leave it.

Building an Alternative Vision

Schools in difficulty are often trapped in feelings of powerlessness, of apparently having tried everything in vain, of being misunderstood by those outside who have quite unrealistic expectations of their pupils' capacities for achievement. Schools are likely to be successful only if they are able to operate in an environment that encourages their efforts to improve.

There are significant numbers of secondary schools characterized often by low levels of pupil attainment on entry, high pupil and staff mobility, a high proportion of pupils excluded from other schools, and with a range of popular schools in the local area. For them, overall and long-term improvement will be extremely difficult in the context of current national policies. It would also be foolish for those outside, including external consultants, to underestimate the pain and messiness involved in a school's change of culture. The insights of 'gurus' such as Michael Fullan and Andy Hargreaves about the management of change are precious, but are easily dissipated by insensitive or hasty application. Part of an external consultant's skill resides in the method and pace with which he or she fosters the growth of 'an alternative vision'. The vision may be held by a small group of staff or by a newly appointed headteacher; in extreme cases, it may not be immediately apparent but will arise from the partnership between those in the school community and an external agency, perhaps the LEA or an external consultant. Though the realization of the vision is likely to be complex and time-consuming, the process of building vision may be summed up in three questions:

- What do you want to happen?
- How will you make it happen?
- How will you know if it's happening?

In contributing to the composition and realization of the vision, the external consultant has an important role in drawing on the experience of other schools in similar difficulties, in matching previous experience to the needs of a particular school, and in sustaining an objective view of the whole process so that progress is recognized, obstacles are anticipated or overcome, and setbacks are honestly acknowledged. It helps, of course, if there are early successes and these are associated with the contribution of the external consultant. School and consultant alike may be reassured if clear targets are set for the short, medium and long term.

A Primary School Perspective

Optimism, a belief that everyone can improve and a deep interest in the processes that lead to school improvement have caused this consultant to develop a special interest in schools that have severe difficulties. The compensation for the high personal demands made by such work is that whereas advice once offered as an LEA inspector often fell on deaf ears, it seems to be welcomed from an independent adviser (although this could be short lived; a consultant is only as good as their last assignment). There is pressure to operate at a constant level of performance, which is stressful, but this is what people expect when they pay for your services. In addition, if the consultant is working in a school in receipt of special measures through the OFSTED inspection system, there is a pressure that may create the danger of a 'quick fix' rather than a deep rooted change that will have a long-term effect on the school culture.

Working as a consultant to schools in difficulty tests one's skills as a problem-solver and creative thinker to the full, but the chance to focus for long periods of time on a limited number of schools is rewarding, not least because of the opportunity it provides to witness the stories of these schools' improvement at first hand. It has also helped identify several key issues that need to be addressed in working with such schools.

From work with primary schools in difficulty, it appears that there are four key areas where consultants can play a particularly key role: promoting teaching and learning; encouraging monitoring and evaluation; supporting leadership and management; and focusing on public relations. In many ways these are similar to the processes already outlined for those working with secondary schools.

Promoting Teaching and Learning

Switching the attention of the head and staff to teaching and learning is a priority, although difficult to achieve. Leaders of schools in difficulty often spend their time on issues related to long-running feuds and power struggles between individuals rather than on processes that will improve the achievement of pupils. Additionally these 'troubled' schools [see Myers and Goldstein in this volume] rarely have the structures in place to support the delivery of the curriculum; for example, policy statements and curriculum plans.

As efforts are made to move the school forwards, endless meetings can become a feature of school life. Staff can easily suspend reality while engaging in such activities and often 'forget' to implement what has been discussed. 'Touching teacher's practice' in the classroom is the real priority that can be neglected if the pressure to get the structures in place is too great. The consultant might need to help postholders to find ways to 'close off the bolt holes' so that individuals among the staff cannot avoid implementing policy agreements. In one school this meant helping the English postholder to set up a series of meetings designed to improve children's writing. After staff analysed three samples from each class, the implications for practice across the school were discussed and action determined. Further sessions required staff to set objectives and plan lessons with two colleagues to improve aspects of writing. This strategy introduced staff to the experience of working collaboratively with peers as well as providing an element of accountability; individuals were committed to carrying out the plans they had made with colleagues. Teachers made changes to their practice and children's writing improved.

Encouraging Monitoring and Evaluation

Achieving a balance between getting structures, systems and approaches agreed and focusing the spotlight on what is happening in teaching and learning in the classrooms is important for schools wanting to improve. Looking directly at practice always brings with it the possible teacher reaction of 'attack my teaching and you attack me'.

Time taken with the whole staff to thrash out the approach to be used for monitoring and evaluating aspects of the work of the school, is time well spent. Developing a collective approach where everyone at some stage will be involved is seen to be effective by those who have tried it. One example of this has been a review of early monitoring activity involving the whole staff with the aim of improving practice.

A way to introduce the monitoring of classroom practice has been for the headteacher to use some agreed criteria as a focus, as in the case where the use of positive reinforcement strategies was implemented as one part of the school's teaching and learning policy. Once a model of monitoring had been demonstrated by the head then the monitoring agenda was extended to one of the curriculum leaders who looked at an aspect of learning related to a curriculum area. In one case this was how independent pupils were in their selection and use of maths resources. Thus, a cascading process was used.

The skills required to monitor and evaluate successfully can and need to be developed; for example, the need to define a key question that the postholder wants to answer in relation to the chosen focus. Some schools have an arrangement with their link inspector or particular consultants. The head, deputy or postholders can then monitor colleagues in partnership with an 'expert'.

The purpose for monitoring and evaluating aspects of the work of the school is to draw conclusions that can guide future developments for the school as a whole, particularly with reference to raising pupils' achievement. Care is needed that the approach taken to interpret findings reflects this purpose rather than using data as ammunition to attack particular teachers. When there is a need to look at the work of individual staff this needs to be made explicit and should be carried out as part of a different agenda, whether as individual staff support and development or as part of a competency procedure.

A key issue to be resolved with regard to monitoring and evaluating aspects of teaching and learning is who should be involved in interpreting the data and making judgments. Some schools have concluded that it is wise to avoid a purely hierarchical approach where only senior staff make the judgments. A more constructive method seems to be to invite the whole staff to interpret the data presented in order to give a school-wide picture rather than to identify individuals; alternatively the staff can be put in teams so all will play a part in an evaluative session at some stage. The concept of the staff taking a collective responsibility for pupils' achievement appears to be a useful route for schools to take.

Supporting Leadership

Supporting the head and other senior staff 'from the wings', helping them to give a more convincing performance as leaders, is a central task of the consultant. It is not what the consultant does but what others, particularly the head, do that is important for the long-term health of the school. Weaknesses in leadership, past and present, are likely to be features of schools in difficulty. Achieving clear definition of the roles, particularly of the headteacher, deputy head, senior management team and of the governing body, is often a major, long-term element of the consultant's work. Indecisiveness on the part of leaders undermines confidence and increases the potential for conflict. The consultant may need to help the headteacher to determine the detail of what might be appropriate tasks for key members of staff, including developing job descriptions that define expectations more specifically and designing alternative staffing structures as part of a long-term approach to matching staffing more closely to school needs. Additionally, discussions may involve helping the head to determine approaches to encourage the governing body to identify their needs and invest in training for themselves in, for example, the recruitment and selection of staff.

If a school has failed its OFSTED inspection, staffing issues often have to be resolved. To demonstrate effective leadership the head and governors are expected to initiate competency procedures in cases where teaching is judged to be poor. The impact of such action on the staff as a whole, who are already demoralized, must not be underestimated. Guilt, confusion about loyalties, feelings of being victims of a 'hit squad' and the unpleasantness that such procedures generate can work against progress being made in the school.

Helping the headteacher to implement plans and follow tasks through to completion so staff get a sense of progress are also essentials, as is helping the head to 'practise fearlessness' (Fullan, 1992): that is, deciding what they will and will not do. Helping senior staff to share leadership by improving methods of working with other staff, and enabling them to develop their skills of monitoring the work of others so they achieve a balance between praise and constructive criticism are all key features of discussions and activity carried by the consultant.

Probably the most taxing of the goals has been to develop the concept of strategic planning in respect of major elements of a school's work. Moving from crisis management to strategically planned ways of working requires more than just a change of approach. Helping senior staff to view the school objectively, to project, to identify a range of possibilities, to make links between cause and effect are just a few of the elements involved. Once this concept is grasped, asking a series of probing questions can help individuals to pinpoint the stages in a process that they need to work through to achieve particular goals.

There is also often a general ignorance among staff of schools in difficulty of normal practices and procedures used by leaders in schools. When these are introduced, their purpose can be misunderstood. For example, a head's action of recording in writing a request for planning sheets has been perceived as victimization by a member of staff, rather than as a more reliable way of communicating with a large number of people. The consultant needs to help heads and others to think through how they will introduce new systems and processes so that they avoid such pitfalls. A goal is often to review with leaders the range of systems, procedures and processes already in place and how these might be made more appropriate and more effective. One possibility is to devise a questionnaire to help staff pinpoint problems with systems for communication.

Focusing on Public Relations

Regaining the respect and confidence of the local community is an important task for the school in difficulty. How the school will demonstrate pupils' achievements needs to be thought through carefully. Acknowledging the achievements of individual children regularly and setting targets is one element of this process. Checking that all groups of pupils are doing equally well needs a system. An achievement event related to an area of the curriculum and involving every child and teacher is a time-consuming but valuable approach to advertising achievement. It develops collaborative ways of working and shows that the school is improving. The consultant's role is to advise and support the curriculum coordinator from a distance so the perception is that the staff and pupils have managed the event themselves.

Key Principles

From our work, we have derived key principles we feel can usefully guide the work of consultants with schools in difficulty. These are:

- every school can improve;
- improvement must ultimately be assessed in terms of improved pupil outcomes;
- every individual in the school has a contribution to make to the improvement;
- start from where the school is currently but help staff to set the goals high;
- help schools to help themselves and guard against creating dependency;
- model good practice; and
- help the head and staff raise their expectations of what is possible and to see beyond the school's four walls.

In all of this work, the consultant's ability to model is fundamental.

The Importance of Modelling

The impact of modelling behaviour can be extremely significant. As a consultant one may model meetings with postholders, at the head's request, where there is discussion of targets that would be achieved by individuals in a particular term. This may be followed one term later by a meeting led by the head who uses a similar approach to set goals with individuals, while the consultant 'sits in' as an observer. The quality of the presentation of the consultant's files and written communications, the way she manages meetings and processes she uses for getting tasks done all can have an effect. Without hearing the consultant 'preaching' about good practice, individuals often adopt ideas and approaches modelled by the consultant. As the school begins to improve, many of those within become 'hungry' for ideas and new approaches.

Conclusion

The external consultant's most important and difficult task is likely to involve giving advice and support to the school as it makes 'the interminable journey from "how?" to "how?"', as one headteacher has put it. Objectivity is essential, so that false dawns and silver linings are both recognized. By virtue of coming from outside the community, the consultant may be able to suggest and refine new roles for individual staff who may feel trapped in a long-established role of cynicism or alienation, which is now expected of them by both senior managers and by colleagues in the staffroom. The consultant may also be able to find common ground for those who have positioned themselves apart, and in so doing broaden the sense of common purpose and cooperation. Evidence of real progress will be made public and celebrated, and will thus challenge the previous mythology of helplessness, whether real or assumed.

Short-term gains should bring the school sufficient confidence to move on to strategic planning. At a time agreed with the school, the external consultant begins the staged process of withdrawal. It is hoped that by this time the school will have developed the capacity to review its own performance and will now be able to manage the continuous process of change.

Reference

FULLAN, M.G. (1992) *What's Worth Fighting for in Headship*, Buckingham, Open University Press.

Part 5

Conceptual Issues

Although most of the authors of the chapters in this section have been involved, in various roles, in trying to bring about school improvement, here they take one step back to consider some of the conceptual complexities of the current focus on ineffectiveness and 'failure'.

In an interesting study of the perceptions of a group of key stakeholders, Caroline Lodge uncovers subtle but important differences in definitions of ineffectiveness, articulated through a range of powerful metaphors. Most of her interviewees appear to have been influenced in their judgments by the current high profile of OFSTED, although some question the judgments made by OFSTED, and all offer other important criteria. Caroline Lodge warns of the danger of the educational agenda being set entirely by ineffectiveness, echoing concerns we can draw from Michael Barber's postscript to his policy chapter.

The fundamental issue of context, raised by Caroline Lodge, is explored in detail by Kate Myers and Harvey Goldstein in their contribution. They describe a political backdrop of public accountability and use of school differences to avoid responsibility, and argue the consequent dangers of publishing comparative information without health warnings. Their caution, that there are no universally applicable targets, and thus there is a need for contextualized targets, is starkly illustrated by three very different types of 'troubled schools'.

David Reynolds elaborates his own understanding on the 'blocks' to change, through drawing on his experience on the governing bodies of two schools under 'special measures'. In common with other authors, he raises the issue of the governing body's contributory role. He views his general reflections, nonetheless, as optimistic. Proposing improvement strategies, Reynolds highlights the importance of school-based data, and micropolitical skills. In concluding, he draws readers' attention to two other possible avenues of exploration. One is that of applied science and medicine. The other is experiences of other countries. In our opinion, however, there are crucial caveats to consider given the very different nature of Taiwanese society.

Ending this section, Louise Stoll and Dean Fink shine a different light on the issue of context, asking why the 'ineffective' schools we hear about are located mainly in working-class neighbourhoods. Taking a cultural perspective, they focus their chapter on the 'unidentified ineffective school', that sits near the top of performance tables and yet adds little value to what its pupils bring with them. Louise Stoll and Dean Fink describe the cultural norms of such 'cruising' schools, demonstrating that they lack the capacity and readiness to change no less than 'failing' schools. Despite offering suggestions for improving cruising schools, Louise Stoll and Dean Fink conclude, somewhat pessimistically, that their mediocrity is perpetuated by the existing system.

Indeed, all of these chapters suggest that the system within which the current debate on ineffectiveness is being held, and the reform structures put in place, contribute to some of the constraints on change in schools and maintaining the status quo.

Chapter 11

What's Wrong With Our Schools? Understanding 'Ineffective' and 'Failing' Schools

Caroline Lodge

Introduction

'WHAT'S WRONG WITH OUR SCHOOLS?' asked a billboard in a South London borough, advertising a local radio programme. It gave two opposite answers: 'nuffink' and 'quite a lot actually'. Each answer contains a tension: the voice of the educated claims problems with our schools, the voice of the inarticulate claims none. Four points may be drawn from this vignette. First, there is an assumption that something *is* wrong with schools. Second, the answers given are quantitative, responding to the question 'how much is wrong?', not exploring what the problems might be. Third, it exposes simple binary thinking: something either is or is not, making more complex judgments hard. Fourth, this debate is being held in public. Much of the debate about ineffective and failing schools is currently carried on in these terms.

My experience suggests that discussions about ineffective or failing schools do not reveal much depth of understanding of those schools. In particular, such discussions avoid clarity about what is meant by ineffectiveness, so that meanings are not shared. Ineffective schools are often lumped together as one type of school, without considering whether they may have different characteristics. The development of strategies likely to help those schools become effective are unlikely to be developed out of such simplistic analysis. In this chapter, I explore how a range of people who work with ineffective schools understand and think about them[1] and discuss:

- how far they draw on the existing research, models and theories about failing and ineffective schools;
- how much the conceptualizing about such schools is framed within the dominant discourses, especially those articulated by policy makers;
- whether these conceptions help with the work of improving our least effective schools; and
- if those who have the job of working with failing or ineffective schools are using what is known about schools in these situations.

The chapter draws on interviews conducted during the early summer of 1996 with eight people working in different roles within education. The chapter begins by considering how far research literature has had an impact on the interviewees' judgments about ineffectiveness. During these interviews it became plain that the Office for Standards in Education (OFSTED) had also had an impact on their judgments and the nature of this impact is explored in the next section. I suggest that judgments about effectiveness are based on values and beliefs about education and schools. The chapter concludes by considering how current debate is affecting judgments about schools and their effectiveness.

Definitions of Ineffective and Failing Schools

The research has described ineffectiveness in a way that goes deeper than the bi-polar. Stoll (1995) indicates several 'lenses' or perspectives through which one can view ineffectiveness. One of these is a cultural lens [see, also, Stoll and Fink in this volume]. Describing five types of school culture, Hargreaves (1995) considers the combination of control and cohesion. Four of the cultures are considered ineffective, and only one effective:

- *formal,* low on cohesion but high on control with an emphasis on academic achievement;
- *welfarist,* low on control and high on cohesion, with a child-centred approach;
- *hothouse,* high on control and cohesion, oppressive, high expectations on involvement and achievement;
- *survivalist,* low on both cohesion and control and close to breakdown; and
- *ideal or effective,* high expectations of work and conduct, demanding and enjoyable for staff and pupils.

Hargreaves suggests that this approach avoids a simplistic continuum from least to most effective and the conceptualization of effectiveness as a list of factors. A third approach differentiates three kinds of ineffective schools: striving, swaying and sliding (Myers, 1995; and chapter by Myers and Goldstein in this volume). Together these perspectives provide a framework for developing a profile of ineffectiveness that is concerned with more than one dimension, that captures more clearly the complexity of school differences, and thus may help identify the focus for improvement strategies.

Mortimore (1995) recently expanded his earlier definition of effectiveness (Mortimore, 1991), referring to its four aspects:

- a specific methodology (added value)
- the characteristics of effectiveness
- the effects of contexts on outcomes
- a belief in the potency of social institutions
  (adapted from Mortimore, 1995).

Using Mortimore's aspects, I shall consider how far those working in education draw on more complex understandings of ineffectiveness, how far they use a simple effective/ineffective conception, and whether the aspects of effectiveness have made an impact on their understanding of ineffective and failing schools.

Understanding Ineffective and Failing Schools

The views of people who work in education are generally not heard or explored, but to investigate their meanings I required access to what people have to say about failing and ineffective schools. As the study was limited by time, the choice of interviewees was restricted to quick access from central London, and to a manageable number of subjects. My original plan was ambitious, and included several teachers. In the event, I only interviewed two secondary headteachers. However, a pilot interview with a primary headteacher reassured me that the key concerns of primary and secondary headteachers related to this topic are not significantly different. My decision to limit the study to those professionally connected to education meant that I did not include parents. They deserve a study of their own as even a small number could not represent the range of their perceptions. Each person was interviewed for about an hour in their place of work. The final choice of interviewees included:

- two secondary headteachers, one working in an outer London suburb (hence HTO), the other in an inner London borough, in a school under 'special measures' (HTI);
- the chief inspector of an outer London borough (LEA);
- a civil servant working in the DfEE (DfEE);
- an HMI (HMI);
- an education journalist from a broadsheet daily newspaper (PR); and
- two academics (ACAD1 and ACAD2).

Each interviewee was asked to define what they meant by an ineffective school, and to suggest the evidence they would use to judge ineffectiveness. They were asked to say what had influenced their thinking about ineffectiveness and why they thought ineffective schools had been given such a high media profile recently. Finally they were asked to comment on how the school's context contributes to its ineffectiveness.

The concept of *in*effectiveness has only found its way into discourse recently and so meanings of ineffectiveness vary and are still being clarified:

> Historically we talked about more or less effective. We wouldn't have said a school was ineffective, but a school was more or less effective . . . But I don't know whether there is a group of more or less effective schools and then there's a group which are ineffective. I just don't know that and I don't think anybody knows that . . . I think it's quite useful to start thinking about ineffective schools as well as effective schools. (ACAD1)

A Specific Methodology

None of the people I interviewed believed that raw indicators, or raw comparisons, revealed a school's ineffectiveness. All eight interviewees drew upon a notion of a continuum:

effective — ineffective — failing

Their main criterion of effectiveness was some kind of measure of pupil outcomes (usually academic attainment) related to a number of other factors illustrated below:

- the prior attainment and abilities of the pupils

  [An ineffective school] is one that fails to make progress with the majority of children, the progress you would expect to make. So I hope that encompasses the fact that schools have different intakes with different capabilities. (HTO)

- comparison with other schools

  An effective school is characterized by high standards, i.e., high achievement in relation to similar schools, and an ineffective school would be poor in relation to schools serving pupils with similar attainment on intake. (HMI)

- the socio-economic status of the intake

  I do think that the two crudish factors which you can use are free school meals and exam results. (PR)

The simple continuum was refined in a second way by adding the dimension of improvement or decline over time.

My perception of a school that was failing or possibly failing might be one where the exam results seemed to be getting worse, where exclusion rates are very high, where attendance rates are low and not getting better. (PR)

A third refinement was to add other continua, here referred to in relation to failing schools:

... one of which is if you have a low proportion of pupils saying they are satisfied with the education they have received, and the other would be that you had picked up the OFSTED criteria for failing schools — poor relationships between pupils and teachers. (ACAD1)

A fourth refinement related to the degree to which the school has capacity for improvement:

> . . . a seriously failing school, that is one which has virtually zero capacity for self-development; in other words, doesn't have any capacity to renew itself. (ACAD2)

For the LEA inspector the quality of 'life and learning' in a school was also important. One headteacher referred to schools' responsibility to 'give the pupils life chances and experiences' which would give them 'some hope of making a success in the world' (HTO). These comments reflect a concern that values other than academic achievement are not lost in making judgments about ineffectiveness.

Those interviewed made a distinction between ineffective and failing schools in relation to a number of factors. Three of those interviewed believed that this difference was only a matter of degree and that the tools of evaluation are not sharp enough 'to allow you to single out from all those schools the bottom 1 per cent' and that decisions about which category a school is in (failing or with serious weaknesses) 'is as much a political judgment as a social scientific one' (ACAD1).

Three of those interviewed explicitly referred to the OFSTED distinctions between schools requiring special measures and those with serious weaknesses when asked to make a distinction between ineffective and failing schools. However, it was the degree to which a school had the capacity to recognize and deal with its own weaknesses that was referred to as a distinction between ineffective and failing schools by four of those interviewed.

In a failing school 'the overwhelming sea of pressures' — i.e., the scale and intractability of problems — had some important implications. Both the journalist and one headteacher referred to the probable need for 'drastic measures' in failing schools. The journalist commented 'they need outside help'. The LEA inspector indicated that they needed longer to recover (having often been in difficulties for a considerable length of time). The approaches to improvement may need to be different for 'schools that are really in serious difficulties [when] the general improvement strategies that we know about don't work' (ACAD2). This view was echoed by the HMI who suggested that some schools have 'an indigenous incapability of dealing with their problem areas', citing dealing with weak teachers as the key example of this. He suggested that some schools are 'so far down that they lose public confidence' and then simply cannot improve. He agreed with both academics that more needs to be known about these schools.

All of those interviewed agreed that there was a category of school that was performing fairly well by national standards, but should be doing significantly better given their intake: that described by Stoll and Fink (1996) as the cruising school [see also Stoll and Fink in this volume]. They commented that inspections were not always identifying them. Although not explicitly stated, the interviewees drew upon an understanding of ineffectiveness that implied a distinction between strolling, struggling and sinking schools. None was explicit about the possibility of an ineffective school on an *improving* trajectory, although it was implied in comments about the work of the DfEE with failing schools.

The 'Characteristics' of Effectiveness

The interviewees' descriptions of the evidence they would use in arriving at a judgment about ineffectiveness are revealing. It appeared that school effectiveness research may have had a limited impact on thinking about ineffectiveness. A recent review of the research has summarized the characteristics of effective schools in a list of eleven factors (Sammons, Hillman and Mortimore, 1995). In Table 11.1 these are compared with the number of times interviewees mentioned their absence as a feature of ineffectiveness.

All interviewed referred to the cluster of characteristics that relate to the quality of teaching. Five of those interviewed referred to inadequate or lack of leadership. Six referred to the role of parents in partnership with the school. Pupils' rights and responsibilities were only referred to by the two headteachers.

There was no systematic application of a list of characteristics of effective schools or attempt to create an alternative list of characteristics of an ineffective school. The extent to which the characteristics identified by school effectiveness research were drawn upon appeared to relate to how closely the individual worked to the chalk face, with the headteachers referring most frequently to the characteristics, followed by the LEA inspector.

The interviewees did not differentiate between the evidence for effectiveness and characteristics of effectiveness. The evidence for ineffectiveness they mentioned is summarized in Table 11.2. What is notable about Table 11.2 is the significant number of characteristics that relate to the affective experience of school: the behaviour, ethos, relationships and morale. It would seem that many of those interviewed considered that a school that does not look out for the well-being of its pupils and its staff is ineffective or failing. While pupil outcomes and associated

Table 11.1 Characteristics of effective schools

Characteristics of effective schools	Mentioned in relation to ineffective schools if absent
professional leadership	5
shared vision and goals	2
learning environment	4
concentration on teaching and learning	2
purposeful teaching	6
high expectations	2
positive reinforcement	1
monitoring progress	2
pupils' rights and responsibilities	2
home–school partnership	6
a learning organization	1

Based on Sammons et al., 1995, p. 8

Table 11.2 Evidence for ineffective schools

Evidence of ineffectiveness	Mentioned by n interviewees
low pupil outcomes	8
poor quality of teaching	7
poor pupil behaviour	6
poor pupil attitudes	5
bad relationships in school	4
poor atmosphere or ethos	3
weak leadership of headteacher	3
low teacher morale	2

poor quality of teaching are important, in making judgments, every person interviewed mentioned evidence relating to other factors.

It was not clear, from the evidence offered, whether ineffective schools were being judged to be significantly different from effective schools. There is a confusion between factors that cause ineffectiveness and those that are outcomes of ineffectiveness. This confusion indicates the need for further research (Reynolds, 1992).

The first academic, the inner London headteacher and the HMI all indicated the limitations of school effectiveness research because they felt that offering ineffective schools models of effective ones to copy does not help schools improve:

> [School effectiveness research] fails to give the glue to make it happen . . . But it's really an art. That's why one can't copy successful schools. You just can't reproduce them like that, time and time again, because successful schools in difficult circumstances are *more* than the features you'd expect to see . . . Which is why one can't fix a school by remote control. (HTI)

> School effectiveness research has been very interesting and very useful, but it has largely confirmed the obvious. That's an important role for research. What it doesn't say too much about is how a poor school turns itself into a good one. (HMI)

There is a growing consensus that it is time to move on from listing characteristics of effectiveness (or indeed of ineffectiveness) to looking at strategies for using the research for school improvement (Reynolds, Sammons, Stoll, Barber and Hillman, 1996) that this small study supports.

The Influence of Context on Schools' Effectiveness

Generally, the interviewees believed that nothing in a school's context inexorably led to ineffectiveness or failure, but that some circumstances made it much harder to achieve effectiveness and to recover from underachievement:

Well, the fact that there are effective schools situated in very difficult contexts shows less successful schools what can be done . . . It isn't easy and there are no quick fixes. But it can be done. But sometimes there are such indigenous problems in the environment and catchment of the schools that it's a very hard job. (HMI)

Ineffective schools are to be found at *every* part of the system. They are to be found in the inner cities, where unfortunately the failing schools tend to be congregated, especially schools containing children of particular backgrounds. (HTI)

Those closest to policy making were concerned that context should not be seen as an explanation or excuse for a school's poor quality. In this they are reflecting government policy that schools are not prisoners of their surroundings. This view was not shared by the outer London headteacher:

Some schools . . . have been characterized as failing, as failures, without taking account of the real social problems that they are facing. (HTO)

Aspects of the context most frequently cited related to parents — their attitude to school and their ability to support their children and the school. The turbulent nature of the context of some schools was also cited as presenting particular difficulties, especially in relation to migrant populations in inner cities. Other factors thought likely to contribute to a difficult context were the country's culture of anti-intellectualism and the lack of effective support by the LEA.

For some, it was the combination of forces within a difficult context that would make it more difficult for schools to be effective, especially when the strategies for improvement were frail, perhaps relying on one or two key people. During the interviews, the closure of Hackney Downs School, which had occurred five months earlier following considerable national media coverage, was referred to in relation to the impact of context on a school. This 'dreadful saga' (ACAD1) appears to be in the process of taking its place as a landmark event, comparable to William Tyndale. The decision by the Education Association to close the school was not regarded as unproblematic, although one of the academics described it as 'the policy of the last resort, the *last* last resort' (ACAD1). The DfEE representative referred to Hackney Downs as proof that 'you can't succeed with every case'. A changing climate was also noted by the second academic who noted that LEAs were now more willing to tackle the difficult problem of closing schools. According to a DfEE paper, five LEA and two independent 'failing' schools were due to close in the summer of 1996, one in January 1997, and 'closure is under discussion at some half dozen other schools' (DfEE, 1996, p. 6).

Silver (1994) has described how the shift in policy about judgments in education is connected to the move away from concentration on social contexts of schooling towards a focus on economic accountability. This shift has produced a great deal of unclear thinking in making judgments about schools, especially about ineffective and failing schools in disadvantaged areas. OFSTED's *Framework* demonstrates this, but so too did those I interviewed.

The issue of the effect of context raised an important point about research tools. The first academic discussed in some detail the uncertainties within OFSTED over this issue:

> You will know of continuing debates about whether OFSTED should or should not contextualize school performance. In the Chief Inspector's Annual Report which came out in February 1996 he remarked that schools had been identified in that way. As he said, 'I have chosen these schools because they were excellent in comparison with schools in comparable circumstances.' But when a month later the *Times Educational Supplement* ran the story saying 'Inspectors to take account of deprivation in judging schools' he wrote a letter to say that 'we haven't got the tools right yet'. And when you look at the OFSTED guidance document [on inspection], it's clear that they haven't got it fully sorted out yet. (ACAD1)

Several of those interviewed, including the headteacher quoted earlier, were keen to separate the 'myth of ethnicity' (LEA) from discussions about context, meaning that they did not believe that low achievement was related to the attitudes of minority ethnic groups. The LEA inspector referred to the findings of the School Matters research (Mortimore, Sammons, Stoll, Lewis and Ecob, 1988), and the recently published OFSTED report on reading (OFSTED, 1996a) to illustrate that research suggests that poor attitudes to school and reading are more likely to be found in the English, Scots, Welsh and Irish group than, for example, among Afro-Caribbeans. The inner-city headteacher agreed with this view.

In discussing the context of ineffective and failing schools, interviewees raised some important policy issues relating to the importance of support from the LEA, the need to take specific action to reduce the odds in areas of great difficulty, the need to train teachers specifically to work in these areas and the need to learn more about the strategies of those schools which were improving despite the odds.

The extent to which social context is considered a factor in judgments about effectiveness is still being contested, not least because we do not yet at national level have the tools to do this. It is an important strand in school effectiveness research (for example Sammons, 1996; Scheerens, 1992; Teddlie and Stringfield, 1993) [see also Myers and Goldstein in this volume].

A Belief in the Potency of Social Institutions

Those who worked most closely with children and schools revealed a belief in the importance of education for the life chances of the children, for the transformational power of education. The inner London headteacher spoke with passion about his belief in the ability of every individual and institution to improve, and of the particular significance of education for 'people from the most vulnerable sections of our community for whom education is the only ladder out of their circumstances'. This view was shared by the LEA inspector and the other headteacher, who defined an ineffective school as:

> ... a school in the end that doesn't give the pupils the right life chances and experiences that allow them to go out with at least some hope of making a success in the world.

The evidence from these interviews suggests that judgments by educational professionals have been influenced 'by criteria defined by the government and its policy-related agencies' (Silver, 1994, p. 107). It also suggests that judgments are being made on other criteria, in particular the extent to which education has personal significance. The potential for education to transform the lives of young people, and especially the lives of those living in the most deprived areas of the country, is clearly still a strongly rooted value and remains a strong influence on judgments about schools. Even the government agencies have had to temper their criteria to take account of some aspects of schools' context, as can be seen, for example, in the revised OFSTED *Handbook* (1994). It is to the impact of OFSTED on judgments about schools that this chapter now turns.

OFSTED's Influence

All the interviewees suggested that the creation of OFSTED and OFSTED's own activities and publications had influenced their thinking on ineffective and failing schools. The 1993 Act made the category of 'failing' school an official one. This was later revised to refer to schools 'requiring special measures'. Media attention and OFSTED's own publications have also concentrated on such schools and their improvement (Wilcox and Gray, 1996). Criteria for judging that a school 'is failing or likely to fail' are laid out in the revised *Framework* (OFSTED, 1995). The judgment relates to a list of characteristics, which is different from the list for judging that a school is acceptable. Precisely how the evidence is weighed to arrive at the judgment about the school is not revealed and is presented as unproblematic.

More recently, OFSTED has created another category of schools: those 'with serious weaknesses' (OFSTED, 1996b). Judgments about these schools are made in a different way. This may be because it is hard to squeeze another category between acceptable and requiring special measures. The indicators do not distinguish between outcomes and the contributory factors that underpin the judgments described in the *Framework*. The indicators for schools with serious weaknesses are more than one of the following:

(i)   unsatisfactory or poor teaching in 25 per cent or more of lessons;
(ii)   pupils' attainment is low and progress poor in relation to pupils in similar schools;
(iii)   absence greater than 10 per cent;
(iv)   significant unsatisfactory features in the leadership and management of the school; and
(v)   poor behaviour.

Generally a school deemed to have serious weaknesses is considered likely to reveal more than one of these features (OFSTED, 1996a) and, from September 1997, inspectors will be required to state whether a school has serious weaknesses.

Those interviewed considered that OFSTED's indicators were a strong influence on their understanding of ineffective and failing schools. It is true that all those interviewed frequently referred to OFSTED. On closer examination, rather than the detail and rationale of OFSTED's judgments, it is the pervasive notion of the judgment itself, and especially the judgment of 'failing', that has been accepted. Given that OFSTED had only been set up four years previously and has modified its strategies several times, it is not surprising that the forms rather than the substance of its judgments have been internalized.

As one might expect, the HMI expressed most satisfaction with OFSTED's judgments: 'We have growing confidence in the probity of inspection findings'. He emphasized the need to differentiate between outcomes and contributory factors, which is stressed in the 1995 *Handbook*. Others interviewed could not distinguish so straightforwardly between them:

> We use exclusion as an indicator and attendance, and both of these are affected by the attitude of the community to discipline and the value of schooling. So in a particularly difficult area there may be little parental support, exclusion will rise and attendance will fall. (DfEE)

The LEA inspector (who has experience as an OFSTED inspector) came closest to reflecting the criteria of OFSTED:

> OFSTED provides a good starting point [for defining 'ineffective' and 'failing']. The evidence base is the classroom in its focus on pupil achievement and other factors follow: management and other dimensions follow. It has sharpened our understanding of what matters. (LEA)

OFSTED's criteria were not accepted without reservations. Several of those interviewed considered that OFSTED's criteria picked up failing schools in the inner cities, but not schools whose underperformance was masked by favourable circumstances — the cruising schools:

> I'm not convinced that the OFSTED definition always captures failure, but they capture a particular kind of failure, which tends to be inner-city schools. (PR)

> I wait for the day, with interest, when OFSTED finds a school to be failing because it's getting 45 per cent A to Cs when it should be getting 70 per cent, because there are schools like that. Although if the OFSTED system was refined, as it should be, then it would find those schools. At the moment it doesn't appear to. (ACAD2)

> I am quite clear that it isn't picking up all of that latter category [i.e., with national average pupil attainment but actually underperforming], but it is picking up a few of them. And you might challenge me by saying, what failing school has got

GCSE results above the national average? And the answer is none. But there are some which come pretty close to that which have been failed. I would like to find a failing grammar school because I am quite sure that there are some. (DfEE)

OFSTED's judgments do not allow for these subtleties and the inconsistent bases for judgment about the need for 'special measures' and 'serious weaknesses' may partly explain this difficulty.

The second academic was concerned about schools' capacity for self-renewal, and doubted that OFSTED's new *Framework* would provide 'evidence of how the school deals with change, deals with policy implementation, deals with professional development of learning' (ACAD2).

Another criticism was the OFSTED's lack of accountability:

I am just not convinced in any way that their opinions are valid or reliable . . . I think it's amazing that we have this incredibly complicated and expensive system and nobody is actually looking to see if it's doing what it's paid to do. (HTO)

The HMI was sure, in contrast, that OFSTED's own quality assurance system was functioning well, and pointed out that HMI's independent visits to failing schools concurred with 96 per cent of the inspection teams' judgments.

While OFSTED may have focused attention on failing schools and those with serious weaknesses, the interpretation of what is meant by these labels, how judgments have been made, and the values lying behind them (beyond the central importance of teaching and pupil achievement) are not shared. It would appear that these conflicting perspectives coexist without occasioning public debate, and despite being rooted in very different sets of values and beliefs about education.

Values and Beliefs About Educational Success

The interviewees' use of metaphors revealed some important values and beliefs underpinning their judgments about schools. Many metaphors were of the kind used in everyday speech (for example 'coming out of the woodwork'), but some metaphors used in relation to ineffective and failing schools stood out as images of violent treatment to a living body:

It's something to do with real determination and passion, real passion, and going to the stake for it. (LEA on the headteacher's leadership)

It's like chemotherapy, if you've got some kind of growth. The chemo has that effect but it also has the potential to save life. (HTI speaking about identifying failing schools)

Who will light them up? (HMI on leaders and teachers in schools who have been in one school for a long time and have 'impaired vision')

. . . continually pulling up the roots. (HTO on LEA officers' interventions in a failing school within the LEA)

Images of martyrdom, treatment for illness, excitement and gardening practice all indicate an organic conception of schools; one which conflicts with the managerial systems construction conveyed by OFSTED. The image of the school organization as an organism, as opposed to a machine, political system or instrument of domination (for example, Morgan, 1986), was widespread and helps us understand how these people visualized processes within the organization, how a school might fall sick, need treatment, even require putting out of its misery. This metaphor has been further exploited by Myers (1995), drawing upon research in other fields and psychoanalytical theory to consider difficulties faced by failing schools.

Three interrelated discourses can be seen to be at work alongside these older images and the humanistic values described. There is a long history of a discourse of failure in the English education system and it is evident in the work of OFSTED, with its 'increasing obsession with failure' (Mortimore, 1996). The discourse of failure has gone hand in hand with the discourse of derision (Ball, 1990). These discourses have been joined by the discourse of effectiveness (as distinct from school effectiveness research) which has meant that there is a convergence of agreement about the necessity of judging performance of the individual school which underpins the OFSTED inspection system. The understanding from the school effectiveness tradition that individual schools make a difference, joined with the understanding that schools must be the site of change, and the creation of schools as units of financial accountability (through Local Management of Schools) have together created a widespread assumption in this country that the school should be the unit of accountability, and of improvement. This assumption was shared by those I interviewed. However, this is not how many other OECD countries make judgments in their education systems [see Kovacs in this volume], although some are moving in this direction. In Sweden, Germany and France pupils are seen as the differentiating factor, as all schools are considered to be more or less equally effective (OECD, 1995).

These discourses may be damaging efforts to improve schools:

> If the entire public debate about education is dominated by ineffectiveness then it creates a misleading impression of the education service. It has a demoralizing effect . . . and the politicians do have to learn that if they focus entirely on ineffectiveness they allow the agenda to be set entirely by ineffectiveness and it will be very difficult for them to get the overall improvements across the system that they want. (ACAD2)

Another effect of this discourse is the official view that it is enough to say that because some schools can succeed in difficult circumstances all schools can. Systemic factors are hidden in the discourses of effectiveness and of failure, which focus on the responsibility of the individual school. The impact of the quasi-market is making it harder for some schools to succeed, thereby contributing to a widening gap between the rich and the poor in inner-city schools (Gewirtz et al., 1995). We can learn more from an approach which asks why some schools are not able to thrive. Understanding the combination of factors operating on some schools would be more likely to encourage improvement than an approach that invokes blame.

These discourses, then, can hide the contribution of other factors to schools' ineffectiveness, especially the contribution of socio-economic context and of factors within the education system itself. The question about context has the potential to challenge the dominant effectiveness discourse, which implies technical solutions to such problems. The practitioners interviewed rejected the technical approach to school improvement:

> But it's really an art. That's why one can't copy successful schools. You just can't reproduce them like that, time and time again, because successful schools in difficult circumstances are *more* than the features you'd expect to see . . . Which is why one can't fix a school by remote control. (HTI)

Conclusions

The more detailed examination of ineffective schools, reflected in different topologies, has largely been ignored in the day-to-day thinking about ineffective schools. This is unwise as policy decisions are not taking into account whether a school is ineffective but improving, struggling with improvements, or quite incapable of generating improvements without significant external support. It was clear to all who commented on policy implications that more research about ineffective schools and how they have improved is needed. Policy has used a rather blunt approach; improvement through continual scrutiny, public exposure and exhortation to emulate the most successful practice, assisted by a sharp dose of action planning and target setting, washed down with the threat of closure.

The fundamental purposes of education are being contested. In my sample of educationalists there was a strong assumption that schools exist to maximize the life chances of individual children. There was an acknowledgment of another purpose: to provide the appropriate skilled workforce to meet the economic needs of the country. While these are not necessarily contradictory, they do not always sit easily together. For example, an emphasis on basic skills needs may be made at the expense of developing a wider range of children's knowledge and abilities.

The right to be part of making a judgment, or to decide what criteria are used, is also, to some extent, contested. These interviews show that professionals are making judgments on wider criteria than raw scores or OFSTED's criteria, and that alternatives to a management-oriented conception of the school are still in use. In other words, those aspects of schools they think are important, but which are not treated as important in official statements, are still influential and they are still basing their judgments on them.

All but one of my interviewees, however, were at least in their 40s. What of the next cohort of headteachers, LEA inspectors, academics and government officials? They are currently the younger teachers in our schools. And what of the parents and children? They will have been exposed to different assumptions, different authority for the judgments and different discourses. They may absorb and accept more of the discourses now in operation. It will be their judgments that will be significant in twenty years. By then, the perspectives on ineffective schools which have been promoted during the period of the Conservative Government may have become established orthodoxy rather than contested opinion.

Note

1   This research was carried out for a dissertation, part of an MA in School Effectiveness and School Improvement at the Institute of Education, University of London.

References

BALL, S.J. (1990) *Politics and Policy Making in Education: Explorations in Policy Sociology*, London: Routledge.

DfEE (1996) 'How weak schools recover: September 1993 to June 1996', *How Weak Schools Recover*, London, Institute of Education: DfEE.

GEWIRTZ, S., BALL, S.J. and BOWE, R. (1995) *Markets, Choice and Equity in Education*, Buckingham: Open University.

HARGREAVES, D.H. (1995) 'School culture, school effectiveness and school improvement', *School Effectiveness and School Improvement*, **6**, 1, pp. 23–46.

MORGAN, G. (1986) *Images of Organization*, London: Sage.

MORTIMORE, P. (1991) 'The nature and findings of research on school effectiveness in the primary sector', in RIDDELL, S. and BROWN, S. (eds) *School Effectiveness Research: Its Messages for School Improvement*, Edinburgh: HMSO.

MORTIMORE, P. (1995) 'School effectiveness — where next?' *Learning From Each Other*, Summary of conference presentation, London, Institute of Education.

MORTIMORE, P. (1996) 'We should inspect our obsession with failure', *The Independent*, Section 2, 25 July, p. 17.

MORTIMORE, P., SAMMONS, P., STOLL, L., LEWIS, D. and ECOB, R. (1988) *School Matters: The Junior Years*, Wells: Open Books. (Reprinted in 1994 by Paul Chapman, London.)

MYERS, K. (1995) 'Intensive Care for the Chronically Sick', Paper presented at European Conference on Educational Research, University of Bath.

OECD (1995) *Schools Under Scrutiny*, Paris: OECD.

OFSTED (1994) *Handbook for the Inspection of Schools (consolidated edition)*, London: HMSO.

OFSTED (1995) *Framework for the Inspection Schools*, London: HMSO.

OFSTED (1996a) *The Teaching of Reading in 45 Inner London Primary Schools: A Report by Her Majesty's Inspectors in Collaboration with the LEAs of Islington, Southwark and Tower Hamlets*, London: OFSTED.

OFSTED (1996b) *Consultation on Arrangements for the Inspection of Maintained Schools from September 1997*, London: OFSTED.

REYNOLDS, D. (1992) 'School effectiveness and school improvement: An updated review of the British literature', in REYNOLDS, D. and CUTTANCE, P. (eds) *School Effectiveness: Research, Policy and Practice*, London: Cassell.

REYNOLDS, D., SAMMONS, P., STOLL, L., BARBER, M. and HILLMAN, J. (1996) 'School effectiveness and school improvement in the UK', *School Effectiveness and School Improvement*, **7**, 2, pp. 133–58.

SAMMONS, P. (1996) 'Complexities in the judgement of school effectiveness', *Education Research and Evaluation*, **2**, 2, pp. 113–49.

SAMMONS, P., HILLMAN, J. and MORTIMORE, P. (1995) *Key Characteristics of Effective Schools: A Review of School Effectiveness Research*, London: Institute of Education for OFSTED.

SCHEERENS, J. (1992) *Effective Schooling: Research, Theory and Practice*, London: Cassell.

SILVER, H. (1994) *Good Schools, Effective Schools: Judgements and Their Histories*, London: Cassell.

STOLL, L. (1995) 'The Challenge and Complexity of the Ineffective School', Paper presented at the Annual General Meeting of the British Educational Research Association, University of Bath.

STOLL, L. and FINK, D. (1996) *Changing Our Schools: Linking School Effectiveness and School Improvement*, Buckingham: Open University Press.

TEDDLIE, C. and STRINGFIELD, S. (1993) *Schools Make a Difference: Lessons Learned from a 10-year Study of School Effects*, New York: Teachers College Press.

WILCOX, B. and GRAY, J. (1996) *Inspecting Schools: Holding Schools to Account and Helping Schools to Improve*, Buckingham: Open University Press.

Chapter 12

The Study and Remediation of Ineffective Schools: Some Further Reflections

David Reynolds

Introduction

The study of school failure, 'ineffective' schools or 'failing' schools has not been an activity that has interested many within the British educational research community historically. With exceptions (e.g., Barber, 1995; Stoll, Myers and Reynolds, 1996; Reynolds, 1991, 1996a) and with the notable exception of the contributors to this book, researchers have preferred to study effective school institutions and assume that this study will help us understand and potentially remediate the ineffective ones (see reviews of this tradition in Reynolds, Bollen, Creemers, Hopkins, Stoll and Lagerweij, 1996; Reynolds, Creemers, Stringfield, Teddlie, Schaffer and Nesselrodt, 1994). Why has this been the case?

First, the early seminal work of Coleman, Campbell, Hobson, McPartlard, Mood, Weinfeld and York (1966) and Jencks, Smith, Ackland, Bane, Cohen, Gintis, Heyns and Micholson (1971) generated in the mid-1960s and 1970s a widespread dissatisfaction with education and a widespread professional and public belief that 'schools make no difference'. Researchers were therefore unwilling to study *failure* and consequently studied *success* because they felt that the study of failure might have further contributed to the overwhelming sense of pessimism about the condition of education.

Second, the association of many in the educational research community with the professional development of teachers on in-service and pre-service courses has historically made researchers unwilling potentially to damage inter-professional relationships by studying professional failure. The needs of Departments of Education within the higher education sector to market themselves in years of declining enrolments and the related more general need not to upset our 'partners' involved with us in teacher education has made researchers reluctant potentially to wound professional self-confidence. This is shown particularly in the case of the absence of research on teacher effectiveness, where the British context shows considerable variability in teacher quality (Reynolds and Farrell, 1996) but a virtually total absence of the teacher effectiveness knowledge base that is a common feature of educational discourse and research in the United States, the Netherlands and Australia (see Creemers, 1994, for a review).

David Reynolds

Third, we have been held back in our understanding of school ineffectiveness by our difficulty in actually attracting 'ineffective' or 'failing' schools into our research studies and the consequent impoverishment of our knowledge. Virtually all the major British and American school effectiveness research studies have suffered from sample attrition and although it is obviously difficult to get reliable information on this matter, one's impressionistic assessment is that the schools that have dropped out were performing more unfavourably on student outcomes, and were in more difficult socio-economic circumstances, than those schools that permitted the research to take place. In the original Reynolds (1976) school effectiveness studies, for example, the one school to drop out of the sample of nine schools was widely seen within its community as ineffective.

In school improvement, too, the samples of schools providing our knowledge base appear to be highly unrepresentative of all schools. Many schools come into improvement projects precisely because of the location of their senior personnel on school improvement or school effectiveness courses — schools sending people on such courses are highly unlikely to be representative of all schools. Many improvement projects, for example the innovatory 'Improving the Quality of Education' project from Cambridge described by Hopkins and colleagues (1994), are additionally based upon 'volunteer' schools that are unlikely to be typical of all schools.

Fourth, since we have lacked for a variety of reasons detailed information about the ineffective schools, and since we have been anxious to celebrate effective schools, we have therefore tended to do a number of things involving the 'back mapping' of the effective schools' correlates or characteristics into the ineffective schools as the proposed solution to the ineffective schools' problems (see descriptions of such ideas and related projects in Reynolds, Bollen, Creemers, Hopkins, Stoll and Lagerweij, 1996). However, these 'effectiveness factors' are of course the processes and structures that have come from studies of schools that have already become effective — such studies do not tell us the school characteristics needed to reach the status of 'effective'. Furthermore, by mentally planning our research to focus upon the sites of effective schools and then operating with a kind of 'school effectiveness deficit model', we may miss those factors (such as poor staff/staff relations, for example) that are present and exist in the ineffective schools but not in the effective schools. Particularly, we may simply look to see the quantity of the 'success' or 'effectiveness' characteristics the ineffective schools may or may not have, without looking to see whether there are separate 'failure' characteristics that exist in the ineffective schools that require different conceptualization, operationalization and measurement [see also Myers and Goldstein in this volume].

The Existing Knowledge Base Reviewed

In other publications, we have outlined what the characteristics of ineffective schools seem to be, based upon the experience of our attempted interventions in them over a number of years (Reynolds, 1991; Reynolds and Packer, 1992; Reynolds, 1996a).

It has been argued that they possess numerous characteristics that may not permit easy improvement, in particular:

- the widespread belief that change is for other people;
- the belief amongst staff that the school should stick to its past methods of operation;
- the reluctance of individual staff to stand out from the prevailing group culture;
- the reluctance of many staff to attempt new things, fearing that they may fail;
- the blaming of factors external to the school by the staff for the failure of the school;
- the absence of any understanding among the majority of the staff about possible alternative policies;
- the belief among the staff that outsiders have little to contribute to turning the school around;
- the presence of numerous personality clashes, feuds and cliques within the staff group, in a setting of generally grossly dysfunctional relationships; and
- the unwillingness or inability of staff in the school to see that its 'presenting' problems of failure mask the 'real' problems of the institution.

Others have also usefully contributed to our knowledge in this area. Rosenholtz (1989) studied the social organization of a sample of schools in Tennessee and generated a typology of two types of school, the one called 'moving' or learning enriched, and the other 'stuck' or learning impoverished. Teddlie and Stringfield (1993) note that in their 'outlier' ineffective schools, selected on the basis of poor levels of value-added academic achievement over time, expectations of pupils' achievements were lower and principals were more involved in activities peripheral to the attainment of the major academic goals. Myers (1994 and 1996) has also speculated upon the 'deep culture' of ineffective schools and usefully explored the importance of their collective myths, which are seen as very pervasive and additionally very destructive and disempowering of change. Stoll, Reynolds and Myers (1996) have also surveyed the various perspectives — and policy remedies — that have been applied to this sector of education, and Barber (1995) has also related the problems of ineffective schools within their local and national policy contexts.

Some Further Evidence on Ineffective Schools

The picture of the schools that one has viewed in the existing literature is not, then, a particularly hopeful one for those expecting it to be an easy task to turn such schools around. The organizational problems of the school (an absence of 'effectiveness' characteristics and the presence of 'failure generating' characteristics) combine with the culture of the school (fatalism, pessimism and a hostility to those outside school factors that might be helpful for change in positive directions) and the relational patterns of staff (cliques, fractiousness) to generate a three-dimensional block upon the possibilities of change.

My more recent experience of ineffective schools in the late 1990s suggests, though, that the above picture may have been a somewhat partial and overly pessimistic one. This experience, derived in part from being a member of the governing body of two schools that have been in receipt of 'special measures' as determined by OFSTED and in part from undertaking consultancy and in-service work with schools other than those in Wales that had formerly formed the totality of my experience, suggests that there are a number of other factors in the organization, culture and ethos of ineffective schools that are of relevance.

One of these factors makes the difficulties of an ineffective school probably even more severe and probably even longer lasting. This is the likelihood that the schools possess governing bodies that have historically both moulded, and subsequently reflect, the 'ineffective' cultural characteristics of the school itself. Both the governing bodies of my experience possessed considerable passivity, a considerable knowledge deficiency about what to do to improve matters, and a very fractured set of interpersonal relations, with these being based upon racial lines in one of the schools studied. In this particular school, the racial balance of the pupils in the school had reached the crucial 'threshold' of being comprised of 35–40 per cent Asian, Oriental and Afro-Caribbean children, the level at which 'white' children often become somewhat threatened and accordingly indulge in racist attacks, racial abuse and the like. The numerous racial incidents in this school became paralleled by considerable racial conflicts between 'Asian' and 'white' governors, which meant that the governors were unable to give a unified response when the school needed leadership to deal with the 'special measures' routine of OFSTED and the associated involvement of local education authority inspectors.

There are, however, a number of features of ineffective schools that may also make their problems more remediable than we have argued hitherto. First, all the available evidence from studies both of 'effective' and of 'ineffective' schools suggests that ineffective schools are not merely possessed of a low 'mean' or average of the teacher behaviours linked to effectiveness, they are also possessed of a much greater 'range' or variation in these behaviours. The work of Teddlie and Stringfield (1993), for example, shows this wider range of teaching behaviours in their ineffective schools and Murphy (1992) has rather nicely noted the symbolic, organizational and cultural 'tightness' that prevails by contrast in effective schools.

It is of course easy to see how ineffective schools may generate this wide range, since they are less likely to have possessed the leadership and management that could generate coherence and cohesion in school organizational response to pupil needs. It is also easy to see how the student academic and social outcomes from these ineffective schools may also be affected by a large within-school range: inconsistency of teachers' standards and behaviours makes the possibility of socialization of young people into 'core' standards and values thoroughly problematic (Reynolds, 1996b).

However, the existence of this range also has the potential for *facilitating* the improvement of ineffective schools, since it means that even within such schools there will be *relatively* good practice. Given that the range of variation by department *within* schools is probably three to four times greater than the average variation *between* schools (Reynolds and Cuttance, 1992), then it is likely that the typical ineffective secondary school will have some departments which have relatively good practice *when compared with all schools of all levels of effectiveness*. It is of course highly likely that there will be problems within the ineffective schools in actually making purposive use of their variation by utilizing the experience and excellence of their effective departments. But the existence of such effectiveness is a potential resource that few have considered to date.

Second, it is important to note that the 'movement' in effectiveness status, which can be obtained from ineffective schools, may be considerably greater than might have been predicted from earlier analyses. Precisely because ineffective schools are highly likely to have been in an unstable, stressed and 'unsteady' state, they may be amenable to rapid improvement in the same way as some of them have been amenable to rapid dissolution and decline. One of the two schools we have recently been involved with was to a considerable degree turned around within three months of the appointment of a new headteacher, whose initial diagnosis of the school's problems was that the school needed, above all, 'order' in the playground and in its corridors so that there was a predisposition to order in the classrooms. This gave teachers who had spent historically much of their within lesson time in simple 'firefighting' as behavioural problems occurred, the chance both to teach academic material again and to rediscover the enjoyment of their 'craft' of teaching. The power of external reinforcers such as market-based competition, the publicity given to schools that have failed and the strong community pressure upon both of the schools to improve were all factors which in both schools made their 'turnaround' a more rapid process than might have been expected from the existing literature.

Third, not all the staff to be found in ineffective schools are the tired, defeated 'old lags' or 'rump of poor practice' that have been so prevalent in past descriptions of the schools. In recent years, the pressures upon teachers in general and in the ineffective schools in particular has encouraged the premature retirement of many of the disillusioned, less competent 'trailing edge' of poor practice that might have comprised maybe up to two thirds or three quarters of the total of the staff in some of the more ineffective schools. Whilst many of these posts have been permanently lost because of the need to cut school budgets, some limited staff replacements have arrived in these schools; staff who are invariably young and invariably ambitious to show that they can survive in difficult circumstances. Indeed, the lack of competent applicants for posts such as that of head of department within such schools invariably means that quite youthful teachers are often given very considerable responsibilities by comparison with what teachers of similar ages would have been given elsewhere in other schools.

In one respect, the arrival of those who are sometimes called the 'Young Turks', or who are sometimes called in American inner-city schools the 'Young

Guns', may pose the ineffective schools problems, since the remaining 'rump' of older, more weary and more fatalistic staff may well not react positively to 'new blood', particularly since many of the 'rump' will themselves have been trying for promotion within these schools for some considerable time without success. Already fragmented staff relations may be made more difficult by such staff changes.

However, the presence in the ineffective schools of some youthful enthusiasm, and some energy allied with some ambition, may generate a rather more positive environment for change than might have been expected from some earlier accounts of this sector.

Do We Have the Technologies to Turn Ineffective Schools Around Successfully?

A generally more optimistic assessment of the prospects of the ineffective schools' 'setting' being improved should lead us naturally to assess those interventions in the lives of such schools that may have positive effects. In past publications, we have simply posed some questions as to what may be appropriate forms of 'remediation' or 'intervention' or 'treatments' in such schools without explaining the knowledge base and experience that led to such questions in the first place. Here, we attempt to flesh out in more detail exactly what the content of successful interventions with ineffective schools might be, utilizing examples of strategies and interventions that have been successfully used in ineffective schools in the last few years.

First, it is likely that ineffective schools need information on how to improve themselves that they haven't got, but all attempts to reach ineffective schools with this information have faced problems because the school organizations themselves are likely to reject the information that they need if it comes in the form of interventions in the life of the school by outsiders, particularly if it were to be through 'university so-called experts'. One successful method has proved to be the 'Trojan horse' technique of reaching the schools, whereby the knowledge the schools need in the fields of school effectiveness, teacher effectiveness and departmental effectiveness is brought to the schools in the form of one of their own members, who is given the knowledge outside school by the 'university so-called experts'. In the Cardiff Change Agents project (Reynolds, Davie and Phillips, 1989), senior personnel from schools, which in many cases were ineffective schools, were admitted to a course which involved one day a week attendance at the local university. These individuals were given bodies of knowledge concerning effective practices and also a wide variety of knowledge bases concerning useful and appropriate interventions in the lives of schools, including psychotherapeutic techniques, group work techniques and behavioural approaches to school management. The teachers themselves took the knowledge bases back to their schools, and found a much more ready acceptance of the knowledge bases amongst their colleagues than would have been the case had the knowledge bases gone to schools through direct university transmission of knowledge to individual schools.

Second, it is highly likely that within ineffective schools are a set of damaged interpersonal relationships, and we have noted above that the ineffective school is likely to possess a large number of cliques, warring factions and fragmented relationships which make coherent organizational responses to its problems very difficult. Staff meetings and general discourse may well show individuals 'playing the person' rather than 'playing the ball' and individuals agreeing or disagreeing with statements and policy proposals not because of the inherent value of the proposal but because of the origin of the proposals in terms of the person or persons that they came from within the school.

In such a setting, the rebuilding of interpersonal relationships is clearly of great importance. One technique is to generate greater unity amongst the staff by using those who are outsiders to a school to provide a common source of hatred: the so-called 'cognitive dissonance' approach whereby individuals are believed to like each other more if they have a common enemy to dislike. One example of the use of this approach is in the role of external persons to a school giving in-service presentations that are calculated to generate a unified response from staff. Arranging for university people to give inservice sessions in hotels, involving provocative lectures after a dinner in which large quantities of alcohol were served to fuel anger with the outsider, would be a classic method of rebuilding relationships by generating a degree of 'fellow feeling' among staff.

Third, the attempt to turn around ineffective schools clearly needs as many reinforcers as possible, given that many of the patterns within such schools may well have been in existence for considerable periods of time. The staff group, although there may be young staff keener on change than their fellow members, may well not provide a very powerful lever for change. The catchment area outside the school may not be heavily involved with the school. In such circumstances, the attempt to turn around such schools needs to find alternative sources of power to use to change the staff as a whole and particularly to change those members of staff who may be particularly ineffective. In these circumstances, pupils and parents have been used to try and improve their schools: in one case, the use of pupil questionnaires for Years 10 and 11 concerning their opinions of their teachers, were introduced into an ineffective school under the guise of encouraging consumer response and evaluating consumer opinions, reasons with which it was hard for staff to argue. Another example from another school was the use of parent questionnaires in which parents were asked to give their opinions on the school in *general*, which of course very often turned into the giving of both global descriptions of things that parents liked or didn't like about the school and very highly *particular* and personalized descriptions of staff they liked and staff that they didn't like within the school. Again, it is virtually impossible for the 'rump' of staff to stop parental surveys, given both the rhetoric and reality of consumerism that pervades educational discussion currently and the clear need for any school (in particular an ineffective school which may well be losing pupil numbers) to protect its intake and therefore protect teachers' jobs.

Fourth, it is highly likely that turning around ineffective schools requires the exercise of a large number of micro-political skills [see also Stoll and Fink in this volume]. In many areas of education it is clear that coalition building, micro-politics and the management of power are key components of school improvement, although of course such techniques receive very little attention either within the discipline of educational management and administration or within school effectiveness currently. If the 'playing of politics' is so crucial in determining the organization of all schools, it is likely to need to play an even greater role within those schools where, for whatever reason, the school has developed an abnormal cultural and organizational response to pupil needs. One way of 'playing politics' is clearly to attempt to bring on, and give enhanced influence to, effective teachers within the school and to increase the proportion of these competent staff by progressively chipping away at the numbers that comprise the 'rump' of poor practice. This rump may comprise two thirds or three quarters of the total staff of some ineffective schools but can very easily be reduced in numbers and in importance by working with its more competent members and giving them enhanced responsibilities. Such responsibilities can be generated through formal promotion or, in the absence of promoted posts or responsibility allowances to give, can be achieved through giving such people informal status by organizing improvement committees or such like.

The playing of politics can be taken further, however. In one school, which improved rapidly over time, the newly arrived headteacher decided to 'play politics' with his staff immediately on arrival at the beginning of the academic year. The usual 'beginning of the year' staff meeting was held, at which all staff were expecting the new headteacher to make clear his intentions about what was to happen to the school. They expected a mission statement and a clear blueprint about what it was that the new person wanted. The new headteacher, though, decided that the best thing he could do was to 'audit' the staff and audit the school's organizational responses, in order to understand enough of what the problems of the school were to propose sensible solutions. The first staff meeting of the year, therefore, was simply an administrative exercise with no clear guidance given about the direction of the mission or the content of change. The headteacher subsequently announced that he was very happy to talk to any members of staff individually about the future direction of the school and said that his door would be open for members of staff to come in and talk to him about what they thought should happen within the school.

Members of staff then, as individuals, began to slip in to see the headteacher, with the first group going in being the 'Young Turks' who were ambitious and who wished for preferment from the new regime. As the old lags saw the 'Young Turks' going in, many of the old lags became somewhat insecure, thinking that the Young Turks would be closeted with the headteacher and communicating what they thought about themselves and their deficiencies. The old lags then started going in to see the headteacher themselves, with the result that by the end of the autumn term virtually every member of staff had been in at least once to see the headteacher and had, to use the headteacher's expression, 'thrown their cards away' by telling the headteacher the background of the school, things about themselves and what the internal processes of the school had been. The headteacher, therefore, was playing a complicated micro-political game, in which he had revealed none of his own beliefs but was waiting for individuals to make clear their own situations and beliefs before telling both individuals and the staff as a whole what his plans were.

Fifth, it is important for coalition building and for gaining a sense of momentum within ineffective schools that goals are chosen that are both easily achievable and achievable in a short time period. Choice of such targets as 'a litter free environment' or 'a graffiti free school', or a focus upon the school attendance rate or suspension rate (where rapid improvements can be made by altering the behaviour of only a small number of pupils) will work much better than choice of 'medium-' or 'long-term' goals such as the school's level of academic achievement, which may take two or three years to influence. With successful attainment of 'low level' targets, competence will be established, confidence will rise and the atmosphere within the school will become more favourable for the major structural and cultural changes that are needed.

Sixth, it is essential that ineffective schools are given the truth about their situations, otherwise known as 'brute sanity' (Fullan, 1991). The need to do this, but the equally important necessity of not alienating the school staff to the situation where they will not respond at all through doing it, is one of the most difficult things to handle within the ineffective school. Successful use of external consultants to *diagnose* with the aid of their specialist expertise, rather than as providers of information about what to *prescribe* on the basis of the diagnosis, is likely to be productive [see chapters by Learmonth and Lowers, and MacBeath]. Such persons can bring in 'value-added' analyses that will show incontrovertibly that a school's performance is not simply due to the quality of the catchment area or the intake but is in reality due to the quality of the school's organization.

Such 'brute sanity' often has a further function apart from truth telling, in that it often flushes out from the 'rump' of staff the views that need to be contradicted and corrected in order for school improvement to occur. On one occasion in an ineffective school, the statement that the school was 'well below the line' in terms of what was being predicted in academic achievement relative to its intake evoked an aggressive protest from one of the leaders of the school 'rump' who complained that the catchment area was so severely deprived that the school had no chance of achieving any more than its present level of GCSE results. The interaction between the outside consultant from higher education and the rump's spokesperson then became so antagonistic that the headteacher had to insist that the discussion was broken off.

The importance of this symbolic 'showdown' as the 'brute reality' of the diagnosis from outside met the different diagnosis from inside the school was considerable. The representative of the rump had clearly lost the argument, and the school staff had been made aware of the school's own role in the generation of failure, but the headteacher could still try to be the leader of *all* the teachers in the school because the diagnosis and truth had been told by someone else other than he. Indeed, as the outside consultant left the meeting of staff at morning breaktime, the headteacher could be heard saying to the staff, 'Whilst I wouldn't agree with everything that Professor X has said, you have to admit that there's something to it, and that the school does need to improve'!

Conclusions: Further Broadening Out Perspectives
on Ineffectiveness

The above somewhat revised, and somewhat more optimistic, picture of ineffect-iveness that more recent experiences with schools suggest, together with what one would regard as the beginning of a technology of 'treatments' that may work in their specific contexts, is clearly of potential importance in broadening the way in which the schools have been seen away from the conventional 'pathology' model that has predominated historically.

Further broadening and enlightening of our perspectives can take place through the further reorientations that are associated with appreciation of two additional bodies of knowledge on:

- the study of other countries' educational philosophies, and their systemic technologies of education; and
- the use of experience and analogies from other non-educational disciplines, such as applied science and medicine.

To take the comparative educational dimension first, it is clear that not all societies have the range of variation in school quality that is so marked in most accounts of the British experience. Data from the International School Effectiveness Research Project (ISERP) shows that while the school/classroom level explains approximately 20 per cent of pupil variation in the United States, and 12 per cent of variation in the UK, in Taiwan it explains only 1–2 per cent (Reynolds and Farrell, 1996). The latter society, and other Pacific Rim societies also, is committed to utiliz-ing a strong 'technology' of education in which teachers are taught in pre-service education to utilize a small number of teaching and schooling strategies which are repetitively and thoroughly taught to all. Likewise, the ways of organizing school-ing are heavily standardized, involving central government provision of children's textbooks, centrally determined assessment methods and content, and central deter-mination of such factors as school goals and 'mission' (see Reynolds and Teddlie, 1996; and Creemers and Reynolds, 1996, for further exploration of this theme).

By contrast, British methods of both teacher development and school organ-ization have traditionally been much more concerned with a voluntaristic approach, in which the technologies of education are chosen by individual teachers and head-teachers from a range of strategies, some of which may be teacher or school gen-erated or 'invented'. Whilst the generation of their own individual methods may be responsible for the 'artistry' of the leading edge of British teachers and schools that has historically been much commented upon, it is possible that it may also be responsible for the 'trailing edge' of British practice also seen in the ineffective schools. Methods utilized in other societies whereby good practices in teaching and in schooling are discovered, codified and routinely transmitted as part of the routine procedures of professional education, may have positive effects, therefore, on our educational variation in general and upon our ineffective schools in particular.

The second body of knowledge that might be useful to us in understanding and remedying ineffective schooling is that derived from the experience and interventions of both applied science and the applied science of medicine. Applied science, for example, attaches enormous importance to the investigation of any failure in its technology, such as bridge failure or the failure of machinery of any kind. Medicine studies sickness and ill health, wishing to examine in detail the characteristics of the problem, its epidemiology, and the possible remediation of the condition (in marked contrast to conventional school effectiveness research which has studied the 'well' or effective schools and assumed that the way to improve the 'sick' or ineffective schools is to give them health producing characteristics, rather than study and remedy their illness).

Whilst it is clear that it is possible to establish cause and effect relationships within the physical sciences that have eluded us so far in the study of education, the insights that other disciplines' strategies of 'problem identification' and 'problem remediation' might give us are potentially useful as we seek to advance the study of school ineffectiveness from its early somewhat simplistic base (see Hargreaves, 1997, for speculations on this theme).

Conclusions

Whilst we noted earlier that the study of 'ineffective' schools has not been central within the educational research community, there are increasing signs of interest in the sector. Some of the earlier, more pessimistic approaches to the schools need to be complemented by a recognition that the schools have potential for improvement, and that we may have a 'technology' of improvement of use to them.

It is clearly crucial that our knowledge of the sector increases further. The present wide range of schools in 'special measures', and the large number of researchers involved in attempts to help such schools, constitutes an experiment of nature where the effects of such interventions on school processes, outcomes and functioning could be measured and codified. It is therefore vitally important that the current wave of policy interventions contribute directly to knowledge as well as to practice.

References

BARBER, M. (1995) 'Shedding light on the dark side of the moon', *Times Educational Supplement*, May 12, pp. 3–4.

COLEMAN, J.S., CAMPBELL, E., HOBSON, C., McPARTLAND, J., MOOD, A., WEINFELD, F. and YORK, R. (1966) *Equality of Educational Opportunity*, Washington: National Center for Educational Studies.

CREEMERS, B. (1994) *The Effective Classroom*, London: Cassell.

CREEMERS, B.P.M. and REYNOLDS, D. (1996) 'Issues and implications of international effectiveness research', *International Journal of Educational Research*, **25**, 3, pp. 257–66.

FULLAN, M.G. (1991) *The New Meaning of Educational Change*, London: Cassell.

HARGREAVES, D. (1997) Paper presented to the symposium on 'Ineffective Schools', Annual Meeting of the International Congress for School Effectiveness and Improvement, Memphis.

HOPKINS, D., AINSCOW, M. and WEST, M. (1994) *School Improvement in an Era of Change*, London: Cassell.

JENCKS, C.S., SMITH, M., ACKLAND, H., BANE, M.J., COHEN, D., GINTIS, H., HEYNS, D. and MICHOLSON, S. (1971) *Inequality*, London: Allen Lane.

MURPHY, J. (1992) 'School effectiveness and school restructuring: Contributions to educational improvement', *School Effectiveness and School Improvement*, **3**, 2, pp. 90–109.

MYERS, K. (1994) 'Why schools in difficulty may find the research on school effectiveness and school improvement inappropriate for their needs', Unpublished EdD Assignment, University of Bristol.

MYERS, K. (1996) *School Improvement in Practice: Schools Make a Difference Project*, London: Falmer Press.

REYNOLDS, D. (1976) 'The delinquent school', in WOODS, P. (ed.) *The Process of Schooling*, London: Routledge and Kegan Paul.

REYNOLDS, D. (1991) 'Changing ineffective schools', in AINSCOW, M. (ed.) *Effective Schools for All*, London: David Fulton.

REYNOLDS, D. (1996a) 'Turning around ineffective schools: Some evidence and some speculations', in GRAY, J., REYNOLDS, D., FITZ-GIBBON, C. and JESSON, D. (eds) *Merging Traditions: The Future of Research on School Effectiveness and School Improvement*, London: Cassell.

REYNOLDS, D. (1996b) 'The effective school: An inaugural lecture', *Evaluation and Research in Education*, **9**, 2, pp. 57–73.

REYNOLDS, D., BOLLEN, R., CREEMERS, B., HOPKINS, D., STOLL, L. and LAGERWEIJ, N. (1996) *Making Good Schools: Linking School Effectiveness and School Improvement*, London: Routledge.

REYNOLDS, D., CREEMERS, B.P.M., STRINGFIELD, S., TEDDLIE, C., SCHAFFER, E. and NESSELRODT, P. (1994) *Advances in School Effectiveness Research and Practice*, Oxford: Pergamon Press.

REYNOLDS, D. and CUTTANCE, P. (1992) *School Effectiveness: Research, Policy and Practice*, London: Cassell.

REYNOLDS, D., DAVIE, R. and PHILLIPS, D. (1989) 'The Cardiff programme — an effective school improvement programme based on school effectiveness research', *International Journal of Educational Research*, **13**, 7, pp. 800–14.

REYNOLDS, D. and FARRELL, S. (1996) *Worlds Apart? A Review of International Studies of Educational Achievement Involving England*, London: HMSO for OFSTED.

REYNOLDS, D. and PACKER, A. (1992) 'School effectiveness and school improvement in the 1990s', in REYNOLDS, D. and CUTTANCE, P. (eds) *School Effectiveness: Research, Policy and Practice*, London: Cassell.

REYNOLDS, D. and TEDDLIE, C. (1996) 'World Class Schools: Some Further Findings', Paper presented to the Annual Meeting of the American Educational Research Association, New York.

ROSENHOLTZ, S. (1989) *Teachers Workplace: The Social Organization of Schools*, New York: Longman.

STOLL, L., MYERS, K. and REYNOLDS, D. (1996) 'Understanding Ineffectiveness', Paper presented at the Annual Meeting of the American Educational Research Association, New York.

TEDDLIE, C. and STRINGFIELD, S. (1993) *Schools Make a Difference: Lessons Learned From a Ten Year Study of School Effects*, New York: Teachers College Press.

Chapter 13

Who's Failing?[1]

Kate Myers and Harvey Goldstein

The Ubiquity of Failure

There seems to be a lot of failure about: failing schools, failing teachers, failing children. Hunting the failing school has become an exciting and rewarding journalistic and political pastime. When the quarry is identified it can be savaged and publicly humiliated. For example, one of the early schools identified by the Office for Standards in Education (OFSTED) as 'failing', was feted under a double page spread in *The Mail on Sunday* under the banner headline, 'Is this the worst school in Britain?' (Brace, 1994). [See Whatford in this volume.]

Failure in some form or another exists in all educational systems: a search for remedies is always necessary and complacency is unacceptable. Nevertheless, in education systems in many parts of the world teachers are under stress, available resources are decreasing and student motivation seems to be lessening in the face of decreasing job opportunities. It should come as no surprise if various parts of the system find it difficult to cope.

In this chapter we look at the political and ideological contexts within which the ethos of failure has blossomed. We propose the term 'troubled and troubling' for schools that for a variety of reasons find themselves in difficulties and characterize three types of 'troubled' schools. We describe what happens to schools that are currently publicly labelled as 'failing' and argue that the performance of such schools cannot be evaluated properly or fairly unless the different contexts in which these schools and their teachers have to work are taken into account. We believe that the information used to judge schools must be reliable, available and relevant. Not all information is, and an indiscriminate principle of 'freedom of information' can be abused in ways that harm rather than help schools and the children who they serve. We are particularly concerned by the way that school effectiveness research has been misused to 'shift the blame'. By making the individual school entirely responsible for its outcomes, central government can abdicate its share of any responsibility for 'failure'.

Political Background

In the last twenty years many educational systems have been exposed to considerable amounts of change. A key feature has been the frequent revisions of style of politicians (from confrontational to receptive) and 'U' turns in policy. Often these have led to low morale amongst teachers and administrators. A number of major initiatives have had a notable impact on state schools in England and Wales. These include the delegation of financial management to individual schools, the National Curriculum, new vocational courses and qualifications, national testing, teacher appraisal, publication of average achievement scores for schools in 'league tables', a semi-independent role for some schools under 'grant maintained' status and the external inspection system administered by the OFSTED. The 'market ideology' underpinning many changes has undoubtedly encouraged a climate in which competition has begun to dominate cooperation. Replacing a planned system with one where local market forces predominate makes it plausible to locate blame with individual schools, and now even parents, through the introduction of parent contracts. Markets operate through competition in which there are winners and losers. Designating schools as 'effective' or 'failing' is a natural consequence.

Labelling

For the recipients of a failing label the results can be dramatic, even catastrophic. Some even describe the process as similar to a bereavement [see, also, Pugh in this volume]. The school may be taken under the direct control of the Department for Education and Employment (DfEE); have their heads and many of the teachers removed; or have an Education Association appointed with the task and powers to try and 'turn them around' or indeed close them down as happened in 1995 with Hackney Downs School in inner London. Alternatively, they may simply drift out of business as parents lose confidence and move their children elsewhere.

Given we have schools that for a variety of reasons are in serious difficulties, we have to find ways of dealing with them. In our view labelling them as 'failing' does not support them [see, also, Kovac's chapter in this volume]. We need to understand the wider context in which such schools exist to understand them and be able to help them. For example, most schools currently identified by OFSTED as 'failing', serve deprived and disadvantaged students. This is not, of course, to argue for complacency or low expectations in disadvantaged environments but it does emphasize the need to contextualize judgments properly. Naming schools as 'failing', often has the effect of lowering morale and obscuring positive aspects. Public humiliation is not the best way to improve matters. (Labelling schools as 'successful' can be problematic too. It can lead to complacency. It can also lead to inordinate pressure to ensure that each year's examination and test results are an improvement on those of the previous year, without any reference to the talents and abilities of the students in each cohort.)

Publishing the average test scores of schools in the form of rankings or league tables has encouraged competition rather than collaboration and cooperation between schools and thereby undermines one of the prerequisites for school improvement — the opportunity and capacity of schools to learn from each other. Along with numerous other reform initiatives that have involved teachers learning, 'unlearning' and 're-learning' new curricula, new teaching strategies and new structures within a very short period of time, some of these changes have fostered a climate of fear and retribution. For many heads and teachers, the combined effect of the changes and related pressures has had a negative impact on their morale, resilience, and self-esteem.

The discussion about failing schools also raises the question of whether this 'problem' has always existed on this scale and we have just chosen to overlook it, or whether the number of schools that could be described in this way has increased only recently. No doubt such schools have always existed and we have neglected to deal with them adequately. Nevertheless an inevitable result of comparisons among schools, whether by publication of crude league tables or even more sophisticated 'value-added' ones, is that there will always be winners and losers. Once the losers are deemed to be 'failing' it is difficult to find ways to help them when the prevailing atmosphere is one of recrimination, and retribution. So the attribution of failure is important and we need to look more closely at what this attribution might mean.

What Do We Mean by 'Failing'?

Any attempt to define 'failure' poses problems, particularly when the terms 'failing' and 'ineffective' are often used interchangeably. For example, are all schools that are not 'effective' therefore 'ineffective' and/or 'failing'? Are there intermediate categories of schools not doing as well as they might but not (yet?) in a serious or even dire state? How should we describe schools that are effective in some areas but not others (Sammons, Thomas and Mortimore, 1995a)?

Some commentators have tried to address this issue (see, for example, Stoll and Fink, 1996; and Barber in this volume) by differentiating between 'struggling' and 'failing' schools. It is reasonable to suppose that most schools might be 'failing' some of their students, some of the time, in some respects. For example a school that is relatively 'effective', for white, middle-class boys may not be so for black, working-class girls and issues of race, gender and social class are particularly pertinent when the question 'effective for whom?' is raised.

OFSTED, defines failing schools according to how far one or several of the following deficiencies are found:

- poor standards of pupil achievement;
- poor quality of education provided;
- inefficiency in the running of the school; and
- poor provision for pupils' spiritual, moral, social and cultural development. (DfEE/OFSTED, 1995)

All these definitions are located within the school.

Troubled and Troubling

Within a market ideology of competition between schools, these attempts to define 'failure' locate blame within the school: they pay little attention to the surrounding context that may contribute to what is interpreted as 'failure'. To avoid making such assumptions we think the terms 'troubled' and 'troubling' schools are more neutral. 'Troubled' schools we argue, are those that are perceived to have serious problems. These schools are 'troubling' because of their effects on children, staff and others who are connected with them.

We have argued that 'troubled' schools are those that are viewed as causing concern and while some schools, rightly, give proper cause for concern it is debatable whether simply blaming, labelling and imposing draconian measures on them helps them improve (indeed by lowering morale such steps may have just the opposite effect). If positive change is to be encouraged we need to find more constructive ways to work with these schools. One of us recently has worked with three such schools (Myers, 1996a). Two particular issues have emerged from this work.

First, the current literature and collective wisdom on school effectiveness and school improvement seems to be of limited use to such schools. This is both for the reasons we have already given and because most of this research was based on schools that were already deemed 'effective' (Reynolds 1995a, 1995b). Although characteristics prevalent in effective schools (Sammons, Hillman and Mortimore, 1995b) may be of background interest to those working in troubled schools, simply being aware of what is missing is of limited practical help for those wanting to rectify their situation. Knowing, for example, that strong leadership is absent, does not provide clues on how to make it exist. In addition, it may be more than the absence of these positive characteristics that causes schools to experience problems. Troubled schools may be actively affected by 'antithetical' characteristics. For example, it is not just that there is no 'strong, purposeful leadership' that contributes to a school's problems and pushes it into the troubled category but the consequences of weak, fragmented and inconsistent leadership (Myers, 1994). Unfortunately, there seems to be little research on the many combinations of characteristics (and how they interact with each other) that can prevail in troubled schools.

Second, every troubled school is different. The reasons they have got to a troubled state are varied. The ways they react to being in such a state are individual. Consequently there is no magic or simple solution to their difficulties. They need different types of support.

Characterizing 'Troubled' Schools

Elsewhere, one of us (Myers, 1996a) has described three distinct categories of troubled schools.

'*Striving*' schools are those that are in trouble but are determined to change and improve. Although the head and staff know there are serious problems to address they do not accept a simple definition of failure. In one head's words:

Curiously, the blow dealt us by HMI (official inspectors) served to concentrate minds and energies on the task in hand. There was a great sense of injustice, of there being 'another agenda' and consequently a great determination to prove our accusers wrong. This engendered the staff cohesiveness so critical to success. (Drake, Mortimore and Dick, 1996, p. 103)

In this 'striving' school, the fact that the vast majority of the staff, united *with* the head to demonstrate that the judgment was wrong proved to be very significant for the school's subsequent improvement. The head exercised strong leadership to make changes and the staff *allowed* her to do so.

'*Swaying*' schools are ones where for a while it may be 'touch and go' whether the school will survive let alone improve in the face of their difficulties. In one school, within a two-year period there was considerable staff turnover including the head and deputy head. Two acting heads ran the school before a permanent appointment eventually was made. During this time the school experienced one pilot and one OFSTED inspection. Staff morale wavered. On occasions staff appeared energized and enthusiastic, but at other times they were demoralized and dejected. In the end 'under new management' and with additional support, the school started to improve.

'*Sliding*' schools are those that seem to have become fixed in a seemingly never-ending downward spiral. One troubled school, that one of us worked with, was not able to find its way out of the spiral. In spite of the enormous amount of financial and human support it was receiving from various quarters it actually deteriorated. Like the 'swaying' school, this school had also experienced considerable staff turnover including most of the senior management team. A number of initiatives were mounted to 'improve' the school, to counter, for example, high student disaffection and improve behaviour but these were rarely carried through consistently because staff were constantly 'firefighting' in response to immediate problems. The cumulative effect of these problems was that the staff became increasingly cynical about whether proposed new initiatives would have any impact. Consequently they became less committed to these initiatives, thus lessening the likelihood of their success. As each initiative failed to deliver an improvement in student behaviour, it became more difficult for the staff *and* the students to believe that *anything* could work. In addition there were serious relationship problems within the senior management team — a lack of agreed and shared goals and dysfunctional transactions amongst them. Dysfunctional relations were also apparent among other staff. A significant number (some of them influential members of the staff group) had worked in the school for a long time. Some were cynical and resistant to any suggested change, often using the assumed teacher union position as a reason why change could not occur. (The teacher union position adopted at school level was not always supported by officials at national level.) There was active conflict between one of the major teacher union groups and the management.

Another group of teachers, mainly recent appointments, consisted of young, energetic, enthusiastic, but not very experienced, staff. They found it a challenge to maintain their enthusiasm in the face of their more cynical colleagues and to cope with inconsistent leadership and support. For some of these teachers, the only alternative to becoming acclimatized to the negative culture was to leave. Many staff had low expectations of students. Among the students there was a culture of ambivalence and even opposition to learning. This disaffection resulted in some appalling behaviour, dissatisfaction and lack of confidence among parents and a poor reputation in the area, low morale among staff and students and poor student outcomes. In short, this school was sliding on a steepening downward spiral. The prevailing myth in this school was one of an institution that could not change.

Myths and Schools

Myths have great importance in our lives and help interpret and fashion events. They give meaning and significance to individuals and, we also suggest, to institutions.

> Myths offer a lens which can be used to see human identity in its social and cultural context . . . (they) convey values and expectations which are always evolving . . . Both Freud and Jung adapted the long classical tradition of allegorical interpretations . . . in order to unlock symbolic, psychic explanations of human consciousness and behaviour. The paradoxical rationality of myth, the potential of figments to disclose the truth about ourselves has become the fruitful premise of much contemporary thinking about the mind and personality . . . Myths define enemies and aliens and in conjuring them up they say who we are and what we want, they tell stories to impose structure and order. (Warner, 1994, pp. 14 and 19)

The problem in the sliding school was that the myths were destructive and disempowering. For many, the 'enemies and aliens' were the outside world, particularly OFSTED and the LEA. For others, even more destructively, they were the students, their parents and senior managers. The enemy was out there. The propensity to blame anyone but ourselves is considered by Senge to be one of seven 'learning disabilities' prevalent in organizations (Senge, 1990). Jung also suggests that positive myths can help overcome our sense of futility. It could be that negative ones reinforce the feelings of futility and become a self-fulfilling prophecy.

In many ways the sliding school was like those Rosenholtz describes as being 'stuck' as opposed to 'moving':

> The deepening detachment, the resigned pessimism, the paralysis of the spirit, and the stagnation of vision, are all present and accounted for in the utterly tragic reality of stuck schools. (Rosenholtz, 1989, p. 159)

However, stuck implies a not moving state whereas this school was moving. Unfortunately the direction was downwards, hence the description of 'sliding'.

Approaches based on collegiality, collaboration and consensus advocated by 'school improvers' because they are characteristics found in schools that are already effective, are extremely difficult to implement when relationships are dysfunctional and there is a high turnover of personnel. Schools have to be in a state of readiness to benefit from this type of approach.

The problem that arises here is how do we support those that are not in such a state of readiness?

Making Judgments: Placing Schools in Context

A useful start is the ability to make informed judgments and to do this there are two general ways in which the performances of schools can be conceptualized.

Contextualizing Targets

One way, which might be termed the absolute definition, is that which occurs when specific, well defined targets are not achieved. For example, a school could set itself the target of achieving an average class size of thirty or less over a year and a relatively straightforward computation could be carried out to decide whether it had succeeded or failed. This is like using simple performance indicators such as average examination results or attendance rates. A school can be deemed to fall short if it is seen to be below a given threshold. That threshold, of course, will have elements both of arbitrariness and judgment in its choice. So-called 'absolute' criteria will necessarily be chosen partly on the basis of existing variations among schools. For example, it would be rare for a definition to be chosen so that no school fell into the category, and likewise it would be rather pointless to choose a threshold that nobody could reach.

Another example is where different targets may be set for each school, but, so as to be realistic, these targets are set in the knowledge of what it is thought any institution is capable of achieving. Thus, for a school which already has an average class size of 30.5 a target of thirty may seem realistic, whereas for one with an average size of thirty-seven such a target may not.

As soon as we begin to try to understand how targets are set and standards for failure come to be defined we see that there really can be no absolute universally applicable targets. To set a target which has a *useful* function requires, among other things, an understanding of where a school already is and how easily it can move to another state. In other words we must contextualize our target setting. This need to contextualize has become relatively well understood in the last few years. When evaluating student achievement at the end of a phase of schooling, the most important method for doing so is now recognized to consist of 'value-added' analysis, whereby the achievements of the same students when they enter school are taken into account. In addition, such factors as income and social background of students' parents are valuable where available. 'Value-added' systems may even have begun to be adopted in several places, and received formal support from the UK government in 1995 (DfEE, 1995).

While the principle of contextualizing educational achievement is now generally recognized among policy makers, it has not been extended widely into debates about school failure. Inspectors, and others such as the media, need to recognize that it is much easier to achieve acceptable behaviour and results in some circumstances than in others. This kind of recognition needs to inform all judgments of 'blame'. By contextualizing information, whether this is for examination results or attendance, it should be possible to recognize good practice better when it occurs, especially under difficult circumstances.

The Purpose of Judgment

A second way in which context affects how we view school performance is in terms of the *purpose* of any judgment that is made. The perceived purpose of any system of judgment alters how the system operates. It may cause those with a stake in not being labelled as 'failing' to distort their behaviour so as to avoid negative judgments. These distortions may be detrimental to the students. For example, in England and Wales where schools' examination results have been published nationally in rankings or league tables, some schools have responded by concentrating their efforts on those students they believe may improve their average examination results, while giving less attention to the rest. Schools in these circumstances have been known to 'collude' with absenteeism and even to find ways of removing low attaining students from their roll. In any high stakes system, it is almost inevitable that this kind of 'gaming' or 'playing the system' will take place. Attempts to judge which schools are 'failing' often pay little heed to the practical consequences of such judgments. As discussed above there are many adverse consequences of being labelled as 'failing' and there may be an overall net loss.

Ranking Schools

Any public ranking of institutions identifies winners and losers. Those at the bottom invariably attract attention as low achievers or 'failures'. Whether the ranking is made in terms of crude, uncontextualized outcomes or with reference to some contextualization as with 'value-added' test scores, there is always a great deal of imprecision in any judgments. There are several reasons for this.

First, the findings are always about a group of students who have completed the stage of schooling being analysed and so it is a previous state of the school that is being judged. The current state may be different. Thus, for example, test scores for 16-year-old students are based on a cohort who will have started at the school several years previously and any inferences may well not apply to succeeding cohorts.

Second, the statistical procedure whereby 'adjustments' are made for background factors and prior attainment will only produce estimates within a margin of error so that a great deal of uncertainty about the exact position of any school will remain. In addition there may well be factors such as household income which influence student achievement. Failure to include these will tend to distort comparisons (Goldstein and Spiegelhalter, 1996).

Public league tables are, of course, entirely relative. It is perfectly possible that, in some sense, all the schools could be performing satisfactorily, given the various conditions under which they are operating. Yet by ranking them, those at the lower end may not be able to escape the 'failure' label. This relativism is often obscured by the language we use. In league tables of academic achievement, especially adjusted ones, schools often attract descriptions of 'effective' or 'ineffective' with no further qualification. This is just one of the undesirable side effects of some 'school effectiveness' research which arises from the loose use of such terms in quite unjustified ways.

Public Accountability and the Fetish of Information

In many industrialized societies there is a strong popular belief that the publication of information about the functioning of public bodies is an overwhelming social good. In the context of school 'failure' or 'success' the role of published information about performance is crucial. It provides data to make judgments or, in market terms, it introduces a common currency by which the 'worth' of institutions can be measured. Yet public disclosure of information cannot be upheld as an absolute principle.

This is recognized by governments, for example, when they reserve the right to withhold information they deem to threaten national 'security'. Likewise, if publication of information is likely to harm individuals unfairly, or to mislead, then there is a case for refusing to publish it. The capacity of performance indicators to reflect reality accurately is extremely limited and their publication may cause inappropriate inferences to be drawn about institutions.

In such circumstances, we would argue, information should not be made available publicly: or it should have warnings attached about the dangers of interpretation so that nobody would wish to take it seriously. This warning would be more than that which appears on tobacco advertisements. It would involve a proper explanation of why the information is suspect and a reassurance that those who publish the information fully accept its limitations. We have elaborated on this elsewhere (Goldstein and Myers, 1996) and drawn attention to the need for guidelines to govern the publication of performance indicators.

Shifting the Blame

In the late 1970s a number of research studies (Edmonds, 1979; Rutter, Maughan, Mortimore and Ouston, 1979) were published which attempted to redress the emphasis of earlier research (Coleman, 1975; Jencks, Smith, Ackland, Bane, Cohen, Gintis, Heyns and Michelson, 1972) on the overriding importance for student achievement of factors extrinsic to the school. This early work was taken up by others

(Mortimore, Sammons, Stoll, Lewis and Ecob, 1988; Nuttall, Goldstein, Prosser and Rasbash, 1989) who embraced the newly developed technique of multi-level modelling to produce valid and efficient analyses of their research data (Aitkin and Longford, 1986). The period of this 'school effectiveness' work up to the early 1990s concentrated on identifying factors associated with school differences after making adjustments for prior achievement. In particular, it paid considerable attention to providing individual school estimates of 'value-added' performance. As we have already indicated, it has been recognized more recently that the provision of rankings or 'league tables' of value-added performances is scientifically dubious due to large measures of uncertainty resulting from small numbers of students, imperfect measurements and failure to take into account all relevant factors (Goldstein and Spiegelhalter, 1996). Recently, the attention of school effectiveness researchers has shifted from the level of the school to that of the classroom and teacher. There has also been a recognition that institutions and teachers may be differentially effective; that is, they may do relatively well with certain types of students and not with others, or in some curriculum areas and not others.

At the same time, there has been some disappointment with the apparently low (typically about 10 per cent) amount of the total variation attributable to schools. Despite this, however, it seems that for certain groups of students, in certain areas, the school effects are much larger, thus giving a further impetus to the study of differential effectiveness. It seems, therefore, that school effectiveness research is entering a new phase of more detailed and indeed more difficult, work which requires careful long-term data gathering and whose benefits will become apparent only after several years. Unfortunately this is neither politically convenient nor expedient. Most politicians want easy solutions preferably in sound-bites and have attempted to use school effectiveness research to both espouse 'quick fixes' and to shift the responsibility for performance from the centre to individual schools.

Indeed there have appeared several academic critiques of school effectiveness work (Hamilton, 1996; Pring, 1996; Elliott, 1996) which have argued that some of the findings of school effectiveness research have been used for political ends to ascribe 'failure' to schools, using league tables, even value-added ones, to identify 'failing' institutions. These critics have pointed to the limitations of current school effectiveness research models and have associated many school effectiveness researchers with such uses.

The ensuing debate (Sammons and Reynolds, 1997) and the refocusing of school effectiveness research onto the finer details of schooling, have helped to put the current research activity into a broader perspective, but have yet to have an impact on the formulation of policy. On the contrary, policy makers of most political persuasions choose to ignore the caveats and focus on the prima facie evidence of school differences as a means of avoiding responsibility themselves and consequently laying the major responsibility for performance and hence for failure at the doors of the schools. Ironically, contextualizing performance, by using adjusted league tables of test scores, for example, may actually strengthen the belief that blame resides in the school by encouraging the view that *all* other factors have been accounted for, and that any residual variation *must* have its origins in the schools. Nevertheless, if it is accepted that responsibility needs to be located some-where, there remains the issue of where. For the sake of argument, suppose that in technical terms we could find an acceptable adjustment procedure, eliminate most of the uncertainty attached to the indicator, disregard the historical nature of the information and rely solidly upon our technical judgments of school differences. Who then is to blame?

If a school or teacher is performing poorly a first priority is to discover the reason why. In some cases personal factors such as acute illness may be involved. In other cases, however, we may need to look outside individual schools or groups of schools into the wider society. Education is not a one-way affair. It is not simply the case that an education system delivers graduates into society, having educated them to fill different roles. Nor is it the case that the performance of people in the workplace or society at large can be causally related directly to their education.

To attribute, say, the poor economic performance of a country to the organ-ization or performance of its education system is to make a logical and empirical blunder. It is just as easy to argue the reverse, namely that a poor economic performance in a nation has a direct effect on its education system in terms of motivation, resource provision or some other feedback mechanism (see Raffe and Willms, 1991). Likewise it is not legitimate to argue that league tables of interna-tional educational performance reflect the quality of national education systems. The attribution of cause and effect is fraught with difficulty in these circumstances, and the mere repetition of one interpretation does not strengthen its plausibility. The fact that so many policy makers of most political persuasions appear to believe that a large number of the ills of society can be blamed on the education system does not make that proposition correspond more closely to the truth.

In view of this, the notion of context needs to be extended to include the general political and social context within which schools operate. For example, in a political system where the structure and content of education is subject to rapid, and perhaps poorly coordinated change, such as happened in England and Wales in the early 1990s, we should expect disruption, low morale and a consequent effect on 'standards'. In such circumstances, it is inappropriate to shift blame to the schools. Likewise, in an economy where there is increasing unemployment and consequently low employment expectations among young people, any effect on educational performance cannot necessarily be laid at the door of schools.

While there are undoubtedly positive aspects to increasing the autonomy of schools, the advantages may be neutralized if this also results in schools being expected to assume total responsibility for their destinies.

Conclusion

There are three main problems with attributing blame to schools that are troubled. First it may not be justified. We have illustrated the complexity of the issues and how difficult it is to disentangle precisely what is going on. It is rarely one person or one event that has caused the problem; it is more likely to be a series of unlucky and unhappy circumstances. These 'troubled' schools are characterized by a complex combination of factors and circumstances which need to be understood to effect improvement. Second, whatever is going on inside the school is often compounded by circumstances beyond the control of the school, for example, the level of support and resourcing, turnover of key personnel, local and national legislation, or the social deprivation of students and their families. Third, and perhaps most important, we have argued that attributing blame does not necessarily help the situation get better. In fact by lowering morale and thereby encouraging staff and students to 'leave a sinking ship' it may have the opposite effect.

Until a significant number of those involved with 'troubled' schools (staff, students, parents, governors, local authority personnel, politicians) accept the need for change and assume responsibility, there is little chance of improvement. But it must be remembered that these problems do not exist in isolation: they are linked to the wider society and need to be seen within that framework. There is an old African saying that 'it takes a village to educate a child'. The education community should take heed of this and find ways of working together to encourage and support those involved with troubled schools, rather than allowing them to be continually criticized and discouraged. The first steps must be to acknowledge: that schools that find themselves in this situation are there for a variety of reasons not necessarily of their own making; that there are no packaged remedies; that diagnosis and support has to be individually based and adequately resourced; and, finally, that real change takes time.

Note

An earlier version of this Chapter appeared as 'Failing schools or a failing system?', in the 1997 ASCD Yearbook, *Rethinking Educational Change with Heart and Mind* (ed. A. Hargreaves).

Acknowledgments

We are extremely grateful to the following for their helpful comments on an early draft: Susan Bailey, Dean Fink, Andy Hargreaves, Peter Mortimore, Abby Riddell, Louise Stoll, Sally Thomas, Chris Watkins.

References

AITKIN, M. and LONGFORD, N. (1986) 'Statistical modelling in school effectiveness studies', *Journal of the Royal Statistical Society*, A, 149, pp. 1–43.
BARBER, M. (1995) *The Dark Side of the Moon: Imagining an End to Failure in Urban Education*, London: TES–Greenwich Education Lecture.
BELL, J. (1961) *Family Group Therapy*, London: Bookstall.

BOTTANI, N. (1994) 'The OECD international education indicators', *Assessment in Education*, 1, pp. 333–50.

BRACE, A. (1994) 'Is this the worst school in Britain?', *Mail on Sunday*, 20 March, p. 9.

COLEMAN, J.S. (1975) 'Methods and results in the IEA studies of the effects of school on learning', *Review of Educational Research*, 45, pp. 335–86.

DfEE (1995) *GCSE to GCE A/AS Value Added — Briefing for Schools and Colleges*, London: Department for Education.

DfEE/OFSTED (1995) *The Improvement of Failing Schools: UK Policy and Practice 1993–1995*, London, OECD UK Seminar, November.

DRAKE, D., MORTIMER, L. and DICK, M. (1996) 'A school's view: St Mark's School', in MYERS, K. (ed.) *School Improvement in Practice: Schools Make a Difference Project*, London: Falmer Press.

EDMONDS, R.R. (1979) 'Effective schools for the urban poor', *Educational Leadership*, **37**, 1, pp. 15–27.

ELLIOTT, J. (1996) 'School effectiveness research and its critics: Alternative visions of schooling', *Cambridge Journal of Education*, **26**, 2, pp. 199–223.

GOLDSTEIN, H. and MYERS, K. (1996) 'Freedom of information: Towards a code of ethics for performance indicators', *Research Intelligence*, 57, pp. 12–16.

GOLDSTEIN, H. and SPIEGELHALTER, D. (1996) 'League tables and their limitations: Statistical issues in comparisons of institutional performance — with discussion', *Journal of the Royal Statistical Society*, A, 159, pp. 385–443.

HAMILTON, D. (1996) 'Fordism by fiat', *Forum*, **38**, 2, pp. 54–6.

HOPKINS, D. and AINSCOW, M. (1993) 'No room for hit squads', *Education*, 16 July, p. 50.

HOPKINS, D., AINSCOW, M. and WEST, M. (1994) *School Improvement in an Era of Change*, London: Cassell.

JENCKS, C., SMITH, M., ACKLAND, H., BANE, M.J., COHEN, D., GINTIS, H., HEYNS, B. and MICHELSON, S. (1972) *Inequality: A Reassessment of the Effect of Family and Schooling in America*, New York: Basic Books.

MORTIMORE, P. (1991) 'The nature and findings of research on school effectiveness in the Primary Sector', in RIDDELL, S. and BROWN, R. (eds) *School Effectiveness Research: Its Messages for School Improvement*, London: The Scottish Office, HMSO.

MORTIMORE, P., SAMMONS, P., STOLL, L., LEWIS, D. and ECOB, R. (1988) *School Matters: The Junior Years*, Wells: Open Books.

MYERS, K. (1994) 'Why schools in difficulty may find the research on school effectiveness and school improvement inappropriate for their needs', Unpublished assignment for Doctor of Education Degree, University of Bristol.

MYERS, K. (1996a) 'School improvement in action: A critical history of a school improvement project', Dissertation submitted in partial fulfillment of the requirements for the Doctor of Education degree, University of Bristol.

MYERS, K. (1996b) *School Improvement in Practice: Schools Make a Difference Project*, London: Falmer Press.

NUTTALL, D.L., GOLDSTEIN, H., PROSSER, R. and RASBASH, J. (1989) 'Differential school effectiveness', *International Journal of Educational Research*, **13**, 7, pp. 769–76.

OBHOLZER, A. and ROBERTS, V.Z. (eds) *The Unconscious at Work: Individual and Organizational Stress in the Human Services*, London: Routledge.

OFSTED (1993) *The Handbook for the Inspection of Schools*, London: HMSO.

OFSTED (1995) *Update*, Fifteenth Issue, July, London: OFSTED.

PASSMORE, B. (1995) 'Heads call time on long hours', *Times Educational Supplement*, 16 June, p. 11.

PRING, R. (1996) 'Educating persons: Putting education back into educational research', *Scottish Educational Review*, **27**, 2, pp. 101–12.

RAFFE, D. and WILLMS, J.D. (1991) 'Schooling the discouraged worker: Local labour-market effects on educational participation', *Sociology*, 23, pp. 559–81.

REYNOLDS, D. (1995a) 'The effective school: Inaugural lecture', *Evaluation and Research in Education*, **9**, 2, pp. 57–73.

REYNOLDS, D. (1995b) 'Some very peculiar practices', *Times Educational Supplement*, 16 June, p. 19.

REYNOLDS, D. and PACKER, A. (1992) 'School effectiveness and school improvement in the 1990s', in REYNOLDS, D. and CUTTANCE, P. (eds) *School Effectiveness: Research, Policy and Practice*, London: Cassell.

ROSENHOLTZ, S. (1989) *Teachers' Workplace: The Social Organization of Schools*, New York: Longman.

RUTTER, M., MAUGHAN, B., MORTIMORE, P. and OUSTON, J. (1979) *Fifteen Thousand Hours: Secondary Schools and Their Effects on Children*, London: Open Books.

SAMMONS, P. and REYNOLDS, D. (1997) 'A partisan evaluation — John Elliott on school effectiveness', *Cambridge Journal of Education*, **27**, 1, pp. 123–36.

SAMMONS, P., THOMAS, S. and MORTIMORE, P. (1995a) 'Accounting for Variations in Academic Effectiveness between Schools and Departments', Paper presented at the European Conference on Educational Research and Annual Conference of the British Educational Research Association, University of Bath, September.

SAMMONS, P., HILLMAN, J. and MORTIMORE, P. (1995b) *Key Characteristics of Effective Schools: A Review of School Effectiveness Research*, London: OFSTED/Institute of Education, University of London.

SENGE, P.M. (1990) *The Fifth Discipline: The Art and Practice of the Learning Organization*, London: Century Business.

STOLL, L. (1995) 'The Complexity and Challenges of Ineffective Schools', Paper presented as part of the symposium, Research into School Effectiveness and School Improvement at the European Conference on Educational Research, University of Bath.

STOLL, L. and FINK, D. (1996) *Changing Our Schools: Linking School Effectiveness and School Improvement*, Buckingham: Open University Press.

THOMAS, S., SAMMONS, P. and MORTIMORE, P. (1995) 'Determining what adds value to student achievement', *Education Leadership International*, **52**, 6, pp. 19–22.

WALROND-SKINNER, S. (1976) *Family Therapy: The Treatment of Natural Systems*, London: Routledge and Kegan Paul.

WARNER, M. (1994) *Managing Monsters: Six Myths of Our Time*, The 1994 Reith Lectures, London: Vintage Books.

Chapter 14

The Cruising School: The Unidentified Ineffective School

Louise Stoll and Dean Fink

With an increase in the public accountability of schools over the last few years there has been growing attention to ineffective schools. In England, publication of league tables of examination results, reports of schools 'requiring special measures' as a result of OFSTED inspections, instances of school closures, and the announcement of the first Education Association to take over the running of Hackney Downs School have promoted discussion of and consternation about 'failing' schools. The very public travails of The Ridings School have further heightened the national preoccupation with ineffective schools. But what is an ineffective school? It would appear that teachers have one view, government another, and various segments of the community still another. We would also suggest that pupils, although seldom asked, would hold different views of ineffectiveness.

The apparent national consensus on the need to eliminate ineffectiveness, however, and the equally pervasive inability to agree on its components, raise many questions. Can ineffectiveness be identified through league tables and external inspections? Why do ineffective schools seem to be preponderantly in working-class neighbourhoods? Is it possible for schools in which most pupils appear to achieve well to be ineffective? Most important, how can ineffective schools be turned around?

In this chapter, we view ineffectiveness through a cultural lens. We suggest that ineffective schools appear in many guises and describe types of ineffective school. Our main focus, however, is on what we have called the *cruising* school (Stoll and Fink, 1996). This is a school which appears to be effective based on accepted measures, but is resting on its laurels, has little capacity to adjust to societal change and is, or is becoming, ineffective for a significant percentage of its pupils. It is our view that this kind of ineffectiveness is far more pervasive than the Hackney Downs and Ridings schools and, in some ways, more challenging to 'turn around'. This chapter, therefore, concludes with some suggestions as to how to get the cruising school *moving*.

What Is Meant by Ineffectiveness?

The topic of ineffective schools is increasingly popular with governments and the popular press. Only recently, however, has the scholarly community attempted to address the concept of 'ineffectiveness' and to gain some insight into its causes and results. Briefly, if we were to draw on the existing knowledge bases of school effectiveness and school improvement, this would lead to two perspectives, or lenses, through which we might consider ineffectiveness.

The School Effectiveness Research Perspective

Taking the position that school effectiveness is ultimately concerned with pupils' progress and development, this view suggests that an ineffective school would be one in which pupils progress less than expected given consideration of initial attainment and background factors. Furthermore, key aspects of pupil achievement and development are not addressed. For example, the school might focus all of its attention on academic results or social development. Complexities arise, however, with such an interpretation when equity or within-school differences are considered. In this situation should the school be considered partially or differentially effective if the achievement of some but not all groups of pupils is boosted, or should this be considered a form of ineffectiveness (Stoll, 1995)?

A derivative of this perspective is that based on the 'statistics of school improvement'. Its proponents argue that it is the stability of school effects over time that is important (Gray, Jesson, Goldstein and Hedger, 1995). Thus, multi-level statistical analysis over a period of time might indicate that an initially effective or ineffective school is declining from year to year. Again, this begs the question of what was used to define initial effectiveness.

School effectiveness research also seeks to describe what an effective school looks like (Mortimore, 1995), and many studies have identified a list of characteristics associated with more effective schools (see reviews by Cotton, 1995; Reynolds, Sammons, Stoll, Barber and Hillman, 1996; Sammons, Hillman and Mortimore, 1995). It is insufficient, however, to take existing research on the characteristics of effective schools and assume that ineffective schools are the opposite of these factors. Furthermore, attempts to improve historically ineffective schools using only factors shown to be present within effective schools have been unsuccessful (Reynolds, 1991). Elsewhere (Stoll and Fink, 1996), we have tried to piece together some characteristics based on the few available studies that included 'ineffective' schools (Mortimore, Sammons, Stoll, Lewis and Ecob, 1986; Rosenholtz, 1989; Teddlie and Stringfield, 1993; Reynolds, 1996; see also Brown, Riddell and Duffield, 1996). These include a lack of vision, unfocused leadership, dysfunctional staff relationships and poor classroom practices. The knowledge base, however, is still limited.

The School Improvement Perspective

A second view of school ineffectiveness focuses on school improvement. Current definitions of school improvement emphasize change management capacity and control; development of specific supportive conditions and strategies; a focus on goals and, particularly, pupil outcomes; and that all schools can get better (van Velzen, Miles, Eckholm, Hameyer and Robin, 1985; Hopkins, Ainscow and West, 1994; Myers, 1996; Stoll and Fink, 1996). In terms of this perspective, an ineffective school could be viewed as one that is controlled by change, rather than controlling it; that lacks appropriate conditions and strategies; is not pupil-outcome oriented; and, for whatever reason, does not attempt to improve. Such a school tends to be locked into crisis planning and makes little attempt to build the capacity to respond to increasingly complex and unpredictable societal changes.

While both of the previous perspectives have the potential to yield important insights into school ineffectiveness, they are limited by their conceptual understanding of schools as rational places in which cause and effect are determinable through rational investigation (Fink and Stoll, forthcoming). They fail to account for the non-rationality and non-linearity which make schools unique social systems. In our efforts to understand the dynamic nature of schools in an increasingly paradoxical and complex world, we have been increasingly drawn to ideas about school culture (Stoll and Fink, 1996).

A Cultural Perspective

School culture is difficult to define. Hargreaves (1995), offering an anthropological definition, describes it as 'the knowledge, beliefs, values, customs, morals, rituals, symbols and language of a group' (p. 25). Schein (1985) considers the essence of school culture to be, 'the deeper level of *basic assumptions* and *beliefs* that are shared by members of an organization, that operate unconsciously, and that define in a basic 'taken-for-granted' fashion an organization's view of itself and its environment' (p. 6). What this means is that each school has a different reality of school life and 'the way we do things around here' (Deal and Kennedy, 1983). School culture is hard to capture because it is largely implicit and we only see surface aspects. Often we only begin to know a school's culture when we break one of its unspoken and often non-rational rules.

Because of their different realities, schools do not have the same readiness for change. This is a problem for those who offer generic knowledge about school improvement, because it provides insufficient detail to variations required in improvement conditions and strategies to meet the needs of different types of schools. Different change strategies, micro-politics, leadership styles, and communication networks may be required to effect change. Indeed, as no two schools are the same, there may be no one best way to approach school improvement, which is likely to frustrate those who seek simple solutions.

For this reason, we have developed a typology of five different school cultures. It is based on the assumption that schools are either getting better or getting worse. The rapidly accelerating pace of change makes standing still impossible. Building on models of school culture developed by Rosenholtz (1989) and Hopkins and colleagues (1994), if school culture is considered on two dimensions, effectiveness–ineffectiveness, and improving–declining, five types of school can be identified

Figure 14.1   A cultural typology

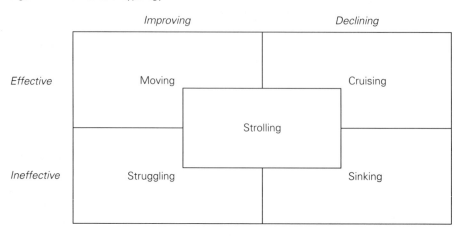

(Stoll and Fink, 1996, see Figure 14.1[1]). The typology provides one way to look at the readiness for change and change capacity of schools with different cultures. While it is somewhat simplistic and no school can be said to be exclusively of one kind or the other, in our work with schools and school leaders we have found it provides a useful way to open up a dialogue about different types of ineffective schools. This model can also operate on various levels: it could be applied to a whole school, to departments, and to policies, practices and programmes within schools. For example, the school's strategies for high achieving pupils might be *moving* while those experienced by 'at risk' pupils might be *sinking*. For the purposes of this chapter we will take a whole school perspective, even though this is somewhat idealized.

In this model, two types of 'ineffective' school are identified:

- The *sinking school* (ineffective and declining) is a failing school. It is not only ineffective; the staff, whether through apathy or ignorance, are not prepared or able to change. It is a school in which isolation, self-reliance, blame and loss of faith are dominating norms, and powerfully inhibit improvement. It will often, although not always, be in socially disadvantaged areas where parents are undemanding and teachers explain away failure by blaming inadequate parenting or unprepared children.
- While the *struggling school* (ineffective, but improving) is ineffective because its current pupil outcomes and school and classroom processes need attention, it is aware of this, and expends considerable energy to improve. Considerable unproductive thrashing about occurs as those in the school community determine the what and how of the change process, and build the climate that will support other improvement conditions and strategies (Stoll and Fink, 1996). There is a willingness, however, to try anything that may make a difference. Ultimately it will succeed because it has the will (Miles, 1987), despite lacking the skill. Sadly, it tends to be viewed as

'failing' or sinking, and this negative attention often acts as a demotivational force in terms of school improvement.

As we have reflected on this model, we have become increasingly concerned by what we view as the unidentified ineffective school.

The Cruising School

The *cruising school* ('effective' but declining) is perceived as effective, or at least more than satisfactory, by teachers and the school's community. It has a carefully constructed camouflage. While it appears to possess many qualities of an effective school, it is usually located in a more affluent area where pupils achieve in spite of teaching quality. League tables and other rankings based on absolute achievement rather than 'value-added' often give the appearance of effectiveness. External perceptions of outside inspectors may also not detect ineffectiveness, and many cruising schools may never be exposed as offering an impoverished diet to their pupils. If, however, schools are to be effective for all children we must raise both the ceiling and the floor. The cruising school lacks the capacity and will to change no less than the sinking school.

Cruising schools may not appear to be ineffective for all pupils, at least based on contemporary models of teaching and learning. The curriculum of cruising schools is generally influenced by the humanist perspective (Brouilette, 1996), which is hyper-rationalistic and fragmented. It is usually predicated on the notion that intelligence is distributed on a normative curve and the role of schools is to place pupils into their appropriate niche. It is generally unsuitable for less academically inclined pupils and unchallenging for the more able. It also contributes little to goals of social justice for 'at risk' pupils. A different and more democratic paradigm suggests that each pupil has a mind and that *each* mind should be developed (Stoll and Fink, 1996). It is a view which suggests that there are multiple intelligences (Gardner, 1983) and that we develop all pupils by using their strengths to build areas in which they are less competent. There is no question this is a more challenging agenda than the 'sort and select' practices of many cruising schools, but it is the only way to strengthen schools for *all* the pupils of *all* the parents. It is for this reason that we suggest that the cruising school is perhaps society's greatest challenge because it has not been identified as ineffective for a significant percentage of its pupils.

The existing system of governance tends to perpetuate mediocrity in the guise of cruising schools. Within a decentralized system, there are many benefits to schools having increased control over their own destinies. A drawback however, is that while more effective schools, free from constraints, can move in their chosen direction without, in some cases, being 'held back' by LEA policies, less effective schools may be left without system-level 'checks and balances' to ensure they do not decline. Given that such schools often do not realize their difficulties until too late, many do not seek help to improve. This is particularly true of cruising schools.

Often, in voluntary projects set up by LEAs and higher education, we have noticed that volunteers tend to be those who least need support. With limited external capacity for resources to be offered as an incentive, uninvolved schools are often those least aware and most needy of support and stimulation (Stoll and Fink, 1996). This does not only refer to schools with difficulties; complacent schools are also at risk. The challenges are how to raise awareness of, engage interest in and encourage commitment to school effectiveness and improvement in *all* schools.

Cultural Norms

One may have to dig even deeper to understand the beliefs and values that underpin the functioning of cruising schools. Through a cultural perspective, it is possible to examine the non-rational side of school change. One particular route to understanding and changing school culture is through exploring cultural norms (Saphier and King, 1985), one piece of the culture puzzle. Fullan (1991) argues that 'educational change depends on what teachers do and think — it's as simple and as complex as that' (p. 117). What they do and think is fundamentally influenced by their beliefs, assumptions and values, which in turn shape norms. Because basic assumptions and values are so deep-seated, uncovering them is hard. By peeling off the next layer of the onion — norms — we see they underlie most aspects of behaviour in schools. Norms are an expression of deeply held values and they influence workplace action. From our experiences in Britain and Canada, and from an understanding of the literature, elsewhere we suggested ten cultural norms that influence the behaviour and actions of those in improving schools (Stoll and Fink, 1996). These include such interconnected norms as shared goals, joint responsibility for school success, collegiality, and shared learning among others. We argued that in terms of change, it is vital to understand underlying values and how they motivate norms and actions, even though they are much more difficult to reach than surface behaviours.

In reflecting on cruising schools, we briefly considered turning these norms of improving schools around and describe declining schools as schools which lacked these norms. It was obvious that such an approach did not fit with our own experience and that of others (Hargreaves, Fullan, Wignall, Stager and Macmillan, 1992; Myers, 1995; Stoll, 1995; Reynolds, 1996; Fink, 1997). In cruising schools, cultural norms have usually remained unexamined and unchallenged for many years. We, therefore, suggest that the following norms more accurately capture the culture of cruising schools. In addition to identifying each norm we provide a catchphrase that captures the essence of the norm.

1. Contentment — 'If it ain't broke don't fix it'

Hargreaves and colleagues (1992) describe a school in which 'context, culture and community are tightly woven together' (p. 26). In effect there is little pressure for change both from within and outside the school. Reynolds (1996) views staff members of such schools as 'cling-ons' because they believe that everything is just fine because 'we have always done it this way' (p. 54), and the community supports this view.

2. Avoidance of Commitment — 'Let's send it to a committee'

Cruising schools have developed an array of strategies to create the appearance of change without really changing anything of substance. Activities such as committee work, school development planning, and staff meetings often provide 'traps' (Odiorne, 1979) in which people create the illusion of pursuing goals but become so enmeshed in activity that they avoid real commitment to change. Another dodge is constantly to seek more information about the change. Since there will never be enough information, this strategy provides an effective excuse for inaction.

3. Goal Diffusion — 'We do our own thing but we do it well'

The culture of cruising schools by definition is usually balkanized (Hargreaves, 1994) or individualistic. Teachers know what is going on in their own departments, phases, or key stages. They may even commit to shared goals in these units but have little knowledge of or commitment to school-wide initiatives. As a teacher one of us interviewed said 'I have a wonderful department where everyone is truly cooperative. I don't know if all the departments within the school or all the departments in other schools can say that.'

4. Reactive — 'Let's wait and see'

Cruising schools rarely get involved in change projects until they must react to top-down mandates or peer pressure from other schools. Rather, they tend to rely on their past achievements and generally positive reputation as a reason for inaction. 'But in times of rapid change of the sort we are encountering in an increasingly postindustrial, postmodern world, these qualities can lead to a caution and a reticence about change which amplifies rather than alleviates the anxieties felt by the school's teachers' (Hargreaves et al., 1992, p. 37)

5. Perpetuating Total Top–Down Leadership — 'It's your job, not mine'

Decision making tends to be hierarchical. Senior managers, through middle managers, direct through memo and fiat. While staff members talk about the need for leadership, they are generally quite content to let someone else assume responsibility for change. This enables them to avoid ownership of changes and to point to a 'lack of leadership' when innovations fail.

6. Conformity — 'Don't rock the boat'

Reynolds (1996) suggests that in ineffective schools there is 'reluctance on the part of individuals in school to stand out from the prevailing group culture, even though they may have wanted to, because of a desire to 'hide' behind the group' (p. 154). Cruising schools which tend to 'rest on their laurels' discourage risk taking and promote conformity. Peer pressure tends to force innovators into line. Rules and regulations substitute for individual judgment and discretion.

7. Nostalgia — 'Things used to be great around here'

Louis and Miles (1990) describe the importance of the 'golden age' mythology as an obstacle to change. It impedes change in two ways:

> First, it typically masks a set of teacher assumptions that are primarily student- (or community-) blaming: The golden age occurred at a time when students wanted to learn and so on . . . Second, the myth typically acts as a barrier to real innovation in the school: It is essentially a conservative view, which emphasizes wanting to go back to the old ways. This is the downside of a stable staff: A stable staff may be necessary for change, but it is more likely to lead to a 'golden age framework'. (p. 187)

Cruising schools plan by looking into the rear view mirror (Stoll and Fink, 1996) to some halcyon days which get better as the years go by.

8. Blaming Others — ' "They" are pushing new ideas down our throats'

The enigmatic 'they' provide a useful target for avoiding change. The 'they' can be government, the local education authority, or the senior management team, who are forcing unproven or inappropriate changes on the school. In some cases this may be true, and the staff is quite justified in its opposition. On other occasions, however, the tendency to blame others, like parents and pupils, for any problems the school experiences may be less justified.

9. Congeniality — 'We all get along'

Cruising schools are 'comfortable pews'. Staff tend to be congenial, but not truly collegial. They also avoid conflict. Change, however, often precipitates conflict and discord before anything useful can happen (Huberman and Miles, 1984). In cruising schools, however, challenges to the status quo are discouraged, ignored or avoided. Controversy and conflict will exist but they are often 'swept under the carpet' for the sake of congeniality and staff harmony.

10. Denial — 'The research and data are biased'

The historian Tuchman (1984) describes people who assess a situation in terms of preconceived fixed notions while ignoring or rejecting any contrary signs — who act 'according to wish while not allowing one to be deflected by the facts' (p. 7) — as 'woodenheaded'. Woodenheadedness is a symptom of the cruising school. While sinking or failing schools fear outside involvement (Reynolds, 1996), cruising schools generally ignore or reject advice and information from outside which is inconsistent with the school's prevailing practices and policies. Evidence that the school is inadequate for significant groups of pupils is often met by denial, criticism of the sources of the data or attacks on the messenger.

How Do You Turn Around a Cruising School?

Since the national focus has been on struggling and sinking or 'failing' schools, the remainder of this chapter addresses the problems presented by the cruising school. The enormity of this challenge is exemplified by a discussion between a male and female head during a leadership seminar one of us conducted. The female was the head of a selective girls grammar school. The male had recently become the head of a selective boys grammar school. Each school did well on league tables, the pupils were apathetic but presented no discipline problems, and the parents were generally supportive. The two heads described their schools as being in a 'time warp'. Little had changed in terms of classroom practice and assessment, school organization and culture for many years. What alarmed the heads in particular was their staffs' apparent indifference, and in some cases unwillingness, to consider new or alternative ways of doing things. Before their present appointments, each head had been responsible for turning around an OFSTED-identified failing school. They agreed that as school leaders, their present schools were far more challenging than their 'failing' schools, because in the 'failing' school the staff and the parents and the school governors at least knew that their schools had problems. The heads attended the seminar in the hope they could get some ideas of how to break through the wall of smugness and self-satisfaction because the strategies for change they had employed in their previous schools were proving inadequate. The vital question posed by these heads, therefore, was if a school is cruising, what can be done to improve it? It is generally agreed that schools facing such difficulties require more external support than those starting from a solid base. What are some of the alternatives, and issues that need to be addressed in different types of cruising schools? From our work we have identified a few of the more pervasive issues which tend to be particularly evident.

Readiness for Change

Perhaps the place to start for school change agents (Fullan, 1993) is to determine a school's readiness for change. The readiness for change and capacity to take ownership are vital to school improvement but harder to achieve in some schools than others. In ineffective schools, facets of their climate may need attention early on before people feel able to participate actively in improvement efforts and concentrate on the real agenda. These fundamental conditions can be summarized within the overall heading of *climate setting* (Stoll and Fink, 1996). Without attention to these fundamental conditions for change at the earliest opportunity, real lasting changes that will impact teaching and learning are highly unlikely. More successful schools devote considerable time to establish trust and openness between staff, pupils and the community before they embark on substantive changes. Recognition of teachers and celebration of their successes is emphasized, and humour encouraged. A school's readiness for change depends to a large extent on individual teachers. Their psychological state may have an impact. Neglect of interpersonal and psychological processes may lead teachers to behave defensively to protect themselves from innovations that might expose their inadequacies (Reynolds, 1996). Valuing individuals and their contributions to others enhances teachers' self-esteem and builds trust. Addressing establishment of communication lines and decision-making procedures are also climate-setting features.

What makes attending to these conditions difficult in cruising schools is that the evidence of ineffectiveness or even difficulty is not as readily apparent as in sinking or struggling schools. Schein (1985) identifies three significant developmental periods in the life of an organization. Depending on the growth stage, cultural function changes, as do the mechanisms likely to bring about change. These periods are birth and early growth, midlife, and maturity and/or stagnation and decline. Cruising schools, by definition, are in the third stage. Discipline, work completion, attendance, for example, which are usually issues in sinking schools may not be problems in cruising schools because of the nature of the school's, intake. Dysfunctional elements, however, have surfaced, but challenge of old assumptions is resisted, and complacency is deeply ingrained. Change processes in this situation are complex, but need to be radical.

Leadership

The role of the headteacher in shaping culture is highly significant. As the heads of the selective grammar schools described previously discovered, cruising schools present a unique leadership challenge for which there are no easy answers.

Since cruising schools are ostensibly effective but declining, they require a 'wake-up call'. Such schools often do not recognize the signs because the pupils usually perform well on tests and examinations. Schein (1985) proposes a variety of strategies for business leaders that could be applied to cruising schools:

- *managed 'revolution' through outsiders* — the hiring of a new head, for example, who brings new values and ideas. Since she or he is not part of the long established culture, the new head will see the school with 'new eyes'. This, of course, is no easy task because structures, recurring processes, age-old symbols and myths have to be 'weakened' before a new leader can introduce their own values;

- *coercive persuasion* — 'the right incentives' are used to make it hard for certain teachers to leave. Meanwhile old values are consistently challenged, and rewards and support given to those who take on new assumptions. 'If psychological safety is sufficient, members of the group can begin to examine and possibly give up some of their cognitive defenses' (p. 294);
- *turnaround* — once those in the school have been persuaded to understand the difficulties associated with past values, norms and actions, a variety of mechanisms are combined, that require participation of all groups and psychological safety. These may include:

  * *managed evolution through hybrids* — accepted 'insiders' with slightly different values, who take on new leadership roles, for example, a respected teacher being appointed deputy head;
  * *planned change and organization development* — use of an organizational development approach to deal with conflicts between and among various subgroups and culture founders;
  * *technological seduction* — new materials or schemes are introduced either as part of a general improvement effort or, specifically, to change teacher behaviour causing re-examination of beliefs and values;
  * *incrementalism* — consistent use made of every opportunity and decision to influence the school in a particular direction.

Cruising schools are in danger of becoming 'boiled frogs'. Senge (1990) describes the parable of the 'boiled frog' in which he explains that a frog dropped into boiling water will jump out whereas a frog placed in luke-warm water which is gradually raised to boiling will sit while the heat is increased and boil to death. In cruising schools, most people think every thing is 'just fine', in fact very comfortable. The initiation of appropriately targeted staff development combined with the creation of a meaningful 'corporate' school development plan (MacGilchrist, Mortimore, Savage and Beresford, 1995) are important strategies. There may be other ways to stop the slide and recapture a culture of continuous improvement. Headteachers must be prepared to provide courageous leadership, and occasionally risk overt action to support the learning of all pupils. Such actions might include confronting unprofessional behaviour or poor teaching practices, swapping around teaching or middle management assignments, modifying timetables or arranging for outside support.

Planting seeds of innovative practice and nurturing their growth can also be useful strategies. One of our colleagues, for example, felt that pupils in the middle stream in his high school were being cheated in their educational experience. He knew that only 75 per cent attended classes regularly and that the same percentage completed their courses. Had he raised the issue at a staff meeting, his staff would have gone into heavy denial and come up with numerous reasons why the parents were sending the wrong pupils to school. This head, instead, went to his five 'best' teachers and suggested they be involved in a 'pilot project' to teach and develop a better course structure for these pupils. He provided some limited financial resources, but time-tabled them to have work-time together and the support of a well-respected deputy. He then let them get on with the task. By the end of the year, 90 per cent of the pupils were attending and over 90 per cent succeeded in completing their course work. By the next year the head had people who would never have volunteered and probably would have resisted teaching these youngsters asking him if they could join the 'project'.

If It Ain't Broke — Break It

Another of our colleagues, head of a cruising school, described his frustration with his staff when he said that if he heard it once he heard it a thousand times, 'if it ain't broke don't fix it' (see section on norms, pp. 194–7). The title of an American management book, *If It Ain't Broke — Break It* (Kriegel and Patten, 1991), suggests a necessary strategy for leaders of cruising schools to get the attention of the people who must effect change. Starting from the premise that every teacher wants to do a good job, and every parent only wants the best for their children, if the school is cruising it is not adding value to the pupils academically, socially or in other important ways. Elements of the school may, in fact, be regressing. All this is masked, however, because pupils arrive in the school with relatively high levels of achievement, and most continue to achieve in spite of the quality of teaching and learning. If 'value-added' measures are employed, however, which demonstrate that pupils are not achieving what one would expect considering the quality of the school's intake, then it could be argued that the pupils are being cheated. Similarly, if achievement data are disaggregated to look at differences between and among groups of pupils and subjects, then those not progressing can be identified. Parent and pupil attitude surveys also can reveal ineffective aspects of the school. A school we worked with in Ontario, for instance, found school activities were well attended but only a segment of its pupil population participated in every activity. In other words, the same pupils sang in the choir, played sports and participated in drama. The survey revealed that at least 25 per cent of the pupil population was uninvolved, disaffected, and angry about the social structure of the school. This is confirmed by results of pupil attitude surveys administered in Britain (Barber, 1996). Typical of a cruising school, the school tried to undermine the credibility of the instrument and denied the message of the results. Had the school's head shared this data with his staff and parents then a 'door' to improvement might be opened. Unfortunately neither the head nor his staff was ready for change. Perhaps the greatest hurdle in a cruising school is for the staff, and sometimes even the head, to recognize that there is room for development.

Changing Structures

Another level for change is to challenge existing structures. Mortimore and colleagues (1988) differentiate between school factors that are 'givens', such as legislated requirements, and 'policy' issues that are discretionary and could be changed or altered. Many 'policy' issues in cruising schools have become 'givens' in the minds of most staff. Structures relate to how schools use time, space, and define roles and relationships. One strategy to 'move' the cruising school is to challenge all structures. For example, hard questions need to be asked to determine if the structure, such as lesson period length, or the allocation of rooms, or roles of subject department heads are 'givens' or 'policy' issues. If they are 'policy' issues, do they any longer make sense? Why must all periods be the same length? Why does the English department always have the rooms on the first floor? Why do we have two playtimes, one for infants and one for juniors? Why do the men occupy the upstairs staffroom? The bottom line is, if the structure no longer makes sense, it should be changed.

The strategy of changing structures is often necessary to promote change, but schools that only restructure are, in Fullan's (1992) words, 'doomed to tinkering'. For substantive change to occur, changing structures is not enough, cruising schools must address their 'if it ain't broke, don't fix it' culture. Structures and cultures are intricately linked (Hargreaves, 1994; Hopkins, Ainscow and West, 1994; Stoll and Fink, 1996). Simply stated, it is difficult to change one without changing the other. For example, one of the greatest barriers to teacher collaboration is time, a structure. It may be necessary to alter teachers' time-tables to allow for joint work. It will also be necessary to address the power centres of the school.

Managing the Micro-politics

Politics is as much part of schooling as learning. Power is everywhere in education (Ball, 1987). Teachers exercise power over their pupils, senior managers exercise power over their teachers, and the smarter teachers know how to manipulate or manoeuvre around senior managers. Politics is about acquiring and using power and influence. At their worst, micro-political environments make a school dysfunctional and prevent positive change (Sarason, 1990). At their best they interact positively to advance the organization's purposes. Cruising schools tend to be intensely micro-political places: because the culture is usually balkanized, departments contend for time, space and financial resources. In sixth forms, they also compete for pupils because greater enrolment means more classes which means more teachers and size of departments tends to dictate influence. Classroom teachers and pastoral support teachers often are involved in micro-political activity. Males and females, people in the arts and staff members interested in sports, management team and staff provide but a few of the micro-political tensions in schools and often in cruising schools. How does one turn political activity into 'positive politics' (Blase, 1988)? Perhaps the first challenge is to recognize the existence of political activity and its manifestations in the school and to understand the legitimate concerns and needs of various departments, subjects, and groups [see, also, Reynolds' chapter in this volume]. Through attention to structural changes, and addressing the cultural norms, school leaders can redirect this energy into more productive activities. The corrosiveness of micro-political activity occurs when it is channelled into in-fighting within the school as opposed to coalescing around school-wide goals.

Macro-politics and Cruising Schools

The challenge of 'turning around' a cruising school, in significant ways, runs counter to prevailing macro-political forces. Sadly we suspect that governmental initiatives of the next decade will be to attend to the mediocrity of the cruising schools created by government policies of the present decade. There is considerable evidence to suggest that the world-wide romance with market approaches to education has created two classes of school; the haves and the have-nots (Whitty, 1997). Overt and covert selection has created schools that are more attractive to the more affluent middle class (Blackmore, 1995). Ironically, 'within English culture, schools judged to be good and hence over-subscribed are more likely to be academically selective schools or formally selective schools with a persisting academic reputation' (Whitty, 1997, p. 14). In other words, parents in a position to choose, select schools that correspond most closely to the academic and social goals they remember from their traditional schools. Rather than promoting diversity and innovation, they reproduce a model of schooling which is of questionable relevance in a postmodern world. The norms of experimentation and risk taking necessary to *move* schools disappear in an environment that promotes security, stability and the maintenance of continuity. The norms of cooperation and collegiality whither and die as schools and teachers fight for pupils and prestige. Rather than focusing on improved teaching and learning, many of these schools tend to put their energies into glossy brochures and public relations exercises. One need only peruse the more influential school management journals or attend prominent management conferences to see how the creation of a public image and the winning of the enrolment competition have superseded teaching and learning as prime topics of managerial concern. As one teacher has stated, the term 'headteacher' is rapidly becoming an oxymoron. The law of unintended consequences holds that for every action there is an unintended consequence. We would suggest that in their single-minded focus on failing schools, choice and market solutions, governments in some countries and states have created an 'unintended consequence'; a more difficult type of ineffective school — the cruising school.

Conclusion

Ineffectiveness is a major challenge for all those concerned with and about school improvement. It is dependent on how the purposes of schooling are perceived, associated definitions of effectiveness, and perspective on the educational process. It is particularly complicated because it comes in many guises, sometimes wearing a mask of 'effectiveness' to the uniformed observer. Its complexity is compounded by the influence of school culture which pervades all improvement efforts and is, itself, intertwined in an elaborate braid with structure, micro-politics, and leadership.

Given contextual differences between schools, similar approaches to improvement are inappropriate. The focus on 'failing' schools, as we have suggested, has deflected attention away from the cruising schools that continue to hide behind the quality of their intake and offer a truly mediocre education. Current accountability measures may 'weed out the truly dreadful' but leave what we consider the most difficult challenge to educational systems unrecognized and unattended. Furthermore, while research attention is now being turned to examining the process of improvement in less effective schools (for example, Robertson and Sammons, 1997) and to understanding how certain schools succeed 'against the odds' (National Commission on Education, 1996), further case studies are desperately needed, especially of cruising schools.

Note

1 The model is described in full in Stoll and Fink (1996).

References

Ball, S. (1987) *Micropolitics of the School*, London: Methuen/Routledge and Kegan Paul.

Barber, M. (1996) *The Learning Game: Arguments for an Education Revolution*, London: Victor Gollancz.

Barth, R. (1990) *Improving Schools from Within: Teachers, Parents, and Principals Can Make the Difference*, San Francisco: Jossey-Bass.

Blackmore, J. (1995) 'Breaking out from a masculinist politics of education', in Limerick, B. and Lingard, B. (eds) *Gender and Changing Educational Management*, Rydalmere, NSW, Australia: Hodder Education.

Blase, J. (1988) 'The teachers' political orientation vis à vis the principal: The micropolitics of the school', *Politics of Education Association Yearbook*, pp. 113–26.

Brouilette, L. (1996) *A Geology of School Reform: The Successive Restructuring of a School District*, New York: State University of New York Press.

Brown, S., Riddell, S. and Duffield, J. (1996) 'Possibilities and problems of small-scale studies to unpack the findings of large-scale school effectiveness', in Gray, J., Reynolds, D., Fitz-Gibbon, C. and Jesson, D. (eds) *Merging Traditions: The Future of Research on School Effectiveness and School Improvement*, London: Cassell.

Cotton, K. (1995) *Effective Schooling Practices: A Research Synthesis: 1995*, Portland, Oregon: Northwest Regional Educational Laboratory.

Deal, T.E. and Kennedy, A. (1983) 'Culture and school performance', *Educational Leadership*, **40**, 5, pp. 140–1.

Fink, D. and Stoll, L. (forthcoming) 'Educational change: Easier said than done', in Hargreaves, A., Fullan, M., Lieberman, A. and Hopkins, D. (eds) *International Handbook of Educational Change*, Leuven: Kluwer.

Fink, D. (1997) 'The attrition of change', Unpublished doctoral dissertation, Open University.

FULLAN, M.G. (1991) *The New Meaning of Educational Change*, New York: Teachers College Press and London: Cassell.

FULLAN, M.G. (1992) *What's Worth Fighting for in Headship*, Buckingham: Open University Press.

FULLAN, M.G. (1993) *Change Forces: Probing the Depths of Educational Reform*, London: Falmer Press.

GARDNER, H. (1983) *Frames of Mind: The Theory of Multiple Intelligences*, New York: Basic Books.

GRAY, J., JESSON, D., GOLDSTEIN, H. and HEDGER, K. (1995) 'The statistics of school improvement: Establishing the agenda', in GRAY, J. and WILCOX, B. (eds) *Good School, Bad School: Evaluating Performance and Encouraging Improvement*, Buckingham: Open University Press.

GRAY, J. and WILCOX, B. (1995) 'The challenge of turning around ineffective schools', in GRAY, J. and WILCOX, B. (eds) *Good School, Bad School: Evaluating Performance and Encouraging Improvement*, Buckingham: Open University Press.

HARGREAVES, A. (1994) *Changing Teachers, Changing Times: Teachers' Work and Culture in the Postmodern Age*, London: Cassell.

HARGREAVES, A., FULLAN, M.G., WIGNALL, R., STAGER, M. and MACMILLAN, R. (1992) *Secondary School Work Cultures and Educational Change*, Toronto: Ministry of Education.

HARGREAVES, D. (1995) 'School culture, school effectiveness and school improvement', *School Effectiveness and School Improvement*, **6**, 1, pp. 23–46.

HOPKINS, D. (1995) 'Towards Effective School Improvement', Paper presented to the Eighth International Congress for School Effectiveness and Improvement, Leewarden, The Netherlands.

HOPKINS, D., AINSCOW, M. and WEST, M. (1994) *School Improvement in an Era of Change*, London: Cassell.

HUBERMAN, M. and MILES, M.B. (1984) *Innovation Up Close*, New York: Plenum.

JANIS, I. (1972) *Victims of Groupthink*, Boston, MA.: Houghton Mifflin.

JOYCE, B.R. and MURPHY, C. (1990) 'Epilogue: The curious complexities of cultural change', in JOYCE, B.R. (ed.) *Changing School Culture Through Staff Development*, Alexandria, VA: Association for Supervision and Curriculum Development.

KRIEGEL, R.J. and PATTEN, L. (1991) *If It Ain't Broke — Break It*, New York: Warner Books.

LITTLE, J.W. (1982) 'Norms of collegiality and experimentation: Workplace conditions of school success', *American Educational Research Journal*, **19**, 3, pp. 325–40.

LITTLE, J.W. (1990) 'The persistence of privacy: Autonomy and initiative in teachers' professional relations', *Teachers College Record*, **91**, 4, pp. 509–36.

LOUIS, K.S. and MILES, M.B. (1990) *Improving the Urban High School: What Works and Why*, London: Cassell.

MACGILCHRIST, B., MORTIMORE, P., SAVAGE, J. and BERESFORD, C. (1995) *Planning Matters*, London: Paul Chapman.

MILES, M.B. (1987) 'Practical Guidelines for Administrators: How to Get There', Paper presented at the Annual Meeting of the American Educational Research Association.

MORTIMORE, P. (1991) 'The nature and findings of research on school effectiveness in the primary sector', in RIDDELL, S. and BROWN, S. (eds) *School Effectiveness Research: Its Messages for School Improvement*, Edinburgh: HMSO.

MORTIMORE, P. (1995) 'Effective schools: Current impact and future potential', The Director's Inaugural Lecture, London, Institute of Education.

MORTIMORE, P., SAMMONS, P., STOLL, L., LEWIS, D. and ECOB, R. (1986) *The Junior School Project: Main Report, Part C, Research and Statistics Branch*, London: Inner London Education Authority.

MORTIMORE, P., SAMMONS, P., STOLL, L., LEWIS, D. and ECOB, R. (1988) *School Matters: The Junior Years*, Somerset: Open Books. (Reprinted, 1994, London, Paul Chapman.)

MYERS, K. (1996) *School Improvement in Practice: Schools Make a Difference Project*, London: Falmer Press.

NATIONAL COMMISSION ON EDUCATION (1996) *Success Against the Odds: Effective Schools in Disadvantaged Areas*, London: Routledge.

ODIORNE, G. (1979) *MBO 11: A System of Managerial Leadership for the 80s*, Belmont, Ca.: Fearon Pitman.

OFSTED (1995) *The Annual Report of Her Majesty's Chief Inspector of Schools: Part 1 — Standards and Quality in Education 1993/94*, London: HMSO.

REYNOLDS, D. (1991) 'Changing ineffective schools', in AINSCOW, M. (ed.) *Effective Schools for All*, London: David Fulton.

REYNOLDS, D. (1996) 'The problem of the ineffective school: Some evidence and some speculations', in GRAY, J., REYNOLDS, D., FITZ-GIBBON, C. and JESSON, D. (eds) *Merging Traditions: The Future of Research on School Effectiveness and School Improvement*, London: Cassell.

REYNOLDS, D., SAMMONS, P., STOLL, L., BARBER, M. and HILLMAN, J. (1996) 'School effectiveness and school improvement in the United Kingdom', *School Effectiveness and School Improvement*, **7**, 2, pp. 133–58.

ROBERTSON, P. and SAMMONS, P. (1997) 'Improving School Effectiveness: A Project in Progress', Paper presented at the Tenth International Congress for School Effectiveness and Improvement, Memphis.

ROSENHOLTZ, S.J. (1989) *Teachers' Workplace: The Social Organization of Schools*, New York: Longman.

SAMMONS, P., HILLMAN, J. and MORTIMORE, P. (1995) *Key Characteristics of Effectiveness: A Review of School Effectiveness Research*, London: Institute of Education and Office for Standards in Education.

SAPHIER, J. and KING, M. (1985) 'Good seeds grow in strong cultures', *Educational Leadership*, **42**, 6, pp. 67–74.

SARASON, S. (1990) *The Predictable Failure of Education Reform*, San Francisco: Jossey-Bass.

SCHEIN, E.H. (1985) *Organizational Culture and Leadership*, San Francisco: Jossey-Bass.

SENGE, P. (1990) *The Fifth Discipline: The Art and Practice of the Learning Organization*, New York: Doubleday.

SISKIN, L.S. (1994) *Realms of Knowledge: Academic Departments in Secondary Schools*, London: Falmer Press.

STOLL, L. (1995) 'The Challenge and Complexity of the Ineffective School', Paper presented at the annual conference of the British Education Research Association, University of Bath.

STOLL, L. and FINK, D. (1996) *Changing Our Schools: Linking School Effectiveness and School Improvement*, Buckingham: Open University Press.

STOLL, L., MYERS, K. and HARRINGTON, J. (1994) 'Linking School Effectiveness and School Improvement through Action Projects', Paper presented at the annual conference of the British Educational Research Association, St Anne's College, Oxford.

TEDDLIE, C. and STRINGFIELD, S. (1993) *Schools Make a Difference: Lessons Learned from a 10 Year Study of School Effects*, New York: Teachers College Press.

Louise Stoll and Dean Fink

TUCHMAN, B. (1984) *The March of Folly*, New York: Alfred A. Knopf.

VAN VELZEN, W., MILES, M., ECKHOLM, M., HAMEYER, U. and ROBIN, D. (1985) *Making School Improvement Work*, Leuven, Belgium: ACCO.

WHITTY, G. (1997) 'Creating quasi-markets in education: A review of recent research on parental choice and school autonomy in three countries', in APPLE, M.W. (ed.) *Review of Research in Education*, Washington, DC: American Educational Research Association.

Part 6

International Perspectives

Despite our primary emphasis being on British education, particularly that in England, we felt an international perspective would help readers to consider the chapters within a broader contextual framework. This final section is composed of two chapters; the first an American perspective from a school effectiveness researcher, Sam Stringfield, and the second provided by Karen Kovacs from the OECD.

Sam Stringfield's chapter adds to conceptual issues discussed in the previous section and, again, alludes to the medical metaphor. Anatomy, as defined in the *New Shorter Oxford English Dictionary*, is 'detailed examination or analysis; structure, organization'. Dissecting the findings of the Louisiana School Effectiveness Study, in which he was involved for a decade, and his three-year evaluation of ten 'promising programs', funded by the US Department of Education, Stringfield identifies student, classroom and school level variables in the first, and 'discontinuity themes' in the second. Many of these are familiar to British educationalists and to the other authors, for example leadership issues, staffing, and that all schools, even those deemed ineffective, have some good teachers. There are, however, important differences between the countries, not least of which are the large amounts of money available for American schools from a range of private and charitable foundations.

Stringfield concludes that for some schools, improvement can be particularly vulnerable to external instability, and that what is needed is reliable routes to success for all schools. He looks outside education to high reliability organizations, citing exemplary characteristics and implications for overcoming ineffectiveness in schools. The idea of High Reliability Schools has recently been taken up in this country as one route to school improvement. The question is, can schools, whose fundamental concern is the progress, achievement and development of young people, within a complex system of human interrelationships, be equated with air traffic control? Or is it merely that the metaphor helps us, in this instance, to understand the consequence if schools are not successful for all pupils?

Karen Kovacs' contribution is, in our opinion, a fitting final chapter for this book. For any reader who has not yet questioned that perhaps there is an alternative to a conception of school failure, Kovacs reminds us that England and Wales are very much in the minority, in terms of policy orientation. Her chapter raises the important issues of definition, context, disadvantage, labelling, problems of measurement, and the need for educational failure to be addressed in a comprehensive way, themes that weave their way through the book. She cautions that very few policies have systematically been monitored or fully evaluated, which makes important comparisons difficult, but comments that while public labelling of failure in some countries may have galvanized schools into action, French experience suggests that designation of schools as Education Priority Zones appears to push parents to send their children to different schools.

Significantly Kovacs also draws attention, although not overtly, to the medical metaphor as she highlights the initial policy choice made by most OECD member countries to tackle educational failure through remedial measures (cure), rather than prevention. One wonders whether a much reduced inspection model, with the remainder of funds put into appropriately targeted staff development activities and other necessary resources to support schools, would be a more cost-effective and preventative model for tackling the issue of schools in difficulty. Furthermore, are at least some of these schools in difficulty *because* of the policy context?

Together these two chapters add an important dimension. They also confirm that action must be taken to address the issue of failure at school, the need for active participation and commitment of teachers, an emphasis on effective and sophisticated teaching and learning strategies, and use of reliable data to inform policy and practice.

Chapter 15

An Anatomy of Ineffectiveness

Sam Stringfield

In the preface to his seventeenth-century classic, *The Anatomy of Melancholy*, Robert Burton declared, 'I write of melancholy, by being busy to avoid melancholy.' Very nearly the same sentence, and exactly the same logic, can be applied to the study of school ineffectiveness.

This chapter is about ineffective schools. By presenting data from the toil of two relatively large-scale, longitudinal studies, plus references to additional studies that have included examinations of school ineffectiveness, I hope to help practical educators and researchers become productively busy in avoiding school ineffectiveness.

Sections of this chapter examine four interrelated issues. The first section explores the reasons for studying ineffectiveness and reasons why this topic has become relevant at this point in our history. The second examines common characteristics among ineffective, 'negative outlier' schools in the Louisiana School Effectiveness Study. Third, common characteristics of failed school improvement efforts from the Special Strategies Studies are examined. Finally, I attempt to draw some lessons regarding the necessary steps for avoiding school ineffectiveness. As has been argued elsewhere, part of the resolution will necessarily involve the hard work of creating much more reliable school organizational structures capable of serving all children.

The Causes of a Rising Field of Research on Ineffective Educating

There is ample anecdotal evidence to suggest that less-than-effective schooling is a problem as old as schools themselves. Social commentators of every age have described the horrors of the typical, or worse-than-average, school. But with the exceptions of fleeting periods of civic-minded reform, societies that have attempted to provide even the most meagre appearance of universal public education have also tolerated significant numbers of manifestly ineffective schools.

Why is the history of formal, scholarly study of ineffective schooling so thin? First, as a matter of logic, there needed to be research demonstrating that some schools were *more* effective, before the existence of such a field made any sense. In the US, for example, arguably the most influential study of the third quarter of this century was *The Coleman Report* (Coleman, Campbell, Hobson, McPartland, Mood, Weinfield and York, 1966). A major theme of that very large study was that schools have no differential effects on student achievement. It has only been with the more recent evolution of the school effects field (e.g., Brookover, Schweitzer, Schneider, Beady, Flood and Wisenbaker, 1978; Mortimore, Sammons, Stoll, Lewis and Ecob, 1988; Levine and Lezotte, 1990; Teddlie and Stringfield, 1993) that the detailed study of outlier schools, effective or ineffective, has made a great deal of sense. If no differential value-added existed, then why should researchers spend their very scarce resources looking for it?

Second, studying ineffectiveness implies an increasing confidence within our field. For years most educators have simply not wanted to talk about ineffective schools. The situation was rather like a family that doesn't talk about its crazy old uncle who lives down the block. If no one thinks he or she can do anything about it, and the situation is inherently embarrassing or sad, isn't it best just to look the other way? But members of our field now believe that we can do something about ineffective schools. Increasing numbers of studies are indicating that meaningful improvements in schools are possible (in the US, see Slavin, Karweit and Madden, 1989; Stringfield et al., 1997). If professionals in the field believe that improvement in underperforming schools is possible, then the time may be ripe for study. If research can help practitioners understand the causes and descriptors of ineffectiveness and can help those same practitioners find methods for improvement, then a level of urgency could be expected toward the creation of such research.

Third, and very importantly, until recently school ineffectiveness did not pose an obvious threat to the economies of developed nations. In the US, for example, the median income of young male high school drop-outs was higher in 1972 than had been the median income of young college graduates a generation earlier[1]. Why study an unpleasant topic? However, as with the research base, this situation has changed dramatically in the last twenty-five years. The annual income of the average young US male high school drop-out has dropped by over 50 per cent in the last twenty-five years (Stringfield, 1995). No more-educated US group has seen such a decline in earning power. A post-industrial, information-driven world economy simply cannot provide highly paid, low-skill jobs the way that an industrial economy could (Reich, 1992). This has created a problem, not just for the poor, but for the affluent who do not wish to be obligated permanently to support the poor. Today Australia, North America, and Europe are all struggling for the first time with the spectre of second-generation young men who are able and willing to work, but who, for lack of job skills, are unemployed. Today, school ineffectiveness is a *very* important policy topic in the US, in the UK, and around the developed world.

In summary, three factors have driven the study of ineffective schooling. First, some schools add more value to students' knowledge levels. Second, schools are capable of planned improvement in their effectiveness. Third, the post-industrial economy requires unprecedented high levels of information-processing abilities of virtually all workers. These three factors have generated a moment at which the demand for understanding school ineffectiveness has risen from almost nothing to a very high level.

The Study of Ineffective Schools in the Louisiana School Effectiveness Study

A school in which students are achieving academically at a much higher (or much lower) level than might be predicted using such standard measures as familial socio-economic status is often described an as 'outlier'. Studies of outlier schools have overwhelmingly concentrated on positive outlier schools. Variously referred to as studies of 'exemplary schools' (Weber, 1971), 'unusually effective schools' (Levine and Lezotte, 1990) and 'high-flying' schools (Anderson, Sears, Pellicer, Riddle, Gardner and Harwell, 1992), these positive outlier studies have made important contributions to the field (for a review, see Stringfield, 1994). Of the studies that have examined both positive and negative outlier schools, the largest and longest running has been the Louisiana School Effectiveness Study (LSES; Teddlie and Stringfield, 1993).

LSES researchers built detailed case studies of eight pairs of demographically matched schools. Each school of a pair served a community virtually identical to the community served by its matched school. However, in one school the students' achievement test scores had been much higher than the scores of the other school. This pattern had continued for at least two years prior to the study. The schools were observed by two person teams for at least three days per school on four separate occasions over six years. The LSES researchers produced a series of articles describing the observed differences between the schools. Hundreds of detailed, low-inference classroom observations of third grade (the US schooling level in which most students are approximately 9 years old), produced quantitative differentiations between more and less effective schools. As noted in Teddlie, Kirby, and Stringfield (1989), classroom practices in ineffective schools (regardless of community socioeconomic status) were characterized by significantly lower rates of student time-on-task, less teacher presentation of new material, lower rates of teacher communication of high academic expectations, fewer instances of positive reinforcement, more classroom interruptions, more discipline problems, and a classroom ambience generally rated as less friendly.

Stringfield and Teddlie (1991) also conducted detailed qualitative analyses of the sixteen case studies. Those analyses added significantly to the quantitative findings. Qualitative differentiations were made at three levels: the student, the classroom, and the school.

At the level of *student activities*, ineffective schools were found to be different from more effective, demographically matched schools in two ways. First, students' on-task rates were either uniformly low, or were markedly uneven. In some schools very few academic tasks were put before any students, and in other schools there were distinct differences in demands made of students. It was not enough that some students be required to make a concerted academic effort. Students in positive outlier schools were often more uniformly engaged in academic work.

The second student-level variable was that in ineffective schools students typically experienced their school-related activities as intellectual anarchy. LSES researchers conducted a great many informal interviews of 9 year old students. In the more effective schools, students could typically tell us what they were being asked to do *and why*. School made intellectual sense to those students. In the ineffective schools, tasks were put before the students in what appeared to the students to be nearly chaotic fashion. When interviewed, students at ineffective schools were much less likely to be aware of *why* they were being asked to do a task, how the task built on prior schoolwork, and how it might be expected to lay a foundation for future work. School is, in large part, about sense making. Students at the ineffective schools were very hard pressed to make sense of their daily, weekly, and yearly tasks. As with the time-on-task differences, these sense-making differences were notable during the 1984–85 school year, and again with new third graders 5 years later. Students were having difficulty constructing meaning from their academic tasks at the ineffective schools.

At the *classroom level*, ineffective schools were characterized by a leisurely pace, minimal moderate- to long-term planning, low or uneven rates of interactive teaching, a preponderance of 'ditto sheets' and other relatively unengaging tasks, and teachers teaching in isolation from one another. One of the most readily observable of the classroom differences was that teachers in ineffective schools often failed to cover all of the district-mandated materials by the year's end. The last few chapters of mathematics books, for example, often went unexamined by students. The classes typically lacked any sense of 'academic push', or drive to help students learn at least a minimal amount of information in a year. These students were not being provided equal 'opportunity to learn'. (For discussion of the power of OTL, see Burstein, 1992.)

Related to this lack of push was a lack of planning. In both the fall of 1984 and 1989 researchers asked teachers how far they imagined their classes would progress by spring. Teachers in the ineffective schools were much less likely to offer a concrete response. In fact, they were less likely to view the question as relevant to their jobs. Instead, many teachers in ineffective schools would report that they were 'following the curriculum' (which often meant that they were following far behind the curriculum). Observers often reported that many teachers in ineffective schools appeared to be 'going through the motions' of teaching, as opposed to planning actively and working with students to get content mastered.

Not surprisingly, going through the motions in a relatively unplanned way resulted in classrooms with low or uneven levels of teacher–student interaction. Stallings (1980) had found that high levels of teacher involvement with students — lecturing, questioning, actively engaging, and checking their work — generally resulted in increased levels of student achievement. In LSES, researchers observed the same teacher-level differences. Those differences were found between teachers *and* between schools.

Teachers in ineffective schools tended to rely on 'ready made' materials. They tended to put tasks in front of students and then require that the students work at them, often in isolation from one another. Observers reported that teachers in ineffective schools were more likely to spend their hours passing out 'ditto sheets' and other pre-produced questions for students to answer at their desks. There was not a single ineffective school in which the majority of classes were characterized by rigorous intellectual give-and-take between teachers and students, or among students.

Finally, ineffective schools were structured such that teachers almost invariably taught in isolation from one another. There was little focus on building a professional knowledge base within the school.

The above classroom-level differences were trends, not universals. Almost every school in LSES had *some* effective teachers. However, at negative outlier schools, the numbers of lackadaisical teachers were disturbingly high.

At the *school level*, ineffective schools were observed to be different from their demographically matched peers along seven dimensions. The first of those was that the schools simply were not academically focused. They were occasionally friendly places, but never places in which there was an obvious, whole organization focus on enhancing students' academic performances.

A second finding was clearly related to the first. At the ineffective schools, observers consistently noted that the school's daily schedule was not an accurate guide to academic time usage. Academic periods often began late and ended early. Some content areas were rarely covered at all. At noon one day at one school, the principal announced over the intercom that after lunch the school would observe 'extended recess'. This apparently not unusual declaration (no-one seemed surprised) meant that all of the students in the entire school played outside all afternoon. A half-day of scheduled academic time was simply lost.

Third, at ineffective schools, resources often worked at cross-purposes. A teacher in a pull-out special education class might be using methods that were completely different from those the student experienced in his or her regular class. In some schools, students were pulled out of their regular reading classes to receive extra help in another subject. This is not to argue that school time-tabling is a simple task. Rather, it is to observe that in otherwise matched schools, these scheduling issues had been worked out in ways that were much clearer for both students and teachers.

Fourth, when researchers interviewed the principals of ineffective schools, the principals rarely discussed the specifics of their schools' curricula. In some cases the principals seemed disinterested in curricula, and in others totally ignorant of the particulars of their school's academic program. These principals defined their jobs bureaucratically, not academically or instructionally.

Fifth, the principals were relatively passive in the recruitment of new teachers, the selection of professional development topics and opportunities for the teachers, and in the performance of teacher evaluations. For a principal not to be vigilant in the selection of new staff and the ongoing professional education of a school's teachers is to maximize the probability of school ineffectiveness. It is notoriously difficult in the US to fire a teacher outright. Yet, when probed, principals in more effective schools would invariably describe multiple situations in which they had, over the years, counselled a former teacher into early retirement, another profession, or another aspect of education. Researchers almost never heard similar stories from the principals of ineffective schools. One of the clearest differentiating points for observers attempting to guess schools' negative outlier status often came when a principal opined, 'All of our teachers are good teachers.' If a half hour later that same observer found herself sitting in a class that was academic anarchy, then researchers knew they were visiting an ineffective school. Principals who did not have an accurate, detailed grasp of their teachers' strengths and weaknesses were ill-positioned to guide school improvement.

In ineffective schools, libraries and other media resources were rarely used to their full potential. In six years of visiting one physically lovely school, observers repeatedly noted that the library was very attractive, always clean and orderly. Over time the observers realized that during most hours of most school days the library was locked safely away from the students.

Finally, ineffective schools rarely had systems of public reward for students' academic excellence. Whereas the principals at more effective schools would often post the recent academic honours achieved by various students outside the schools' offices, such school-level recognition of academic efforts were rare in ineffective schools.[2]

Characteristics of Failed School Improvement Efforts From the *Special Strategies Studies*

The *Special Strategies Studies* (Stringfield et al., 1997; Stringfield, Millsap and Herman, in press) were a large-scale research effort funded by the US Department of Education. The goal of the studies was to understand better the potential of 'promising programs' for improving the education of disadvantaged children. Ten separate designs for improving the academic achievements of poor and minority students were studied in a total of twenty-five schools, with each school being carefully monitored for three years. Detailed qualitative case studies of each school were produced. These were supported by less detailed studies of an additional twenty replicate schools. Schools were nominated into *Special Strategies Studies* by members of the various program development teams and others involved in the particular designs. Third party verification of the schools' reputations as exemplars of their specific designs were obtained in twenty-three of twenty-five longitudinal cases before the fieldwork began. Outcome data were contrasted with data from the very large, longitudinal *Prospects* data set (Puma, Jones, Rock and Fernandez, 1993)[3].

The longitudinal nature of the study meant that the research team was able to observe several schools as they moved — deliberately or otherwise — away from some of the relatively promising school improvement designs. These came to be described as 'destabilized schools' (Nesselrodt, Schaffer, and Stringfield, 1997). The research team identified ten themes, each of which was shared by at least two of the schools that either discontinued the specific program or, more often, continued it in name but with no ongoing impact on students' academic lives. These ten are described below.

Eight of the twenty-five longitudinal sites experienced difficulties sustaining *funding* for their chosen 'promising program'. The difficulty was occasionally program specific (e.g., an implementation grant ended). Equally often, the whole school or district (e.g., the governing body) discovered a fiscal short-fall and implemented austerity measures. Whole school austerity measures inevitably resulted in cuts to programs long before cuts in staff. It was always the case that after the fiscal crisis, it was easier to start a new program than to regenerate enthusiasm for the old, gutted one. The effects of fiscal crises were invariably conservative, in that the crisis ended with curricula and instruction looking more like the way things were before school improvement was attempted than the way things were during the change effort.

Eight schools experienced difficulty obtaining or sustaining *teacher commitment* to the reform. In some cases, teachers were allowed either to undertake the reform or not, depending on their personal predilection toward change in general and the particular effort. Inevitably, the long-term net effect on the schools was 'no change'. By contrast, schools that had sustained whole school change typically had taken a faculty vote to commit to the change.

Six schools suffered through *leadership crises* of one sort or another. The leadership might be at the level of the school district superintendent or a within-school informal teacher leader, though most often it was the principal. Whenever a group of reluctant-to-change teachers suspected wavering on the part of the principal or superintendent, the eventual net effect on the school was that the school returned to the old way of doing things.

Six schools experienced difficulties with *curriculum alignment*. Either the new curriculum did not map well onto the district's or state's testing objectives, or it conflicted with a previously existing curriculum component that was fiercely defended by one constituency curriculum component. If the conflict was not clearly and forcefully resolved, the school eventually returned to the old ways.

Five schools had one of two problems related to *staffing*. At the simplest, a school was located in such a remote site (or a location otherwise deemed by young teachers to be unappealing) that the school had difficulty recruiting competent staff. The second, and more common staffing problem, related to the skills of existing staff. Such programs as Paideia (Adler, 1982) and Success for All (Slavin et al., 1996) require many teachers to master whole ranges of new skills. In some cases, teachers were not provided with adequate initial or long-term professional development. In others, it was not completely clear that some teachers possessed the combination of intellectual flexibility and motivation necessary to master the new skills. In a few cases, it was simply not clear that a teacher had the intellectual wherewithal to engage in 'higher order' discussion, let alone lead such a discussion.

Efforts at reform in three schools were essentially scuttled by *racial disharmony* among the teachers and/or administrators. Both the reality and perceptions of racism remain substantial problems in the United States. In one school, many of the black faculty fervently believed that the white principal displayed an active preference for white teachers. In a second school, the promising program was described by some minority teachers as the program of 'a white researcher from a white university'. In a third, unresolved differences among teachers on topics not related to race came to be viewed as undiscussable because they fell along racial lines. In each case, the presence of unresolved, and often undiscussed, powerfully held racial tensions overrode efforts to implement programs that were succeeding in other multiracial schools. The problem was not the presence of diverse racial groups. The problem was the inability of a group of adults to deal forthrightly with issues that arose from different perceptions of the meaning of race.

Three of the schools and their reform efforts were hobbled by *parents'* or the *larger public's perceptions* of the school or program. In at least two cases, the communities viewed the schools as unsafe and hostile environments. The great majority of the parents at those schools refused to visit the schools, let alone become involved in the programs. Other parents worried that a specific program targeted at underachieving students would stigmatize their child. These parents' concern was that the child would come to be viewed by future teachers as unintelligent, and that these teachers would 'write off' their child. As with the race issue above, these were perception problems that were dealt with successfully at other schools. In each case the real problem was a failure of the school and program to deal with the public's perceptions of the program and the problem.

Three schools either eliminated or fatally altered promising programs for *other 'political' reasons.* While no site was involved in deep community controversy over a strategy itself, superintendents were fired or principals removed to meet political issues that stretched beyond the school. If the principal or superintendent had been a strong supporter of the program, his/her loss (for reasons unrelated to the program) often signalled the decline of the program.

At two of the schools, the *physical facilities* were ill suited for the specific reform. Banks of computers, for example, require additional electrical wiring, air conditioning, and, in many neighborhoods, bars on windows. In another case, a high school was temporarily relocated to allow for extensive renovations. Perceived inequalities among the faculty [staff] regarding the allocation of space for the promising program versus non-program teachers caused ill will. The perception by non-program teachers that they got less desirable space caused a rift that never completely healed.

Finally, three schools suffered from one or more *management, communication, and scheduling problems.* Failure to resolve scheduling problems simply rendered a school change effort empty. Schools that could not overcome challenges related to student deportment [behaviour] were equally unsuccessful at implementing more demanding reforms.

Over the three years of *Special Strategies Studies* data gathering, every school in the study faced one or more of these ten potentially destabilizing issues. On occasion, this worked. Researchers recorded some examples of schools taking the 'problems are our friends' tack — that is, enthusiastically taking on each problem as a way both to make things better and build *esprit de corps*, noted by Louis and Miles (1990). A greater number of schools simply muddled through as best they could; and in several cases, one or more unresolved problems simply killed reforms that were working well in other schools.

The major point here can be derived from combining the information on ineffective schools with the information on attempted improvements. The ten destabilizing elements are, almost by definition, more prevalent in ineffective schools. Therefore, the task of moving ineffective schools to relative effectiveness becomes particularly challenging. At the very least, these are schools whose improvement efforts are highly vulnerable to external instability. Improvement in ineffective schools will require the careful, steady guidance of a diversity of supporting persons and institutions.

Needed: Highly Reliable Supports for Schools Becoming More Effective

As noted in LSES, ineffective schools often have *some* very good individual teachers. The schools simply are not able to deliver *consistently* good curricula and instruction. Similarly, the destabilizing forces noted in *Special Strategies Studies* could be viewed as threats, not to the validity of the various promising programs, but to the reliability of implementation and institutionalization.

For example, the Coalition of Essential Schools (CES; Sizer, 1984, 1996) has a history of interpreting local examples of inability to implement the goals of CES, not as a failure of the initiative, but as an indication of the size of the challenges associated with implementation (see MacMullen, 1996). An alternate interpretation of the same data would be that the particular reform has not yet put *reliable* implementation supports in place. Schools need *reliable* routes to success, not just theoretical routes.

There exists a literature of non-school organizations that have achieved remarkable levels of reliability, and on common characteristics of highly reliable organizations as they might apply to schools (Stringfield, 1995, in press). A brief discussion of each characteristic of High Reliability Organizations (HROs) follows, with implications for overcoming school ineffectiveness.

High reliability requires clarity regarding goals
No organization is highly reliable in a large number of areas at once. A near-paramount goal must be obtaining very high academic achievement levels for all students.

HROs evolve where there is a perception, held by the public and the organization's employees, that failures to achieve the organization's core goals would be disastrous
Not 'unfortunate', or 'a pity', the perception must be that failure would be *disastrous*. As discussed in the first section of this paper, the citizenry of the US is coming to view universal educational attainment as a much higher goal than at any time in our history. The potential to improve schooling reliability in the US has never before been so high.

HROs build powerful databases on dimensions highly relevant to their ability to achieve core goals
The data sets are relevant to core goals, are data-rich (with multiple cross-checks on key dimensions), are available in real time (e.g., when they would be useful to

a specific teacher, as opposed to at the convenience of the school system), and are regularly cross-checked by multiple concerned groups.[4] HROs gather data relevant to short- and long-term goals, and to the ongoing processes necessary to achieve them. Focusing on achieving these specific results, all aimed towards a few simple but challenging goals, is what keeps HROs reliable. Gathering diverse data relevant to core goals has also frequently been noted as a component of continuously improving schools (e.g., Schmoker, 1996).

High-reliability organizations are alert to surprises or lapses
Small failures that can cascade into major failures must be monitored carefully. All of us make dozens of mistakes a day. We succeed by catching those mistakes that could cascade into major problems before the cascades gain too much momentum. The clear goals and databases noted above become two of many tools necessary to ensure that all students achieve a reasonable percentage of their potentials. They help assure that when a student is falling behind he is quickly noted, and his problems addressed.

HROs extend formal, logical decision analysis as far as extant knowledge allows
Life in classrooms and schools is a continuous buzz. Lortie (1975) estimated that the average teacher is involved in over 1,200 different interactions with students and peers each school day. The only practical way to have any energy available to apply serious attention to potentially cascading problems is to achieve automaticity in many of the day's more repetitive tasks. That is, most things need to become routinized as a mental labour-saving mechanism. Exactly the same is true in other cognitively demanding fields, such as air traffic control. Furthermore, as in air traffic control or operation of hospital emergency rooms, it becomes critical that teams of professionals know, not just how they would act individually, but how the entire team will act. Standard Operating Procedures become devices which save the inevitably over-taxed intellectual skills of professionals operating in real time.

HROs also have initiatives that actively identify flaws and find improvements to Standard Operating Procedures
To say the least, this is a characteristic that was not shared by the majority of the negative outlier schools in LSES.

HROs recruit extensively, retrain constantly, and take performance evaluations seriously
Again, the contrast with ineffective schools is clear. The intellectual capacities of the professionals within an organization are invariably the organization's most valuable resources. Failure actively and continuously to strive to maximize those scarce resources is to guarantee unreliability, and eventually, ineffectiveness.

In HROs, monitoring is mutual without counterproductive loss of overall autonomy and confidence
Reliability cannot be achieved with each employee going into their room (classroom or office) and simply 'doing his or her job'. Reliability requires mutual

monitoring among professionals, and shared upgrading of skills. To become more reliable, schools do not have to move to physically 'open' classrooms; but they do have to move to open visitation, shared planning and teaching, and open discussion of 'what matters'.

HROs are hierarchically structured, but during times of peak load, HROs display a second layer of behavior that emphasizes collegial decision making regardless of rank

In every school every day, people of diverse ranks see things that need addressing. For example, it is patently ridiculous to pretend that a child who is falling behind in their reading skills is not being noticed by several people in a school. Like almost all other organizations, almost all schools and school districts have a formal hierarchical structure. The important thing is to allow the formal structure to 'go flat' when important information is gathered by a person who is not at the top.

HROs are invariably valued by their supervising organizations

A disturbingly common theme among the ineffective schools in the LSES was how rarely ineffective schools were visited by district personnel. It is human nature to try to avoid failure, but, at the same time, the route to success goes through multi-person attention to problems.

In HROs, short-term efficiency takes a back seat to very high reliability

Throughout *Special Strategies Studies*, chest-beating declarations by school boards or principals that they were going to 'bite the bullet' and 'make the tough cuts' and 'cut the fat' almost invariably had the unintended consequence of debilitating reform efforts. This is not to say that HROs cannot be run very efficiently; they can. It is to say that, in practice, where high reliability has been an achieved goal, attempts to make deep, arbitrary cuts in the name of efficiency have been successfully overruled. Thoughtful, long-term efficiency is a valuable, achievable goal. Short-term draconian cuts substantially reduce organizations' reliability, and those cuts kill school improvement efforts.

Summary

In a manner much less literary than Robert Burton's of three centuries ago, I write of school ineffectiveness, so that by being busy studying it I may help others avoid school ineffectiveness. Today, for the first time, we are evolving a research base on more and less effective schools, and on the conditions and actions necessary to create more effective schools. A few scholars have already begun the scientific design and implementation of more effective schooling for all students. The first reliable routes from a reasonably mapped terrain of ineffective schooling to an even better-mapped area of effective schooling have been drawn. While the maps must be improved, and while ever better routes must be explored and developed, we can look forward with a great deal of optimism knowing enough seriously to take on the historically unimaginable tasks of eradicating functional illiteracy and inadequate mathematical skills from virtually all school children, regardless of background. We can do this in our lifetimes. Then perhaps we can all avoid melancholy, without having to write about it.

Notes

1 In constant (inflation-adjusted) dollars.
2 Similar, though less detailed, descriptions of a smaller set of negative outlier schools have been provided by Venezky and Winfield (1979).
3 Prospects was a five-year, 40,000 student, longitudinal study designed to test the efficiency of additional federal support ('Chapter 1') on students' academic achievements.
4 The initial design of the Louisiana School Effectiveness Study called for a 'double blind', e.g., neither schools nor observers were to know whether any particular school was a positive or negative outlier. Furthermore, the schools were not to know that the study involved an outlier design. A letter to all schools in advance of our first data-gathering cycle inadvertently mentioned the outlier design. One of the more darkly amusing findings of the study was that the great majority of schools honestly believed that they were 'positive outliers'. In general, faculties of negative outlier schools have not gathered and analysed data in ways that allow them to understand that they are performing less well than their sociologically similar peer schools.

References

ADLER, M. (1982) *The Paideia Proposal: An Educational Manifesto*, New York: Macmillan.

ANDERSON, L., SEARS, J., PELLICER, L., RIDDLE, M., GARDNER, C. and HARWELL, D. (1992) *A Study of the Characteristics and Qualities of 'High-Flying' Compensatory Programs in South Carolina as Examined Through the Framework of the SERVE Model for Effective Compensatory Programs*, Columbia, SC, Department of Educational Leadership and Policies, University of South Carolina.

BROOKOVER, W.B., SCHWEITZER, J.H., SCHNEIDER, J.M., BEADY, C.H., FLOOD, P.K. and WISENBAKER, J.M. (1978) 'Elementary school social climate and school achievement', *American Educational Research Journal*, **15**, 2, pp. 301–18.

BURSTEIN, L. (ed.) (1992) *The IEA Study of Mathematics III: Student Growth and Classroom Processes*, New York: Pergamon.

COLEMAN, J., CAMPBELL, E., HOBSON, C., McPARTLAND, J., MOOD, A., WEINFIELD, F. and YORK, R. (1966) *Equality of Educational Opportunity*, Washington, DC: US Office of Education.

LEVINE, D. and LEZOTTE, L. (1990) *Unusually Effective Schools*, Madison, WI: National Center for Effective Schools R and D.

LORTIE, D.C. (1975) *School Teacher*, Chicago: University of Chicago Press.

LOUIS, K.S. and MILES, M.B. (1990) *Improving the Urban High School: What Works and Why*, New York: Teachers College Press.

MACMULLEN, M. (1996) *Taking Stock of a School Reform Effort: A Research Collection and Analysis*, (Occasional Paper No. 2), Providence, Rhode Island, Brown University.

MORTIMORE, P., SAMMONS, P., STOLL, L., LEWIS, D. and ECOB, R. (1988) *School Matters: The Junior Years*, Somerset: Open Books. (Reprinted 1994 by Paul Chapman, London.)

NESSELRODT, P., SCHAFFER, E. and STRINGFIELD, S. (1997) 'An examination of the disruption of Special Strategies Programs', in STRINGFIELD, S., MILLSAP, M., HERMAN, R., YODER, N., BRIGHAM, N., NESSELRODT, P., SCHAFFER, E., KARWEIT, N., LEVIN, M. and STEVENS, R. (eds) *Special Strategies Studies Final Report*, Washington, DC: US Department of Education.

PUMA, M., JONES, C., ROCK, D. and FERNANDEZ, R. (1993) *Prospects: The Congressionally Mandated Study of Educational Growth and Opportunity: Interim Report*, Washington, DC: US Department of Education.

REICH, R.B. (1992) *The Work of Nations*, New York: Random House.

SCHMOKER, M. (1996) *Results: The Key to Continuous School Improvement*, Alexandria, VA: Association for Supervision and Curriculum Development.

SIZER, T.R. (1984) *Horace's Compromise: The Dilemma of the American High School*, Boston: Houghton Mifflin.

SIZER, T.R. (1996) *Horace's Hope*, New York: Houghton Mifflin.

SLAVIN, R.E., KARWEIT, N.L. and MADDEN, N.A. (eds) (1989) *Effective Programs for Students at Risk*, Boston: Allyn and Bacon.

SLAVIN, R.E., MADDEN, N.A., DOLAN, L.J., WASIK, B.A., ROSS, S., SMITH, L. and DIANDA, M. (1996) 'Success for all: A summary of research', *Journal of Education for Students Placed at Risk*, **1**, 1, pp. 41–76.

STALLINGS, J.A. (1980) 'Allocated academic learning time revisited, or beyond time on task', *Educational Researcher*, **9**, 11, pp. 11–16.

STRINGFIELD, S. (1994) 'Outlier studies of school effectiveness', in REYNOLDS, D., CREEMERS, B., NESSELRODT, P., SCHAFFER, E., STRINGFIELD, S. and TEDDLIE, C. (eds) *Advances in School Effectiveness Research*, Oxford: Pergamon.

STRINGFIELD, S. (1995) 'Attempts to enhance students' learning: A search for valid programs and highly reliable implementation techniques', *School Effectiveness and School Improvement*, **6**, 1, pp. 67–96.

STRINGFIELD, S. (in press) 'Underlying the chaos of factors explaining exemplary US elementary schools: The case for high reliability organizations', in TOWNSEND, T. (ed.) *Restructuring and Quality: Problems and Possibilities for Tomorrow's Schools*, London: Routledge.

STRINGFIELD, S., MILLSAP, M. and HERMAN, R. (in press) 'Using "promising programs" to improve educational processes and student outcomes', in HARGREAVES, A., FULLAN, M., LIEBERMAN, A. and HOPKINS, D. (eds) *International Handbook of Educational Change*, Hingham, MA: Kluwer.

STRINGFIELD, S., MILLSAP, M., HERMAN, R., YODER, N., BRIGHAM, N., NESSELRODT, P., SCHAFFER, E., KARWEIT, N., LEVIN, M. and STEVENS, R. (1997) *Special Strategies Studies Final Report*, Washington, DC: US Department of Education.

STRINGFIELD, S. and TEDDLIE, C. (1991) 'Observers as predictors of schools' multi-year outlier status', *Elementary School Journal*, **91**, 4, pp. 357–76.

TEDDLIE, C., KIRBY, P. and STRINGFIELD, S. (1989) 'Effective vs. ineffective schools: Observable differences in the classroom', *American Journal of Education*, **97**, 3, pp. 221–36.

TEDDLIE, C. and STRINGFIELD, S. (1993) *Schools Make a Difference: Lessons Learned from a 10-Year Study of School Effects*, New York: Teachers College Press.

VENEZKY, R.L. and WINFIELD, L.F. (1979) 'Schools that succeed beyond expectations in reading' (Technical Report No. 1), *Studies in Education*, Newark, University of Delaware. (ERIC Document Reproduction Service No. ED 177 484.)

WEBER, G. (1971) *Inner City Children Can Be Taught to Read: Four Successful Schools*, (Occasional Paper No. 18), Washington, DC: Council for Basic Education.

Chapter 16

Combating Failure at School: An International Perspective

Karen Kovacs

Introduction

In 1994, the Organisation for Economic Co-operation and Development (OECD[1]) launched a three-year activity on educational failure. The most important outcomes were four country-hosted seminars, in which national representatives exchanged points of view about key issues for policy development in this area. A final report drew together previous OECD work on this topic; expert and country contributions; as well as case studies and statistical analyses related to failure in different national contexts. The conclusions of this work will be disseminated in two OECD publications (forthcoming, 1997a and 1997b). This chapter presents the main findings of the activity on 'Combating Failure at School' and therefore draws on the knowledge and expertise of all those who participated in it.[2] The views expressed here, however, are those of the author and do not necessarily represent the point of view of member governments.

An Old Problem in a New Context

Although there is a great diversity of views among countries as to what form 'failure' takes and how it may be defined, there is a common worry that education systems are underperforming, leading to a significant level of underachievement by young people, and thus threatening economic competitiveness and social cohesion. The reasons for this perception of failure seem to be two-fold:

1   Structural adjustment has brought about a fundamental change in the relationship between education and the labour market. The knowledge and qualifications thresholds for jobs have risen; so have youth unemployment rates and earnings differentials related to levels of educational attainment (OECD, 1994). In addition, as a result of rapid technological change, the skills needed to function competently in everyday adult life are very different today than they were one or two decades ago.

2   Globalization of the world economy has brought about a fundamental policy shift in education. While in the post-war period, the focus was on

the quantitative expansion of learning opportunities, today it has shifted — in most countries — to improvement in the quality and accountability of educational outcomes. Behind this policy shift lies the need to have a well-prepared and flexible labour force in order to remain competitive.

The renewed emphasis on 'combating failure' in many OECD countries re-flects a concern about the increasingly punitive nature of low educational and skills attainment in post-industrial, service and information economies: 'more than ever before, failure at school begets social failure, which in turn threatens social integration' (Eurydice, 1994, p. 9). Recent studies show that while some 15–20 per cent of young people in these countries leave secondary school without the necessary skills and qualifications to enter into the labour market (OECD, 1994), one third of the adult population in seven advanced economies performs at levels of literacy and numeracy which are below those needed for employment (OECD and Statistics Canada, 1995). There is also a heavy financial burden for educational systems themselves. For example, in 1984, France estimated it allocated 30 per cent of its education budget to costs arising from failure at school (due to grade repeaters and drop-outs), and the French Community of Belgium has estimated its educational expenditure could be cut by around 10 per cent if the practice of grade retention was abolished (see Eurydice, 1994).

Despite the different guises that failure takes in diverse educational cultures, policy-makers face a similar challenge: improving strategies for tackling the problem. In order to do so, educational authorities need to address four key issues:

1 a recognition of the problem;
2 a clear understanding of its multi-faceted nature;
3 strengthening the quantitative knowledge base for policy development in this area; and
4 identifying best practice in order to improve dissemination of 'what works' in combating failure.

This chapter begins with a brief discussion of these four key issues. It then centres on the last two issues, by examining specific indicators of failure and comparing different country approaches to overcome it. Finally, it draws out general policy considerations and challenges for addressing failure. Although the discussion which follows is based on experience in OECD countries, the policy implications are intended to be more widely applicable.

Key Issues for Addressing Failure

It is important to start by commenting on the argument that the concept of failure is unhelpful because it makes the problem worse, by stigmatizing a student or organization and therefore destroying their morale and self-confidence or reputation. In the case of individual students, there is an obvious need not to damage their potentially fragile confidence by labelling them in a way that they will find oppressive. The labelling of institutional failure is the cause of much controversy. The argument advanced in those countries where schools have been publicly labelled as 'failing', is that such schools have lost their ability to improve themselves, and indeed often refuse to accept they could do any better. In these circumstances, the argument runs, the shock of being publicly labelled 'failing' is a necessary first step towards galvanizing the school into action.

Although there are some signs that this approach is working in those OECD countries where it has been adopted, there is also evidence, for example from Education Priority Zones (ZEPs) in France, that designation of a school as part of a priority zone may prompt parents to send their children elsewhere. Because of this, some countries (e.g., Australia, Denmark, Finland and Italy, among others) prefer to refer to measures for the 'success' of students and schools. Independently of whether policies intended to raise the level of achievement are framed in positive or negative terms, large numbers of students leaving a country's education system with poor or no qualifications must, by any standards, be considered a failure.

Recognition of the Problem

Acknowledging the existence of such problems is the first step towards solving them, and action at an earlier rather than later stage may well be more cost-effective as well as advantageous academically. From this point of view, failure can actually be a positive concept. It is worth quoting a rather similar point made in the OECD Report *Our Children at Risk* (OECD, 1995a): 'The concept of *at risk* is an optimistic one if it moves the debate forward by recognising the transactional nature of much learning. In the educational context this means that the right educational experiences over time can help to compensate for disadvantage and optimise the chances of success of all pupils' (p. 19). Similarly, facing up to failure is the necessary, positive prelude to the development of policies for helping the students affected by it.

Understanding the Problem's Multi-faceted Nature

Successful policy development also requires an understanding of the complex nature of this phenomenon. Failure is the product of the interaction of many variables:

- *psychological* — student based (various forms of special educational need, adolescent developmental problems);
- *socio-cultural* — related to students' homes and social background (ethnic minority or migrant background, low income, etc.); and
- *institutional* — school based (inappropriate teaching methods, inadequate resources, poor curriculum).

Researchers have attempted to provide overarching explanations of educational failure by stressing the 'causal effect' of such psychological, socio-cultural or institutional variables; and these three approaches have had an impact on the development of different policy trends.

Psychological explanations

The first attempts to understand the low educational attainment of some students were framed in *psychological* terms. There are two main variants of such psychological explanations: genetic and psycho-affective. The genetic explanation is the longest standing explanation of failure at school. This relates school achievement to cognitive factors, which it claims are inherited but are also affected by the child's early environment. The development of IQ tests has stimulated renewed debate in recent years, following various attempts to restate a cause–effect link of inheritance and social behaviour. The psycho-affective approach explains learning difficulties of slow learners in relation to conflicts within the family. Both of these explanations gave rise to separate provision of remedial education.

Socio-cultural explanations

On the other hand, *socio-cultural* explanations have claimed that the root of educational failure lies in the 'cultural disadvantage' of specific social groups. Furthermore, they have argued that since schools do not respond to the special needs of these groups, they reproduce social inequality and, by doing so, schools themselves help to increase the initial 'disadvantages' of such students. These explanations, which developed in opposition to the psychological theories, correspondingly gave rise to a policy approach for addressing the social factors associated with failure at school: compensatory programmes.

Institutional explanations

Finally, more recent explanations of failure — *centred on the school* — have looked at what happens inside the institution in terms of relationships and processes; and have identified teacher expectations, their interaction with students and school leadership as key factors for determining educational outcomes. In particular, an influential school effectiveness paradigm has developed as a reaction to the literature on genetics and the socio-cultural approach. While this paradigm has attracted considerable interest amongst policy makers, it has its limitations: there is no single, universally applicable set of effective school characteristics,[3] and a review of the literature suggests that school factors account for, at most, some 25 per cent of the variance in student performance. Although this is still significant in policy terms, it does put the effort to change schools into perspective. School-based explanations have given rise to three types of measures for addressing failure: integration of assessment into the teaching process; differentiated learning; and school improvement.

Policy implications of explanations

Today, there is a shared recognition among researchers that no single explanation of educational failure can be satisfactory. It has been accepted that failure is a multi-dimensional problem, which can be viewed from different perspectives: psychological, social and institutional. This realization has had two consequences, which are crucial for policy development in this area:

- an emphasis on the relative nature of failure, since it is a phenomenon which is closely associated with the general culture of a society and, especially, with its educational culture and organization; and
- an acknowledgment that no single policy can be suitable to address different dimensions and contexts of failure.

Need to Develop Quantitative Evidence

Conceptual clarification cannot, however, by itself improve the approaches for tackling educational failure. There is also an urgent need to develop reliable indicators of failure. Even though there exists a vast research literature on this topic, such indicators are scanty since: the problem is defined differently in different countries; some of its manifestations do not easily lend themselves to quantitative analysis; and international comparisons of educational outcomes have only recently become an important policy focus. But conceptual and methodological hurdles (regarding the interpretation and comparability of the data) must not stop the effort to strengthen the quantitative knowledge base on the various dimensions of failure, as well as on the outcomes of different measures for improving the academic performance of students. Availability of comparable information on educational achievement — gathered both at the national and international levels — is crucial for developing better policies in this field, as good policies depend on reliable data, and efficient resource targeting depends on the right evidence.

Identification of Good Practice

Lastly, successful policy making implies disseminating best practice. Research, as well as country experience, have shown that this depends on effective monitoring and evaluation of 'what works'. In the field of combating failure, however, very few policies have been systematically monitored or fully evaluated. Comparing what countries are doing to identify, prevent and remedy different aspects of failure constitutes a necessary step for evaluating the adequacy of the different solutions developed to overcome this problem. Furthermore, the latter is a necessary condition for disseminating those policies for the success of all students, while bearing in mind the difficulties of generalizing from experiences that are often context bound.

Lessons from Indicators of Failure

Although many factors have been associated with educational failure in different OECD member states, only a few have been surveyed on a sufficiently comparable basis for an analysis of the findings to be possible across countries. It has also been extremely difficult to develop indicators for different manifestations of failure in the OECD area. Furthermore, evaluating the progress made in addressing low student achievement in diverse national contexts has not proved to be an easy task.

These three issues will be discussed here, by examining the main conclusions of a 'statistical portrait' of failure, created on the basis of existing data sources (national and international).[4] Even though the indicators developed for this portrait[5] address failure *indirectly*, the findings reported below make it possible to draw important policy lessons about:

- specific factors related to failure;
- different manifestations of the problem, such as early school leaving and failure to acquire the knowledge and skills needed for successful entry into the labour market; and
- the outcomes of different measures intended to address divergence in student performance.

Specific Factors Related to Failure

Different factors have been used to account for the 'vulnerability' of students to failure. Evidence on student achievement in the OECD area makes it possible to draw the following conclusions about three of these factors:

1 *Young people who belong to a disadvantaged socio-economic group are at significant risk of failing in all countries.* Social differences continue to be an important source of disparities for student achievement, notwithstanding the considerable efforts undertaken by the education systems to guarantee 'equal opportunities' for all. In the absence of a reliable (and internationally comparable) SES indicator, it is virtually impossible to assess what progress has been made — in different countries — in reducing the risk of failure arising from this source. For example, to what extent has the development of mass secondary education in nearly all OECD member states reduced the risk of failure for the most disadvantaged pupils? Are there countries which, as a result of their educational structures or teaching practices, are more successful than others in compensating for a disadvantaged social background? Have the widening income disparities and high levels of unemployment — recorded in several OECD member governments over the past decade — further exposed the most vulnerable social groups to failure?

2 *Differences between the sexes are more acute in the weakest group of pupils than in the rest of the population.* In most countries, there are more boys than girls in the group of pupils with the lowest reading scores, but

the reverse is true of mathematics and science subjects. Although a tendency has been observed over the past few decades for gender differences to become less marked, *major differences remain at both ends of the distribution.* Clearly efforts to combat such differences have not yet borne fruit.

3   The education systems in many OECD member states are confronted with *the specific problem of students from an immigrant background, whose mother tongue is different from the language of the classroom.* The linguistic handicap experienced by these students is often compounded by a second, socio-economic handicap. The size, ethnic origin, and social status of these minorities differ from one country to the next, so that comparisons are difficult. However, there is a trend that might warrant a more detailed analysis. Under some education systems (in British Columbia, for example), there seems to be less risk of poor reading skills being associated with membership of a linguistic minority, even though the minorities in question do not seem to enjoy any better social status than those in other countries (such as New Zealand, France or Sweden). *The special structures that have been set up to facilitate the integration of these pupils may well be more effective in some cases than in others.* Different characteristics of the immigrant population would, however, have to be taken into account when making such comparisons.

Manifestations of Failure

Economic competitiveness has led educational authorities to focus on two important manifestations of failure: early school leaving; and the fact that a significant proportion of students finish compulsory education without having acquired the necessary skills to enter into the labour market. But, paradoxically, obtaining reliable data on these problems — that are nationally representative and/or internationally comparable — is particularly difficult.

The limitations of statistics concerning the school drop-out rate and the number of pupils obtaining secondary leaving certificates make it difficult to gauge the dimensions of this phenomenon. However, an analysis of educational indicators for the OECD region, as well as of a recent survey on adult literacy in some OECD countries reflects three important findings:

1   The greatest risks of marginalization, unemployment, or low income are no longer confined to those who have failed to complete primary or lower secondary education. In most countries, it now seems that it is not until young people have completed at least upper secondary education that their chances of finding employment significantly improve.
2   Amongst those who drop out of school, approximately twice as many cite reasons over which they had no control (institutional pressures, economic need and family reasons) as those who say they left out of personal choice (boredom, lack of interest in education, desire to take up employment).

3   Even if students who leave before the end of compulsory school do obtain jobs fairly quickly, these are often only short-lived or low paid. They may be enough to tempt them away from education, especially in areas of high unemployment, but often turn out to be dead ends. Furthermore, a characteristic likely to be common to all early school leavers is poor motivation towards formal education. This reduces the chance that they will re-enter education later in their lives. In addition, indifference or resistance to education is an economic liability at a time when the labour market increasingly requires a continual updating of skills and competences of the labour force.

The identification of those students whose foundation skills are insufficient for their social and productive integration into modern society has not proved easy either. However, an International Adult Literacy Survey (IALS), carried out in seven OECD countries, has produced disquieting evidence in this respect. Data from IALS show that the reading and numeracy skills young people actually need in order to be able to solve the problems with which they are confronted in their everyday lives, or at the workplace, correspond to the level expected — in principle — from people having completed upper secondary education. Yet, in virtually all countries surveyed, there is a significant proportion of people with upper secondary qualifications (and in some cases even with post-secondary qualifications) whose reading skills are below this level. This calls into question the real value of the qualifications obtained. The findings justify the efforts undertaken in some countries (for example, the United Kingdom and the United States) to specify more closely the standards or levels of skills young people need to have attained by the time they finish compulsory education.

Measures of Address Divergence in Achievement

Regardless of the source of the difficulties some pupils experience with the proposed curricula, there is a great difference — in all OECD education systems — between the level attained by the weakest 25 per cent of students and the level attained by the strongest 25 per cent of students in the same grade. *Generally, the difference is equivalent to more than two years of schooling irrespective of the subject considered; and in some countries, it amounts to as much as five years of schooling.* In order to address this divergence in achievement, OECD countries have adopted three main measures:

- *first*, granting slower students more time in which to learn, by requiring them *to repeat one or more grades*. Available data suggest that this approach shifts the gap without actually reducing it;
- *second*, guiding students towards different curricula or streams according to their ability. In countries where this approach has been adopted in the most consistent manner (Germany, Switzerland and the Netherlands), it

would seem that more students considered to be 'at risk' succeed in obtaining upper secondary qualifications, and therefore may have less difficulty in finding employment. At the same time, however, differences between schools are accentuated, insofar as the weakest students (who are often also from a disadvantaged background and/or belong to a linguistic minority) tend to be concentrated in certain schools. The aggregation effects of this approach may have a negative impact, by widening the gap between lowest and highest achievers;

* *third*, maintaining all students in a common curriculum for as long as possible, by setting up remedial measures to help the weakest students. The Scandinavian education systems are a good example of this model, characterized by high levels of care and attention for children with special educational needs, automatic promotion to the next grade until the age of 12 or 14, lower secondary education based essentially on the comprehensive model, and very little difference between schools in terms of their performance. The results recorded for Sweden by IALS suggest that an approach based on the Swedish model could reduce the marginalization effects associated with failure at school, provided it is applied consistently over a long period and is coupled with an active adult continuing training policy.

Lessons from Policy Practice

Education systems have attempted to address the different dimensions of failure through a broad range of policies. The purpose here is to review selected country examples in order to understand the underlying rationales of different approaches. Policies aimed at the system and school levels, as well as various forms of programme assistance, are considered.

Systemic Reforms

An apparent initial choice in dealing with educational failure is whether to tackle it through remedial measures or prevention. Most country policies actually identified for combating failure tend to fall into the remedial category. Remedial measures take the form of programmes which can be fairly closely targeted at specific problems or groups, and are easier to track and evaluate with respect to these targets. Such measures also are more transparent, in that they are seen as attacking the immediate issue. The evident drawback is they do not prevent failure in the first place and do not address the causes of failure within the system. It is this latter point that has led to a rethinking of policy approach.

While there has been a tendency to address failure specifically through targeted programmes (for the reasons identified), authorities are giving new attention to action which is systemic in reach and orientation. This approach is a means to tackle those aspects of structures and practices that are not supportive of success for all and, at worst, actually contribute to failure. There are acknowledged difficulties in this respect with systemic approaches: they may be more expensive, applying to all schools and programmes; and improvements generated through systemic reform may provide most benefits to those young people who are already doing well. Thus, in practice, most countries will use a combination of both approaches.

Improving the provision of pre-school education, the extension of compulsory schooling, and curriculum reform are three examples of system-level intervention strategies applied to tackle different dimensions of failure.

Early years of education

While there is clear evidence that pupils who receive pre-school education start primary school with a discernible advantage over other pupils, it remains a matter of debate how long this effect persists. At this early stage of a child's development, however, it may be unrealistic to try and distinguish a distinct educational benefit. First, young children learn in an holistic way, oblivious of boundaries between education and other forms of achievement. Second, education is concerned with more than academic achievement: acquisition of social, moral and cultural values is generally recognized as of great importance, and trying to measure the impact of this type of pre-school education into later life is problematic. Third, one of the great gains from the early years of education is the development of aspiration, motivation and self-esteem, which are intangible benefits.

Although the provision of early childhood education has increased in most OECD countries, strengthening the knowledge base for this level of schooling is needed in order to meet the expanding demand, while assuring the quality and effectiveness of such programmes. The evidence shows that the early years of schooling — including pre-school education and early intervention programmes at the primary level — are crucial for foundation learning, especially in the case of disadvantaged children (OECD, 1996a).

Extension of compulsory schooling

High rates of participation in education have made it possible to extend the age for compulsory schooling. Although the upper limit is still 14 years in four OECD member countries, it has been raised to 15 in ten countries, 16 in twelve countries, and there are two countries where this limit is higher (17 years in the United States and 18 in Belgium). Although the proportion of young people actually remaining at school until the age of 17 or 18 can exceed 80 or 90 per cent, even in countries where the upper limit for compulsory schooling is 16 or below, the education systems with a higher upper limit succeed in keeping more young people at school until the end of upper secondary education. This argues for raising the age for completing compulsory education in those countries where it is lowest.

Curriculum reform

This manifests itself in a variety of ways, and it is helpful to identify three aspects: content, ethos and structure. Regarding *reform of content*, one of the more comprehensive examples of this in recent years has been the National Curriculum phased in since 1988 in England and Wales, designed as a deliberate response to concerns about school standards. Substantial curriculum reforms have also taken place in Finland, Norway, Portugal and Sweden, but these have been less detailed, less comprehensive or less rapid. The curriculum reform in the UK provides a lesson in the practical difficulties of engineering so wide ranging a change.

Such a far-reaching exercise will be a relatively rare event in most countries (although a number of east European countries have revised their curricula extensively after the dissolution of the Eastern Bloc). More usual is a limited reform measure addressing a particular subject or theme; for instance, all OECD education systems in recent years have had to accommodate the need to teach information technology. The OECD Report *Changing the Subject* (1996b) examines the way in which many countries have altered the teaching of mathematics, technology and science to meet new demands, often impelled by worries about economic competitiveness. But content reform can be expensive. It can also be controversial, especially if it affects a culturally sensitive area like language, and it can provide a solution to only a relatively limited range of problems.

A second curricular approach to the problem of failure is *a change to the ethos or objectives of the curriculum*. A good example of this is the reworking of the Japanese curriculum initiated in recent years in response to concerns that excessive rigidity, narrowness of curriculum and limited teaching style were causing students to drop out of the upper secondary system. The priority was to change underlying attitudes about the purpose of education, and so make schools more attractive to students, engaging their enthusiasm and giving them a sense of fulfilment. This required a more open-minded and flexible approach on the part of teachers and schools to cater for the diversity of students' abilities, interests, concerns and career paths, reinforced by a series of specific measures to broaden curricula, widen learning opportunities and introduce a more participatory approach to lessons. While organizational changes were a part of this reform package, including the introduction of a new 'integrated course' and measures to restrict grade repetition, the key element was a change in the objectives and ethos of the system.

A third curricular response to the problem of low pupil achievement is *reform of structure*: of the administration of the educational system, of examinations and accreditation systems, of scholastic structures, and so on. This kind of change is familiar to all education systems. Recent examples have been the restructuring of education into cycles of learning[6] in Belgium (French Community) and Spain, and the restructuring of the baccalaureate in France and Spain.

Although this three-fold distinction between different types of curricular reform is helpful for descriptive purposes, when it comes to practical implementation the boundaries are not so clear cut. A recent OECD Report (OECD, 1996b) observes the growing awareness amongst policy makers of a need to approach such reforms in an holistic way, so that curriculum changes also encompass teacher education, new approaches to student assessment, and new instruction materials.

School Level Interventions

School-level interventions are based on the premise that schools are responsible for the standards their pupils achieve and are capable of improving them. School improvement has become the main policy focus of measures addressing failure in the component nations of the UK (although there are considerable differences between the four of these), New Zealand and Australia. Some US states and Canadian provinces have also embraced this approach.

While there is evidence that other factors profoundly affect pupil achievement — prior learning and, above all, social factors — policies to improve school effectiveness offer a relatively direct means of affecting pupil outcomes. They also serve the additional purpose of promoting the accountability of educational institutions, in an age of concern over educational standards and pressures on public budgets.

The ability of schools to make a difference will depend to a considerable extent on the degree of autonomy they enjoy, particularly in financial, staffing and curricular matters. In the countries where the focus on school failure is strongest — New Zealand and the United Kingdom — the degree of autonomy is very great, engineered in the former by the abolition of regional education boards, and in the latter by the mandatory delegation of funding and responsibility from local education authorities. It seems likely that the bestowing of greater autonomy on schools will develop in tandem with expectations of greater school accountability. One example is the recent pilot experiment in Denmark by which premises and staffing decisions were delegated to seven pilot institutions required them to demonstrate, in exchange, greater user satisfaction as measured by an external institute.

Although those countries that have pioneered the institutional approach have in some cases made provision for dramatic intervention, in practice a spectrum of intervention exists, and the preference has been to rely on a mixture of deterrence, persuasion and support. Common to all of these is the requirement that the school produces an action plan for recovery. In decreasing order of severity, the means of intervention are:

- School closure. UK ministers used their powers to close the one school in England in which they intervened, after a review judged it beyond recovery. Similar powers in New Zealand have not yet been used.
- To take control of the school. Powers exist in New Zealand for central government to replace the school board with a single commissioner; in England and Wales, for the appointment of an 'education association' (a group of at least five people) to assume the responsibilities of the school's governing body. In practice, these powers have been used very sparingly: three times in five years in New Zealand, and only once in England and Wales. However, the possibility of central government intervention in itself

provides a powerful incentive for the school to regenerate itself. At the time of writing, in England in particular, ministers have quite explicitly used these powers principally as a deterrent, and have limited themselves to only one (highly publicized) intervention, despite the identification of some 200 'failing schools'. According to the Conservative Government, the pattern of recovery emerging at these 'failing schools' appeared to justify this restrained approach [see Michael Stark's chapter]. A similar form of intervention exists in Kentucky, where a fall of more than 5 per cent in a school's test results leads to its designation as a school 'in crisis'. This triggers the suspension of the tenure of its staff and the appointment of specially trained 'Kentucky distinguished educators' who evaluate the staff and decide whether they should remain, be transferred to other schools, or be dismissed.

- The school is effectively put on probation, and allowed a chance to improve itself. In New Zealand, an adverse report on a school leads to a warning and return visits by inspectors. In England and Wales, provided central government considers the recovery plan adequate, the school is allowed to implement it and inspectors return every term to monitor progress. In Kentucky, a fall in test results of less than 5 per cent does not trigger intervention, but an improvement plan must be produced and the school has access to a special school improvement fund.

- A 'quality assurance' model, as exists in Scotland, where national standards and performance indicators are published by the inspectorate, and a sample of schools are visited each year, leading to a published report with recommendations. There is a repeat visit by inspectors twelve to eighteen months later, with further visits if the school causes concern, but no powers of intervention.

Although school improvement has been recognized as an important policy issue by all OECD member states, some of them favour concentrating on policies aiming to improve the education system as a whole. In the context of this debate, three tensions are evident. One is the tension between promoting success through self-improvement on the one hand, and inspiring fear through the threat of intervention on the other. Allied to this is the possible tension between a culture of trust implicit in self-improvement, and the element of control that clearly exists in such approaches. A third tension is that between the 'top–down' and 'bottom–up' approaches to improvement.

Programme Assistance

Programmes to overcome educational failure take two main forms: *targeted projects* and *network development*. The former are the traditional response of government to an educational problem through provision of extra resources for a specific purpose, sometimes made subject to a bidding system, and usually with an evaluation mechanism attached. OECD countries have used such intervention projects at differing levels:

- *regional*: for example, the 500+ Priority Education Zones (ZEPs) in France, which provide additional staff and remedial measures in areas where social conditions are judged to constitute a 'risk factor';
- *institutional*: for example, Northern Ireland's 'Raising School Standards Initiative', which has provided extra resources to some 100 schools with particular disadvantages, under the condition they present action plans for their own improvement;
- *pupil-targeted*: the many examples of this kind of initiative include special measures taken in Ireland and Portugal to help 'traveller children'; Australia's 'National Equity Programme for Schools' (NEPS) which, through programmes agreed with education authorities, provides funds for specific 'target groups' of pupils at risk of failure, largely because of their social background; and the New Zealand government's special programmes to meet the special needs of Pacific Island and Maori pupils.

An alternative approach has become popular, however: the *network approach*. This seems to have been practised quite extensively at the institutional level, with the development of school improvement networks in the US and the UK, whose establishment has often been facilitated by academic institutions. Increasingly, there are examples of it being used by OECD member governments. Italy's 'Quality in Schools' initiative is based on networks of schools — organized around a 'pivot school' — to promote teacher training and reduce the schools' sense of isolation. Local networks of schools are also a component of Australia's 'National Schools Network' and New Zealand's 'Schools Support Project'.

The targeted project approach has obvious advantages for governments. If the problem is an acute one, which excites public attention, a targeted project meets public demand for the government to do something direct and immediate. 'Reading recovery' projects, pioneered in New Zealand, have been adopted in a number of OECD countries under just such political circumstances. Governments can, if they wish to do so, constitute projects so that they can exercise close control over them by attaching conditions to funding. This element of direct control makes it relatively easy to evaluate progress, and to alter or shape the development of the project in the light of experience.

The network approach has the advantage of offering a different mode of involvement to those who deliver the intervention; usually teachers, ancillary pedagogical staff and inspectors. While projects tend to adopt a top–down approach, networks tend to be more collaborative and participative. This makes them particularly valuable for the purpose of professional development, since it is a feature of the teaching profession that teachers particularly value the direct experience of other teachers in similar circumstances. By encouraging contact and debate, a network can create a 'wave' effect, encouraging subsidiary voluntary activities by participants. The

Italian 'Quality in Schools' project particularly emphasizes the value of the spontaneous participation of schools and its effect on raising the motivation of teachers. This can make networks a cost-effective form of intervention. The drawback to a network approach — from the policy maker's viewpoint — is that it may be less easy to track the activity as it develops; and the internal dynamics of networks can also divert their activities away from the areas on which the programme was designed to concentrate. However, there is some country experience, for example the 'Education Priorities Programme' in the Netherlands, where steps have been taken to 'steer' networks of schools.

General Policy Considerations and Challenges

Overcoming failure requires a sustained and long-term effort to meet the needs of all students, especially low achievers, through different combinations of three main approaches — systemic, institutional and programmatic — which are determined by specific national contexts. In spite of the wide range of measures adopted across countries, there are some general policy considerations for the development of such measures.

Educational Reform Needs to Raise Public Awareness

A fundamental barrier to addressing failure at school is public misperception. This can take various forms, such as cultural attachment to measures of scholastic achievement that mask failure during the schooling process, or to beliefs which reinforce it. Examples of the former are the importance that public opinion in Spain and, even more so, in Japan attaches to university entrance exams. Examples of the latter arise in countries, such as Belgium, where slow learners repeat one or several years of study, in spite of the evidence that grade repeating has a negative effect on student performance (particularly in the case of disadvantaged students).

While such misperceptions can hinder the implementation of measures to combat failure, they can be overcome. Factors which have proved significant in this respect include:

- findings of an inspectorate which informs opinion (the Academies of France, the Office for Standards in Education in the UK and the Education Review Office of New Zealand are examples of such institutions);
- reports of investigative commissions which raise public awareness about the social and economic consequences of failure (such as Japan's National Council on Educational Reform and the Ontario Royal Commission on Learning); and
- the availability of information on student achievement, at a national and international level.

Successful Initiatives Depend on a Clear Understanding of the Respective Roles of National, Provincial/State, Municipal and School Levels

This is particularly, but not exclusively, true of multidisciplinary initiatives such as pre-school provision. Also, pressures for school accountability must be matched by appropriate measurements and the authority to implement change. In particular, performance data need to be viewed against the local context within which the school works, and schools must be given the freedom — over finance and staffing, for example — to make decisions to improve the quality of the education they provide. The onus for initiating action, however, should lie with the authority with overall responsibility for running the system. A national framework for the implementation of local measures for combating failure is necessary in order to avoid policy fragmentation, and the feedback between the system and school levels needs to be ongoing.

Combating Failure Requires an 'Holistic' Approach

The factors that cause failure are deeply intertwined: factors within the education system — curriculum, structure, certification, accountability, quality of teaching, school-level factors — and factors outside, notably the socio-economic backgrounds of students. Individual initiatives can have effect — targeted programmes, for instance, or institutional improvement — but to be most effective, strategies addressing failure must work within the framework of an 'holistic approach' to the problem. They have to be integrated with parallel social and economic initiatives for social equality, implemented at the national, regional and local levels (OECD, 1996c).

In the last decades, the creation of genuinely equal opportunities across different branches and institutional settings of education and training have been promoted through various types of compensatory policies directed at specific schools (priority areas), student populations (multicultural policies), or individual pupils (remedial courses). Although the separate provision of special education programmes and compensatory measures might be called for in certain contexts, experience has proven that 'they may well become much more effective once embedded in the mainstream culture of the system' (OECD, forthcoming, 1997c).

The Active Participation of Teachers and Parents Is Crucial to Tackling Failure

Policy makers need the support of different actors involved in education: parents and students themselves; school leaders and teachers; families and communities. The active participation of the teacher is particularly important. Teachers need to take a part in identifying failure and devising ways of addressing it; this should be seen as a key facet of their professional development. Ideally, teacher organizations should place themselves in the vanguard of such initiatives, which will be in the long-term interests of their members. This needs to be supported by policy action to improve the professional conditions of teachers, and reward those who teach in less favoured areas, subjects and branches.

Regarding parental involvement in education, it is worthwhile to mention a growing trend in this respect in many countries. Two key methods of involving parents in schools can be found: reforms that aim to include parents in school governance (Denmark, England and Wales, and Spain are good examples), and systems that enable parents better to support their children's learning — either at home or in school — by assisting them in extra-curricular activities or, even in some countries, in the classroom (two countries which pursue this policy, especially regarding disadvantaged students, are France and Ireland). An effort should be made to evaluate the effect of these different approaches on student outcomes, particularly for those sectors of the population with learning difficulties (OECD, 1997).

A Variety of Support Systems Are Needed to Combat Failure

Developing supportive frameworks for children from birth through to their integration into the workplace should be one of the main aims of policy action in this field (OECD, 1995a, p. 144). Wider provision of a high-quality pre-school education is crucial for pupils at risk to acquire the basic skills during their primary years. The transition points throughout the whole schooling process also have to be facilitated; particularly the transition from school to work, since drop-out rates increase in the later years of education.

The role of educational and career guidance is also very important in this respect. While it has been acknowledged that 'poor guidance' can be especially harmful in the case of the least advantaged students (by reinforcing damaging stereotypes), it has been recognized that it is precisely this sector of the student population which could potentially benefit most from 'efficient guidance services' (for a fuller discussion on this topic, see OECD, 1996d).

Effective Action Against Failure Requires an Increasingly Sophisticated Range of Pedagogical Techniques

The recognition that teaching is the core requirement for the realization of a high-quality education for all is not new. Yet an urgent need persists to reduce the lag between advances in pedagogy and their application in the classroom. More flexible means of supporting students should replace such rigid approaches as grade repetition, and the mastery of differentiated teaching and formative assessment by teachers is crucial for improving student achievement. Furthermore, the role and function of the teacher has to be conceptualized in a new way: she or he cannot continue to be a 'knowledge transmitter' who helps students to obtain a diploma for life. Rather, the teacher has to become an 'attentive guide' who stimulates the curiosity, perseverance, flexibility and adaptability needed by students in order to advance through different learning pathways; successfully complete diverse learning itineraries, and continue learning throughout a lifetime. Consequently, much importance should be attached to initial teacher education and in-service professional development for teachers; and to effective classroom practices, targeted towards individual school needs and circumstances. Particular attention needs to be devoted to 'individualized' approaches for socializing and educating those at risk, which implies adapting curriculum, pedagogy and school organization to meet a wide range of ability (a strong argument about this issue is made in OECD, 1995a).

Improving Policy Development in this Area Requires Sensitive Evaluation Mechanisms

The focus on the quality of educational outcomes has led to the establishment of mechanisms for the evaluation of schools, and the performance of teachers and students. The main policy reasons for establishing such evaluation mechanisms are closely related to measures addressing educational failure: school accountability and improvement; monitoring the progress of reforms aiming to raise national standards; and increasing the understanding of the factors which create successful schools. In practice, school evaluation has meant implementing some kind of inspection process, as well as the development of performance indicators in order to 'measure' institutional effectiveness. The evidence shows that, even if inspection can be beneficial shortly before or after it takes place, long-term and continuous improvement requires investment in staff development programmes as well as the creation of a culture of evaluation among the main educational actors. Experience in different national contexts also shows that a continuous self-review can be especially effective for 'failing schools' (OECD, 1995b).

Conclusion

At a time when the role of education as an equalizing institution has again come to the forefront, addressing the needs of students with diverse learning abilities has become a major challenge for all education systems. This is precisely the focus of efforts at combating educational failure. Meeting this challenge implies looking ahead: in the twenty-first century, success at school will not be measured by the number of years studied or the attainment of a diploma for life. The *successful students* of tomorrow will be those who have acquired the knowledge, skills and motivation required to continue learning throughout a lifetime; *successful teachers* will be those most able to guide their students through different learning pathways; and *successful schools* will be those institutions which, together with other partners, provide the most adequate environment for both — students and teachers — to attain these objectives.

Notes

1 The Organisation for Economic Co-operation and Development (OECD) is an inter-governmental organization which today encompasses twenty-nine democratic nations with advanced market economies from North America, Western Europe and the Pacific Rim. The Organisation also has a series of activities with non-member states, including developing countries; rapidly growing economies in Asia and Latin America; central and eastern European countries; and the New Independent States of the former Soviet Union.

   The OECD was founded in 1960 with the aim of promoting policies to: achieve the highest sustainable economic growth and employment; contribute to economic and social welfare throughout the OECD area; stimulate and harmonize its members' efforts in favour of developing countries; and contribute to the expansion of world trade on a multi-lateral, non-discriminatory basis.

   It is a forum permitting member governments to study and formulate the best policies possible in the economic and social spheres. One of the principal missions of the OECD is to assist member countries to develop effective policies for human resource development. A single directorate, the Directorate for Education, Employment, Labour and Social Affairs, brings together a range of policy areas that address the human side of economic development. Most importantly, it considers how policies in these areas interact to influence the opportunities for individuals to work and to learn in today's integrated and knowledge intensive economies.

2 The project was undertaken under the supervision of Abrar Hasan. Costas Soumelis, Alan Wagner and John Lowe were responsible for the initial stages of the activity. Simon James assisted in drafting the final report, which profited from the insightful comments of OECD colleagues.

3 For a discussion on the development of measures related to different aspects of school performance, see Foster, Gomm and Hammersley (1996).

4 Three data sources were used to construct a 'statistical portrait' of failure, within the framework of the OECD activity on 'Combating Failure at School':

   - national data of OECD member states collected through the OECD project on International Indicators of Education Systems (INES) with the joint effort of UNESCO and Eurostat;
   - the 1994 International Adult Literacy Survey (IALS), based on representative samples of approximately 3,000 adults, aged 16 to 65, in each of the seven countries which have participated to date (Germany, the Netherlands, Sweden, Switzerland, Canada and the United States); and
   - the 1991 Survey of Reading and Literacy of 14-year-olds, carried out by the International Association for the Evaluation of Educational Achievement (IEA) in thirty-two countries (nineteen of which are OECD Member countries).

5 The following consultants did the statistical analyses: Aletta Grisay, David Neice, Hiko Jungklaus and Edwyn Leuven.

6 The idea of 'cycles' is that of longer units than single year groups: children of the same age may be in different stages of the cycle. Primary school in France and Belgium is based on cycles.

References

EURYDICE (1994) *Measures to Combat Failure at School: A Challenge for the Construction of Europe*, Bruxelles: European Commission.

FOSTER, P., GOMM, R. and HAMMERSLEY, M. (1996) *Constructing Educational Inequality: An Assessment of Research of School Processes*, London: Falmer Press.

OECD (1994) *The OECD Jobs Study*, Paris: Organisation for Economic Co-operation and Development.

OECD (1995a) *Our Children at Risk*, Paris: Organisation for Economic Co-operation and Development.

OECD (1995b) *Schools Under Scrutiny*, Paris: Organisation for Economic Co-operation and Development.

OECD (1996a) *Lifelong Learning for All*, Paris: Organisation for Economic Co-operation and Development.

OECD (1996b) *Changing the Subject*, Paris: Organisation for Economic Co-operation and Development.

OECD (1996c) *Successful Services for Our Children and Families at Risk*, Paris: Organisation for Economic Co-operation and Development.

OECD (1996d) *Mapping the Future: Young People and Career Guidance*, Paris: Organisation for Economic Co-operation and Development.

OECD (1997) *Parents and Partners on Schooling*, Paris: Organisation for Economic Co-operation and Development.

OECD (forthcoming, 1997a) *Education at a Glance Analysis* (chapter on failure at school), Paris: Organisation for Economic Co-operation and Development.

OECD (forthcoming, 1997b) *Combating Failure at School: Dimensions of the Problem, Country Experiences and Policy Implications*, Paris: Organisation for Economic Co-operation and Development.

OECD (forthcoming, 1997c) *Equity and Quality in Education*, Paris: Organisation for Economic Co-operation and Development.

OECD AND STATISTICS CANADA (1995) *Literacy, Economy and Society: Results of the First International Adult Literacy Survey, Paris and Ottawa*. Paris: Organisation for Economic Co-operation and Development.

Notes on Contributors

Michael Barber is on secondment from his post as Dean of New Initiatives and Professor of Education at the University of London Institute of Education as Head of the DfEE's Standards and Effectiveness Unit. He was a secondary school teacher before becoming a research officer then Education Officer (from 1989–1993) for the National Union of Teachers. He was also chairman of the London borough of Hackney's education committee, and from 1993 to 1995, Professor of Education and Director of the Centre for Successful Schools at Keele University. His research focuses mainly on school effectiveness, school improvement, and their implications for policy. He has published widely and speaks regularly on radio and television about education policy. Among his publications are *The National Curriculum: A Study in Policy* and *The Learning Game: Arguments for an Education Revolution.*

John Beresford was appointed as Research Officer to the Cambridge University School of Education IQEA (School Improvement) project in October 1994 after twenty-four years as a primary school teacher. He has worked extensively on school improvement projects in East Anglia, Barking and Dagenham, Humberside, Nottinghamshire and Derbyshire. He has had articles published on LMS and teacher professionalism as well as school improvement topics. He is currently studying for a PhD at Nottingham University on pupil views of effective teaching and learning.

Vivien Cutler has always worked in the inner city. After graduating from philosophy and politics she taught in Glasgow primary schools then moved to London on an ILEA secondment. After working initially for special needs and humanities departments, she broadened her role to include curriculum and pastoral care management. In 1988, she became head of a mixed school in Tower Hamlets. She was appointed to Highbury Grove, an Islington boys school, in 1994.

Dean Fink is an international leadership consultant and a fellow of the University of Lincolnshire/Humberside. A former superintendent and principal with the Halton Board of Education in Ontario, Canada, he has taught at all levels of education from primary to graduate school, and has been a senior manager at primary and secondary levels. In the past three years, he has worked in sixteen different countries, conducting workshops with LEAs and schools in Britain and Ireland. He has published articles on school effectiveness, leadership and change in schools, as well as co-authoring *Change Our Schools* with Louise Stoll.

Harvey Goldstein has been Professor of Statistical Methods at the Institute of Education, University of London, since 1977. He is a chartered statistician, and has been editor of the *Royal Statistical Society's Journal, Series A*. He was elected a member of the International Statistical Institute in 1987, a fellow of the Royal Society of Arts in 1991, and a fellow of the British Academy in 1996. He has two main foci of his research interests. The first is the use of statistical modelling techniques in the construction and analysis of educational tests. He has also explored the ideas of criterion referenced assessment, comparability of assessments, and the interaction of assessment modes and purposes of assessment. The second major research interest is in the methodology of multilevel modelling. The major text on multilevel modelling is his book *Multilevel Statistical Models*.

Alma Harris is Co-Director of the Centre for Teacher and School Development at the University of Nottingham. Her professional interests are in the areas of teacher and school development, school improvement and educational management. A founding member of the Centre for School Improvement at Bath University, she is also an associate of the International School Effectiveness and Improvement Centre (ISEIC) at the Institute of Eduction, University of London. Previously she worked as a teacher, research officer and university lecturer. Recent research includes a DfEE School Improvement Project and she is currently co-directing the DfEE project *Effective Teaching and Learning in Work-Related Contexts*. Books include *School Effectiveness and School Improvement: A Practical Guide* and *Organisational Effectiveness and Improvement*.

David Hopkins is Professor and Chair of the School of Education, University of Nottingham. He has previously worked as a tutor at the University of Cambridge, Institute of Education, an Outward Bound instructor and school teacher. He has a PhD from Simon Fraser University, British Columbia, consults widely on issues of school improvement and teacher quality, and continues to be inspired by the learning experiences of his young children, Jeroen, Jessica and Dylan. Recent books include *Evaluation for School Development*; *The Empowered School* (with David Hargreaves); *School Improvement in an Era of Change*; and *Models of Learning — Tools for Teaching*.

Karen Kovacs is currently Administrator in the Education and Training Division, OECD. From 1983 to 1988 she was head of an educational research department and Professor of Sociology at the National University of Mexico: she then did research on comparative education and on the Mexican political system at the Colegio de Mexico. Between 1989 and 1994, Ms Kovacs held different positions in the Mexican government. She was General Director for Strategic Planning and adviser to the Minister of Foreign Affairs. Subsequently, she became General Director for International Relations in the Ministry of Education.

James Learmonth started out as a teacher of English and drama in London comprehensive schools. He was headteacher of a mixed community school in Tower

Hamlets and then joined HMI, working mostly in urban schools. He became Chief Inspector in Richmond LEA in 1989. For the last three years he has worked in the UK and USA as an adviser and trainer, and is an OFSTED registered inspector. He is currently an Associate of ISEIC at the Institute of Education, University of London, and has recently taken a post in School Development at Canterbury Christ Church.

Caroline Lodge worked for twenty-four years in urban secondary schools in Coventry and London, as a history teacher, head of department, head of year, deputy head, and finally as the headteacher of an inner London mixed comprehensive. She is the Manager of the Centre for Training and Development for the National Professional Qualification in Headship (NPQH) at the Institute of Education in London. In the past she has written about gender, sex education, pastoral care and the education of refugees.

Kathy Lowers has spent thirty-three years working in primary education as a teacher, headteacher, LEA primary inspector and, currently, an independent consultant. A strong commitment to the right of working class pupils to an education of quality has been the driving force behind her work. Besides supporting schools in difficulty she offers a variety of management courses and is involved in the trials of the new qualification for headship (NPQH). She is an Associate of ISEIC at the Institute of Education.

John MacBeath is Director of the Quality in Education Centre at the University of Strathclyde. Over the past six years he has been involved in research and consultancy for a wide range of bodies, including the Scottish Office Education and Industry Department, the Prince's Trust, the National Union of Teachers, OECD, UNESCO, and the European Commission. Much of Professor MacBeath's recent work has been in school self-evaluation, development planning and school improvement. He has worked closely with education authorities through out Britain, with national and international governments and institutions, and is on the Government's Standards Task Force. Recent publications include *Schools Speak for Themselves: Towards a Framework of Self-Evaluation* and contributions to *Success Against the Odds*. He is co-director with Peter Mortimore of the SOEID-funded Improving School Effectiveness Project.

Kate Myers is Professor of Professional Development in Education at Keele University. Previously she was course leader for the Doctor of Education Programme and an Associate Director of ISEIC at the Institute of Education, University of London. She has been a teacher, ILEA coordinator of the Schools' Council's Sex Differentiation Project, an advisory teacher, director of the SCDC/EOC Equal Opportunities Project, senior inspector and project manager of the Schools Make A Difference (SMAD) project in Hammersmith and Fulham. Publications include *Genderwatch!*, *School Improvement in Practice*, *The Intelligent School* (forthcoming, with Barbara MacGilchrist and Jane Reed), and regular contributions to the *TES* and *Education Journal*.

Steven Pugh sold advertising space before becoming a teacher in 1981. He taught history in mainstream schools in Tower Hamlets and Plymouth before going to work with EBD pupils in 1985. In 1990 he became head of the secondary age behaviour support service in Derby before taking up the headship at Brookside. He is presently head of Derbyshire's service for disaffected pupils.

David Reynolds is Professor of Education at the University of Newcastle upon Tyne. He has researched, written and practised in the areas of school effectiveness, school improvement and educational policy for over twenty years, and is currently interested in international school effectiveness research and in generating more reliable school improvement (with Sam Stringfield). He is co-editor of the journal *School Improvement and School Effectiveness* and currently outgoing chair of the International Congress for School Effectiveness and School Improvement. Recent publications include *Merging Traditions: The Future of Research on School Effectiveness* and *School Improvement* and *Making Good Schools*.

Michael Stark is Head of School Effectiveness, in the Standards and Effectiveness Unit at the Department for Education and Employment in London. He advises the Secretary of State on the independent inspection of schools, failing schools, and performance measurement, action planning and development planning. In 1987 he transferred to the Department for Education and set up the new School Teachers' Pay Committee. He has held a range of senior posts at the Department and has been Head of School Effectiveness since January 1994.

Louise Stoll is Coordinating Director of the International School Effectiveness and Improvement Centre (ISEIC) at the Institute of Education. She is involved in partnership improvement projects with schools and LEAs, and set up the School Improvement Network. Current research includes the Improving School Effectiveness Project for SOEID. Previously she was a primary teacher, researcher on *School Matters* and worked on the Halton Effective Schools Project in Canada. Her publications include *School Matters* (with Peter Mortimore and colleagues) and *Changing Our Schools* (with Dean Fink). She has presented and consulted in many countries.

Sam Stringfield is a Principal Research Scientist at the Johns Hopkins University Center for the Social Organization of Schools in Baltimore, USA. The author of over seventy articles, chapters and books, Dr Stringfield is the founding co-editor of the *Journal of Education for Students Placed At Risk (JESPAR)*. His two most recent projects concern designs for improving programmes within schools (*The Special Strategies Studies*) and for improving whole schools (*Bold Plans for School Restructuring*).

Linda Turner has spent all her teaching career in Oldham Education Authority. She has worked in a wide range of schools ranging from a small, all-English, infant school in the suburbs to a large, multicultural primary school with nursery in the inner city area. She has had two deputy headships and two headships and a period of secondment to the local authority to develop Newly Qualified Teacher Training. She has recently been appointed as School Development Adviser in Oldham.

Rob Watling is a Research Associate at the School of Education, University of Nottingham. His recent research into educational policy issues has examined school exclusion, the importance of class size, and the role of multimedia technology in improving access to Higher Education courses. He coordinated the analysis of findings on the Waltham Forest AIP evaluation, and is currently working on a variety of school improvement projects in the East Midlands.

Christine Whatford began her career as a teacher of history at Elliott School (under the ILEA) where, after also being head of history, head of house and senior teacher, she became deputy headteacher. From 1983 to 1989, she was the headteacher of Abbey Wood School in South London. Christine Whatford has been the Director of Education in the London borough of Hammersmith and Fulham since 1989.

Index